THE CECIL OF CHELWOOD PAPERS

THE BRITISH LIBRARY CATALOGUE

OF

ADDITIONS

TO THE

MANUSCRIPTS

THE
CECIL OF CHELWOOD
PAPERS

ADDITIONAL MANUSCRIPTS
51071 – 51204

THE BRITISH LIBRARY
1991

© 1991 The British Library Board

Published by
The British Library
Great Russell Street
London WC1B 3DG

British Library Cataloguing in Publication Data
  British Library
    The British Library catalogue of additions to the
    manuscripts : the Cecil of Chelwood papers : additional
    manuscripts 51071–51204.
    1. Manuscripts
    I. Title
    018.131

  ISBN 0-7123-0152-6

Printed in England on permanent paper ∞ by
St Edmundsbury Press, Bury St Edmunds, Suffolk

PREFACE

This catalogue of the papers of Robert Cecil, first and last Viscount Cecil of Chelwood, presented by him to the British Museum in 1954, is the work of Dr A.N.E.D. Schofield, sometime Curator in the Department of Manuscripts.

The Cecil of Chelwood papers cover the period from the First World War until about 1950, and, as might be expected of the papers of one of its creators and most prominent supporters, include especially material relating to the formation and history of the League of Nations. A proportion of the papers, especially those relating to Cabinet business, were reserved from public use under the thirty year rule until 1968.

This catalogue is a milestone in the history of the Department of Manuscripts, since it is the first to be produced using automation both for the descriptions and the index, and to be delivered to the printer in digital form. The resolution of the inevitable problems thrown up by this pioneering project has been the considerable achievement of Miss Rachel Stockdale of this Department, and of Messrs Andrew Bennett, Tony Glynos and David Grinyer of Computing and Telecommunications. As a result of their labours the production of successive volumes of the *Summary Catalogue* and of the various special catalogues will, it is anticipated, proceed both more rapidly and more economically.

T.A.J. BURNETT
Manuscripts Librarian

TABLE OF CONTENTS

	PAGE
Preface	v
Descriptions	1
Index	23

DESCRIPTIONS

THE CECIL OF CHELWOOD PAPERS

51071-51204. Correspondence and papers of Edgar Algernon Robert Gascoyne-Cecil, Viscount Cecil of Chelwood 1923, (b.1864, d.1958), statesman and promoter of the League of Nations; 1893-1953, n.d. A large proportion of the present collection consists of *typewritten* material. The collection was used by Cecil in *A Great Experiment* (1941) and *All the Way* (1949), and it has frequently been cited by others in books and articles of subsequent date. For a description of other papers of Cecil in the possession of the Marquess of Salisbury at Hatfield House, see Cameron Hazlehurst and Christine Woodland, *A Guide to the Papers of British Cabinet Ministers, 1900-1951*, Royal Historical Society, Guides and Handbooks, Supplementary Series, No. 1 (1974), p. 32. Presented by Lord Cecil in 1954.

Paper. One hundred and thirty-four volumes. British Library arrangement. Classified as follows:—

A.   Special Correspondence: 51071-51157.

B.   General Correspondence: 51158-51192.

C.   Literary Manuscripts, etc.: 51193-51204.

A. Special Correspondence

51071 A. Cecil of Chelwood Papers. Vol. I A (ff. 111). Correspondence with Arthur James Balfour, 1st Earl of Balfour, Prime Minister; 1906-1930. A copy of an official telegram from Cecil to Balfour, 1919, is at Add. 51104, f. 24. Some of the original letters of Cecil and copies of Balfour's letters, exchanged during this correspondence, are at Add. 49737, ff. 40, 97, 122, 140; Add. 49738, ff. 155, 243, (Balfour Papers). The letter from Balfour, dated 12 Sept. 1917, at Add. 51071 A, f. 40, was printed by Blanche E. C. Dugdale in *Arthur James Balfour, First Earl of Balfour* (1936), vol. ii, p. 174, presumably from the copy in the Balfour Papers at Add. 49738, f. 155.

51071 B. Cecil of Chelwood Papers. Vol. I B (ff. 152). Correspondence with Sir Arthur Herbert Drummond Ramsay Steel-Maitland, 1st Bart.; 1911-1927.

51072. Cecil of Chelwood Papers. Vol. II (ff. 274).
1. ff. 1-49. Correspondence with Evelyn Baring, 1st Earl of Cromer; 1908, 1909.
2. ff. 50-108. Correspondence with Walter Hume Long, 1st Viscount Long; 1908-1918.
3. ff. 109-158v. Letters from George Frederick Stewart Bowles, M.P.; 1906-1909.
4. ff. 159-213v. Letters from Edward George Brunker, of the Free Trade Union; 1908, 1909.
5. ff. 214-274. Correspondence with Leopold Charles Maurice Stennett Amery, P.C.; 1912-1945.

51073. CECIL OF CHELWOOD PAPERS. Vol. III (ff. 195). Correspondence with:—
1. ff. 1-39. Herbert Henry Asquith, 1st Earl of Oxford and Asquith, Prime Minister; 1913-1922.
2. ff. 40-58. Emma Alice Margaret Asquith, wife of the preceding; 1922-1944.
3. ff. 59-96. Edward Grey, Viscount Grey of Falloden; 1914-1929.
4. ff. 97-195. Sir Winston Leonard Spencer Churchill, K.G., Prime Minister; 1910-1952. The letter dated 1 Sept. 1944 from Churchill to Cecil (f. 186) and Cecil's reply dated 5 Sept. (f. 188) were quoted in full by Cecil, *All the Way*, pp. 234, 235.

51074. CECIL OF CHELWOOD PAPERS. Vol. IV (ff. 197). Case submitted for legal opinions concerning the provision of £100,000 for the building of public elementary schools under the Appropriation Act, 1907, together with (ff. 12-163) a memorandum by Sir Reginald Playfair Hills, barrister-at-law, (ff. 164-171v) opinions by William Otto Adolph Julius Danckwerts, K.C. and Hills, and (ff. 172-196) miscellaneous papers relating to schools in Wales; 1905-1908. Mostly *copies*.

51075 A, B. CECIL OF CHELWOOD PAPERS. Vol. V A, B. Memoranda and other papers relating to domestic politics; 1893-[1930?]. Partly *drafts, copies* and *printed*.
Two volumes.

51075 A. Vol. V A (ff. 129). 1893-1912.

51075 B. Vol. V B (ff. 141). 1908-[1930?]. Included are (ff. 2-33) a selection of papers concerning Women's Franchise (Conciliation Bill), 1908-[1913?], and (ff. 81-119) papers relating to the Hitchin Parliamentary Election of 1922; however some items in the lists of contents at ff. 1 and 80 are wanting from these sections.

51076. CECIL OF CHELWOOD PAPERS. Vol. VI (ff. 153). Correspondence with:—
1. ff. 1-77. David Lloyd George, 1st Earl Lloyd George; 1915-1943. Including (ff. 66, 67) letters from his daughter, Megan Lloyd George, M.P. and (f. 77) from his second wife, Frances Louise, *née* Stevenson.
2. ff. 78-153. Field-Marshal Jan Christiaan Smuts, South African Prime Minister; 1918-1948.

51077. CECIL OF CHELWOOD PAPERS. Vol. VII (ff. 305). Correspondence with George Nathanial Curzon, Marquess Curzon of Kedleston; 1910-1925.

51078, 51079. CECIL OF CHELWOOD PAPERS. Vols. VIII, IX. Correspondence with Sir Joseph Austen Chamberlain; 1918-1936. Two volumes.

    51078. Vol. VIII (ff. 163). 1918-June 1926.

    51079. Vol. IX (ff. 238). July 1926-1936.

51080. CECIL OF CHELWOOD PAPERS. Vol. X (ff. 282). Correspondence with Stanley Baldwin, 1st Earl Baldwin, Prime Minister; 1923-1939. Cecil's letter of resignation, 9 Aug. 1927, at ff. 209-217 (cf. the imperfect draft at ff. 206-208 and the version subsequently released to the Press at ff. 226-228), together with Baldwin's reply, 29 Aug. 1927, (ff. 220-225) were printed in Cecil, *A Great Experiment* (1941), Appendix II, pp. 358-366. Copies of official telegrams from Cecil to Baldwin, 1927, are at Add. 51104, ff. 85, 88, 92.

51081. CECIL OF CHELWOOD PAPERS. Vol. XI (ff. 235). Correspondence with:—
1.   ff. 1-142. James Ramsay MacDonald, Prime Minister; 1923-1934, also (ff. 90-94, 115) with his son, Malcolm John MacDonald, P.C.; 1930, 1931.
2.   ff. 143-233. Arthur Henderson, P.C., M.P.; 1929-1934, also (ff. 234, 235) with his son, Arthur Henderson, Baron Rowley; 1937.

51082. CECIL OF CHELWOOD PAPERS. Vol. XII (ff. 295). Correspondence with:—
1.   ff. 1-62. Rufus Daniel Isaacs, 1st Marquess of Reading; 1925-1931.
2.   ff. 63-295. John Allsebrook Simon, 1st Viscount Simon; 1931-1945. See also the letter at Add. 51188, f. 279.

51083. CECIL OF CHELWOOD PAPERS. Vol. XIII (ff. 196). Correspondence with:—
1.   ff. 1-47. Samuel John Gurney Hoare, 1st Viscount Templewood; 1918-1945.
2.   ff. 48-196. Robert Anthony Eden, 1st Earl of Avon; 1932-1945.

51084. CECIL OF CHELWOOD PAPERS. Vol. XIV (ff. 253).
Correspondence with Edward Frederick Lindley Wood, Baron Irwin, 3rd Viscount (1934) and 1st Earl Halifax; 1926-1942.

51085, 51086. CECIL OF CHELWOOD PAPERS. Vols. XV, XVI.
Correspondence with James Edward Hubert Gascoyne-Cecil, 4th Marquess of Salisbury; 1906-1945. See also Add. 51104, ff. 97-253 *passim* for copies of official telegrams between Salisbury and Cecil, 1927.
Two volumes.

51085. Vol. XV (ff. 186). 1906-1926.

51086. Vol. XVI (ff. 231). 1927-1945.

51087. CECIL OF CHELWOOD PAPERS. Vol. XVII (ff. 266).
Correspondence with:—
1. ff. 1-177. Robert Arthur James Gascoyne-Cecil, Viscount Cranborne, 5th Marquess of Salisbury; 1922-1945.
2. ff. 178-266. Arthur Neville Chamberlain, Prime Minister; 1937-1939.

51088. CECIL OF CHELWOOD PAPERS. Vol. XVIII (ff. 115).
Correspondence with Maurice Pascal Alers Hankey, 1st Baron Hankey; 1916-1943. Copies of official telegrams between Hankey and Cecil, 1927, are at Add. 51104, ff. 87, 91-96.

51089. CECIL OF CHELWOOD PAPERS. Vol. XIX (ff. 178).
Correspondence with Sir Alexander George Montagu Cadogan, G.C.M.G.; 1923-1944.

51090. CECIL OF CHELWOOD PAPERS. Vol. XX (ff. 138).
Correspondence with:—
1. ff. 1-42v. Frederick Scott Oliver, of Messrs. Debenham and Freebody, barrister-at-law and author; 1912-1918.
2. ff. 43-90. Sir Walford Harmood Montague Selby, K.C.M.G.; 1918-1944.
3. ff. 91-138v. Sir Cecil James Barrington Hurst, G.C.M.G.; 1925-1944.

51091. CECIL OF CHELWOOD PAPERS. Vol. XXI (ff. 211). Correspondence with:—
1. ff. 1-144v. Sir Maurice Drummond Peterson, G.C.M.G.; 1932-1943.
2. ff. 145-211. Sir Mansfeldt de Cardonnel Findlay, G.B.E.; 1918. Copies of official telegrams from Findlay to Cecil, 1918, are at Add. 51104, ff. 1-4, 6-10.

51092. CECIL OF CHELWOOD PAPERS. Vol. XXII (ff. 316). Correspondence with Frederick Dixon, Editor of *The Christian Science Monitor*, Boston, U.S.A.; 1915-1923. Including (ff. 23-288) memoranda and telegrams sent by Dixon through Frederick Leay, Consul-General in Boston, to Sir Guy Harold Locock of the Foreign Office and circulated there. A partial list of contents is at ff. 1-12.

51093-51101. CECIL OF CHELWOOD PAPERS. Vols. XXIII-XXXI. Miscellaneous correspondence, mainly official, concerning foreign affairs; 1915-1934. Including records, mostly by Cecil, of conversations with important persons.
Nine volumes.

51093. Vol. XXIII (ff. 208). [June 1915?]-July 1918.

51094. Vol. XXIV (ff. 180). Aug. 1918-June 1919.

51095. Vol. XXV (ff. 199). 1920-July 1923.

51096. Vol. XXVI (ff. 171). Aug. 1923-Feb. 1924.

51097. Vol. XXVII (ff. 219). March 1924-1925.

51098. Vol. XXVIII (ff. 178). Jan. 1926-Feb. 1927.

51099. Vol. XXIX (ff. 201). March 1927-1929.

51100. Vol. XXX (ff. 216). 1930-June 1932.

51101. Vol. XXXI (ff. 203). July 1932-1934.

51102. CECIL OF CHELWOOD PAPERS. Vol. XXXII (ff. 155). Cabinet memoranda and other papers concerning foreign and home affairs, mostly headed or annotated 'War Cabinet', 'Cabinet', or 'For Cabinet'; 1916-1927. *Copies.* Partly *printed.* Memoranda submitted to the Prime Minister, 1926, apparently for circulation to the Cabinet, are at Add. 51080, ff. 175-183.

Included are:—

1. ff. 1-10. 'Memorandum on proposals for diminishing the occasion of future wars', two copies of the paper submitted to the War Cabinet by Cecil in 1916, one headed 'War Cabinet Paper P. 18 (ex G.T. 484)'. Printed by Cecil, *A Great Experiment*, pp. 353-357.

2. ff. 13-64. Summarised extracts from War Cabinet Minutes, mostly relating to Russia; 1 Nov.-13 March 1918. Related material will be found in Add. 51105, ff. 43-78.

3. ff. 72-90. Draft Convention for the League of Nations, apparently subsequent to the submission to the War Cabinet of the Draft Convention by Lord Phillimore's Committee, 20 March 1918, (cf. the footnote on f. 85) and probably after the circulation to the War Cabinet of Cecil's proposals of 17 Dec. 1918. See D. H. Miller, *The Drafting of the Covenant* (1928), vol. i, pp. 3, 38. Other drafts for the Covenant of the League will be found in Add. 51116.

51103. CECIL OF CHELWOOD PAPERS. Vol. XXXIII (ff. 104). Committee of Imperial Defence and Sub-Committee on the Disarmament Conference (Three Party Committee): memoranda, some by Cecil, relating to the work of the Committee and Sub-Committee, together with papers circulated by the Sub-Committee; 1922-1931. *Copies.* Partly *printed.* Other material on disarmament will be found in Add. 51104, ff. 74-254; 51118-51122.

51104. CECIL OF CHELWOOD PAPERS. Vol. XXXIV (ff. 262). Foreign Office telegrams; 1918-1931. Including (ff. 74-254 *passim*) many relating to negotiations at Geneva for international disarmament and to the Conference for the Limitation of Naval Armament held there in 1927. Mostly *printed copies* for official circulation.

51105. CECIL OF CHELWOOD PAPERS. Vol. XXXV (ff. 189). Foreign Office and other memoranda, some by Cecil; 1915-1919. Mostly *copies*. Partly *printed*. Included are (ff. 185-189) minutes of meetings at the Foreign Office, with Cecil as chairman, concerning the formation of the League of Nations and the application of the League's mandatory principle, 1 and 20 Jan. 1919.

51106-51109. CECIL OF CHELWOOD PAPERS. Vols. XXXVI-XXXIX. Correspondence with Philip John Noel-Baker, formerly Baker, P.C., M.P., Baron Noel-Baker; 1921-1948. Further correspondence of Noel-Baker, within this period and mostly on behalf of Cecil is at Add. 51095, f. 196; 51100, f. 108; 51106, ff. 74-206 *passim* ; 51113, ff. 15-24; 51114, ff. 4-30v, 103; 51115, ff. 3-189 *passim*; 51143, ff. 92, 175, 180.
Four volumes.

51106. Vol. XXXVI (ff. 253). 1921-1927.

51107. Vol. XXXVII (ff. 292). 1928-1932.

51108. Vol. XXXVIII (ff. 181). 1933-1938.

51109. Vol. XXXIX (ff. 201). 1939-1948.

51110-51112. CECIL OF CHELWOOD PAPERS. Vols. XL-XLII. Correspondence with James Eric Drummond, 16th Earl of Perth, Secretary-General of the League of Nations; 1921-1948.
Three volumes.

51110. Vol. XL (ff. 211). 1921-1925.

51111. Vol. XLI (ff. 125). 1926-1929.

51112. Vol. XLII (ff. 213). 1930-1948.

51113. CECIL OF CHELWOOD PAPERS. Vol. XLIII (ff. 251). Correspondence with:—
1. ff. 1-114v. James Arthur Salter, Baron Salter; 1918-1945.
2. ff. 115-157v. Major Anthony Buxton, of the League of Nations Secretariate; 1923-1944.
3. ff. 158-203. Air Vice-Marshal William Foster MacNeece, afterwards MacNeece Foster, British Air Representative to the League of Nations Council; 1926-1941. Copies of official telegrams between MacNeece and the Air Ministry, 1927, are at Add. 51104, ff. 78, 81, 82, 90.

4.   ff. 204-251. Arthur Sweetser, of the League of Nations Secretariate, afterwards President of the Woodrow Wilson Foundation; 1923-1945.

51114. CECIL OF CHELWOOD PAPERS. Vol. XLIV (ff. 155). Correspondence with Francis Paul Walters, of the Secretariate of the League of Nations; 1922-1945. Including (ff. 4-30v, 103) correspondence with Philip John Noel-Baker, mostly on Lord Cecil's account, 1922, 1923, and preceded (f. 1) by a copy of a letter from Walters to [John Leslie?] Roberts, [of the British delegation to the Peace Conference in Paris and afterwards of the Secretariate of the League of Nations?], 1919.

51115. CECIL OF CHELWOOD PAPERS. Vol. XLV (ff. 235). Correspondence with Erik Colban, of the League of Nations Secretariate, Norwegian diplomatist; 1922-1943. Including (ff. 3-189 *passim*) correspondence of Colban with Philip John Noel-Baker, mostly on Cecil's account, 1922-1924.

51116, 51117. CECIL OF CHELWOOD PAPERS. Vols. XLVI, XLVII. Papers relating to the drafting and subsequent amendment of the Covenant of the League of Nations; 1919-1938.
Two volumes.

51116. CECIL OF CHELWOOD PAPERS. Vol. XLVI (ff. 141). Drafts for the Covenant; Jan.-June 1919. Mostly *printed*, with MS. additions. Partly *French*. Including (ff. 118-135) an official League of Nations file containing three such drafts. At f.20 is a copy of President Woodrow Wilson's third or 'second Paris' draft, signed by him. For an account of these various drafts, see D. H. Miller, *op. cit.*, where many of the texts are printed.

51117. CECIL OF CHELWOOD PAPERS. Vol. XLVII (ff. 88). Minutes, etc., of meetings of the Commission of the League and of its Sub-Committee, Feb., March 1919, followed (ff. 69-88) by memoranda, mostly by Cecil, on the Covenant; 1919-1938. *Copies*. Partly *printed*.

51118-51120. CECIL OF CHELWOOD PAPERS. Vols. XLVIII-L. Conference for the Limitation of Naval Armament, Geneva 1927.
Three volumes.

51118. CECIL OF CHELWOOD PAPERS. Vol. XLVIII (ff. 99). Minutes, Final and Draft, of the 1st-13th Conferences of the British Empire Delegations; 19 June-4 Aug. 1927. *Printed.*

51119. CECIL OF CHELWOOD PAPERS. Vol. XLIX (ff. 209). Verbatim reports of the 1st-3rd Plenary Sessions with related papers; 20 June-4 Aug. 1927. *Printed.*

51120. CECIL OF CHELWOOD PAPERS. Vol. L (ff. 183). Provisional minutes of the 1st, 3rd-9th sessions of the Technical Committee; 22 June-8 July 1927. Also of the 2nd and 3rd sessions of the Executive Committee; 8, 9 July 1927. *Printed.*

51121. CECIL OF CHELWOOD PAPERS. Vol. LI (ff. 268).
1. ff. 1-14. Minutes, etc., of the First Meeting of the Technical Sub-Committee on the Limitation of Armaments; Paris, 27 Jan. 1919. *Printed.*
2. ff. 15-268. Foreign Office and other memoranda and papers, including some by Cecil and from the British delegation at Geneva but mostly unattributed, relating to negotiations for the international limitation of armaments; 1922-1933. Mostly *copies*. Partly *printed*, with MS additions. Partly *French*. Another copy of Cecil's note 'President Coolidge's Proposal for a Separate Naval Conference, 14 Feb. 1927' (ff. 104-107) will be found, marked 'Cabinet', at Add. 51102, ff. 116-119.

51122. CECIL OF CHELWOOD PAPERS. Vol. LII (ff. 137). *Preliminary report on the Conference for the Reduction and Limitation of Armaments at Geneva, 1932-1934,* prepared by Arthur Henderson P.C., M.P.; *circa* 1935. Published posthumously in 1936. *Imperfect. Printed.*

51123. CECIL OF CHELWOOD PAPERS. Vol. LIII (ff. 204). League of Nations, Verbatim Reports of meetings; 1922-1932. *Printed*, with MS. additions.
1. ff. 1-33. Third Assembly, 19th Plenary Meeting; 27 Sept 1922.
2. ff. 34-62. Eleventh Ordinary Session of the Assembly, 24th Meeting; 4 Oct. 1930.
3. ff. 63-198. Extraordinary Session of the Assembly, General Commission, 4th-7th Meetings; 8, 11 March 1932.
4. ff. 199-204. Extraordinary Session of the Assembly, 4th Meeting; 11 March 1932.

51124. CECIL OF CHELWOOD PAPERS. Vol. LIV (ff. 200). League of Nations and Foreign Office memoranda and papers, mostly concerning the dissolution of the League and the transfer of certain of its functions, etc., to the United Nations; 1944-1946. Including (ff. 50-200) Provisional Records of the 1st to 7th meetings of the 21st (final) Ordinary Session of the League, 8-18 April 1946, and (ff. 127-131, 167-168) Reports on the 101st and 102nd sessions of the Supervisory Commission of the League, 10 and 12 April 1946. *Printed.* Partly *French.*

51125-51128. CECIL OF CHELWOOD PAPERS. Vols. LV-LVIII. Foreign Office, League of Nations and other memoranda and papers, including some by Cecil but mostly unattributed, concerning international affairs and the work of the League, excluding disarmament; 1920-1932. Mostly *copies.* Partly *printed.* Partly *French.*
Four volumes.

51125. Vol. LV (ff. 293). 1920-Aug. 1923.

51126. Vol. LVI (ff. 258). Sept.-Dec. 1923.

51127. Vol. LVII (ff. 254). 1924-1931.

51128. Vol. LVIII (ff. 219). 1932-1939.

51129, 51130. CECIL OF CHELWOOD PAPERS. Vols. LIX, LX. International High Commission for Refugees (Jewish and other) coming from Germany: reports of the Commission and papers relating to its work; 1933-1938. Mostly *copies.* Partly *printed.* Partly *French.*
Two volumes.

51129. Vol. LIX (ff. 83). Dec. 1933, April 1934.

51130. Vol. LX (ff. 176). May 1934-1938.

51131. CECIL OF CHELWOOD PAPERS. Vol. LXI (ff. 273). Diaries, notes, itineraries, etc., relating to visits and tours abroad by Cecil; 1917-1937. Mostly *copies*. Partly *printed*.
1.   ff. 1-4. Notes of a visit to the British forces in France; Oct. or Nov. 1917.
2.   ff. 5-99. Diary as a member of the British Delegation to the Peace Conference in Paris; 6-10 Jan. 1919.
3.   ff. 100-126. Diary of the first meeting of the Assembly of the League of Nations; 15 Nov.-6 Dec. 1920.
4.   ff. 127-206. Diary of a tour to the United States; 21 March-28 April 1923.
5.   ff. 207-219. Diary of a Scandinavian tour, preceded (f. 208) by an itinerary; 16 May-3 June 1924.
6.   ff. 220-225. Itinerary of a tour, on behalf of the League of Nations Union, to Paris, Madrid, Frankfurt and Berlin; 16 May-5 June 1929. Followed by a printed report submitted to the Committee of the Union.
7.   ff. 226-227. Itinerary of a tour to Vienna, Prague and Heidelberg; 20-31 June 1931.
8.   f. 228. List of engagements during a visit to Brussels; 12-17 May 1934.
9.   ff. 229-231. Diary of a visit to Paris; 14, 15 Dec. 1935.
10. ff. 232-273. Note of a visit to Washington; 13-15 Nov. 1937. See also Add. 51169, f. 54; 51171, f. 229; 51177, ff. 75, 76, 154, 155; 51178, ff. 14-20, for similar material.

51132-51135. CECIL OF CHELWOOD PAPERS. Vols. LXII-LXV. Correspondence with George Gilbert Aimé Murray, O.M, mostly as Chairman of the League of Nations Union; 1922-1952. Original letters from Cecil to Murray will be found in the Murray Papers at the Bodleian Library, Oxford.
   Four volumes.

   51132. Vol. LXII (ff. 269). 1922-1937.

   51133. Vol. LXIII (ff. 263). 1938-1941.

   51134. Vol. LXIV (ff. 273). 1942-1947.

   51135. Vol. LXV (ff. 276). 1948-1952.

51136. CECIL OF CHELWOOD PAPERS. Vol. LXVI (ff. 235). Correspondence with:—
1.   ff. 1-125v. James Clerk Maxwell Garnett, Secretary of the League of Nations Union; 1923-1945.
2.   f. 126-235. Major A. J. C. Freshwater, M.C., T.D., Secretary of the League of Nations Union; 1935-1943.

51137. CECIL OF CHELWOOD PAPERS. Vol. LXVII (ff. 224).
Correspondence with:—
1. ff. 1-175. Herbert Sutton Syrett, solicitor, Chairman, League of Nations Union, City of London branch; 1935-1945.
2. ff. 176-224. Vincent Duncan-Jones, Secretary of the Peace Penny Fund; 1938, 1939.

51138. CECIL OF CHELWOOD PAPERS. Vol. LXVIII (ff. 188). Correspondence with David Davies, 1st Baron Davies, President of the League of Nations Union, Welsh Council; 1923-1943. Memoranda relating to his visits to Paris and Switzerland, 1939, are at Add. 51184, ff. 217-228, 229-233.

51139. CECIL OF CHELWOOD PAPERS. Vol. LXIX (ff. 226).
Correspondence with:—
1. ff. 1-83v. Roger Grey, 10th Earl of Stamford; 1934-1945.
2. ff. 84-226v. Victor Alexander George Robert Bulwer-Lytton, 2nd Earl of Lytton; 1922-1946. See Add. 51188, ff. 31-33 for further correspondence.

51140. CECIL OF CHELWOOD PAPERS. Vol. LXX (ff. 247).
Correspondence with:—
1. ff. 1-75. Sir Norman Angell, author and journalist; 1924-1943.
2. ff. 76-208v. William Arnold-Forster, writer on international affairs; 1930-1948.
3. ff. 209-247. Noel Edmund Noel-Buxton, formerly Buxton, 1st Baron Noel-Buxton; 1928-1944.

51141. CECIL OF CHELWOOD PAPERS. Vol. LXXI (ff. 362).
Correspondence with:—
1. ff. 1-261. Dame Kathleen D'Olier Courtney, D.B.E.; 1930-1946.
2. ff. 262-315. Eleanor Rathbone, M.P.; 1913-1944.
3. ff. 316-362. Aubrey Nigel Henry Molyneux Herbert, M.P.; 1920, 1922, and his widow, Mary Herbert; 1943-1945.

51142. CECIL OF CHELWOOD PAPERS. Vol. LXXII (ff. 271).
Correspondence with:—
1. ff. 1-59. Dame Adelaide Lord Livingstone, D.B.E.; 1934-1944.
2. ff. 60v-92. Miss Freda White, writer on international affairs; 1935-1941.
3. ff. 93-151v. Miss Edith Ellis, Secretary of the League of Nations Union, Scarborough District; 1935-1945.
4. ff. 152-219. Miss Gertrude Ward, Secretary of the League of Nations Union, Sheffield District; 1935-1945.

5.   ff. 220-271. Katherine Marjorie Stewart-Murray, Duchess of Atholl; 1936-1944.

51143. CECIL OF CHELWOOD PAPERS. Vol. LXXIII (ff. 192).
Correspondence with:—
1.   ff. 1-83v. Pierre Cot, French statesman; 1932-1943.
2.   ff. 84-192v. Louis Dolivet, Secretary, International Peace Campaign; 1936-1944.

51144. CECIL OF CHELWOOD PAPERS. Vol. LXXIV (ff. 205).
Correspondence with:—
1.   ff. 1-88v. Thomas William Lamont, American banker; 1923-1944.
2.   ff. 89-132v. Florence Haskell Lamont, wife of the preceding; 1923-1941.
3.   ff. 133-205. Nicholas Murray Butler, President of Columbia University; 1925-1945.

51145. CECIL OF CHELWOOD PAPERS. Vol. LXXV (ff. 169).
Correspondence with:—
1.   ff. 1-77. Otto Lehmann-Russbüldt, German author; [1933?]-1939.
2.   ff. 78-128. Dr. Ernst Künstler, of Danzig; 1934-1936.
3.   ff. 129-169. Dr. Emil Müller-Sturmheim, Austrian journalist; 1938, 1939.

51146-51149. CECIL OF CHELWOOD PAPERS. Vols. LXXVI-LXXIX.
League of Nations Union, miscellaneous papers; 1928-1945. Mostly *printed*.
   Four volumes.

51146. CECIL OF CHELWOOD PAPERS. Vol. LXXVI (ff. 164).
Papers relating to the work of the Executive and other Committees; 1928-1943.

51147, 51148. CECIL OF CHELWOOD PAPERS. Vols. LXXVII, LXXVIII. Memoranda, etc.; 1930-1943. Partly *French*.

51147. Vol. LXXVII (ff. 120). 1930-1937.

51148. Vol. LXXVIII (ff. 174). 1938-1943.

51149. CECIL OF CHELWOOD PAPERS. Vol. LXXIX (ff. 213). Papers of the Executive Committee relating to the Dumbarton Oaks proposals and the establishment of the United Nations; 1944, 1945.

51150. CECIL OF CHELWOOD PAPERS. Vol. LXXX (ff. 98). Papers concerning the British Commonwealth Relations Conference in Toronto, Sept. 1933, organised by the Canadian Institute for International Affairs, preceded (ff. 1-60) by papers of the Chatham House Preparatory Committee in London; March-Sept. 1933. *Copies*. Partly *printed*. See Add. 51168, ff. 16-160 *passim* for related correspondence.

51151. CECIL OF CHELWOOD PAPERS. Vol. LXXXI (ff. 207). London International Assembly: minutes, agenda, reports, etc.; 1941-1943. Mostly *printed*. Partly *French*.

51152. CECIL OF CHELWOOD PAPERS. Vol. LXXXII (ff. 317). Correspondence with Thomas C. Foley, Secretary of the Pedestrians' Association; 1929-1945.

51153. CECIL OF CHELWOOD PAPERS. Vol. LXXXIII (ff. 173). Memoranda and other papers of the Pedestrians' Association; 1929-1943. *Copies*. Partly *printed*.

51154 A. CECIL OF CHELWOOD PAPERS. Vol. LXXXIV A (ff. 172). Correspondence with:—
1. ff. 1-125v. Cosmo Gordon Lang, Baron Lang, Archbishop of York and (1928) Canterbury; 1909-1944.
2. ff. 126-172. William Temple, Archbishop of York and (1942) Canterbury; 1931-1936.

51154 B. CECIL OF CHELWOOD PAPERS. Vol. LXXXIV B (ff. 179). Correspondence with:—
1.   ff. 1-81v. William Temple, Archbishop of York and (1942) Canterbury; 1937-1943.
2.   ff. 82-179. George Kennedy Allen Bell, Bishop of Chichester; 1931-1944. The text of the address given by Cecil to the World Conference on Faith and Order in Edinburgh, Aug. 1937, (ff. 24-28) was mostly printed in *All the Way*, pp. 230-233.

51155. CECIL OF CHELWOOD PAPERS. Vol. LXXXV (ff. 169). Draft reports, minutes and other papers of the Archbishops' Commission on the Relations between Church and State; 1931-1934. Partly *printed*.

51156. CECIL OF CHELWOOD PAPERS. Vol. LXXXVI (ff. 233).
1.   ff. 1-38. Correspondence with Geoffrey George Dawson, formerly Robinson, Editor of *The Times*; 1923-1940.
2.   ff. 39-125. Letters addressed to the Editor of *The Times*; 1907-1918. *Copies*, *drafts* and *printed*.
3.   ff. 126-182. Correspondence with Henry Wickham Steed, Editor of *The Times*; 1932-1944.
4.   ff. 183-233. Correspondence with Robert John Thurlow (*al.* Jonathan) Griffin, author; 1935-1938.

51157. CECIL OF CHELWOOD PAPERS. Vol. LXXXVII (ff. 316). Correspondence with:—
1.   ff. 1-65v. His brother, Hugh Richard Heathcote Gascoyne-Cecil, Baron Quickswood; 1908-1944.
2.   ff. 66-123. His brother-in-law, William Waldegrave Palmer, 2nd Earl of Selborne; 1909-1937.
3.   ff. 124-174. His sister, Beatrix Maud Palmer, wife of the preceding; 1909-1945.
4.   ff. 175-230. His niece, Ann Katherine Swynford Lambton, Professor of Persian, University of London; 1936-1945.
5.   ff. 231-316v. His cousin, Blanche Elizabeth Campbell Dugdale, *née* Balfour, wife of Edgar Trevelyan Stratford Dugdale, of the League of Nations Union; 1921-1946.

B. GENERAL CORRESPONDENCE

51158-51192. CECIL OF CHELWOOD PAPERS. Vols. LXXXVIII-CXXII. General correspondence, chronologically arranged; 1904-1953, n.d.
Thirty-five volumes.

51158. Vol. LXXXVIII (ff. 289). 1904-1908.

51159. Vol. LXXXIX (ff. 282). 1909.

51160. Vol. XC (ff. 283). June 1910-June 1913.

51161. Vol. XCI (ff. 251). July 1913-June 1915.

51162. Vol. XCII (ff. 168). Nov. 1915-March 1921.

51163. Vol. XCIII (ff. 195). April 1921-Dec. 1923.

51164. Vol. XCIV (ff. 177). Jan. 1924-Oct. 1926.

51165. Vol. XCV (ff. 203). Nov. 1926-Dec. 1927.

51166. Vol. XCVI (ff. 165). 1928, 1929.

51167. Vol. XCVII (ff. 195). Jan. 1930-Feb. 1932.

51168. Vol. XCVIII (ff. 164). Aug. 1932-Dec. 1933.

51169. Vol. XCIX (ff. 265). 1934.

51170. Vol. C (ff. 254). Jan.-July 1935.

51171. Vol. CI (ff. 239). Aug.-Dec. 1935.

51172. Vol. CII (ff. 214). Jan.-March 1936.

51173. Vol. CIII (ff. 263). April-Aug. 1936.

51174. Vol. CIV (ff. 232). Sept.-Dec. 1936.

51175. Vol. CV (ff. 220). Jan.-May 1937.

51176. Vol. CVI (ff. 175). June-July 1937.

51177. Vol. CVII (ff. 214). Aug.-Oct. 1937.

51178. Vol. CVIII (ff. 204). Nov. 1937-Jan. 1938.

51179. Vol. CIX (ff. 252). Feb.-May 1938.

51180. Vol. CX (ff. 176). June-July 1938.

51181. Vol. CXI (ff. 209). Aug.-Oct. 1938.

51182. Vol. CXII (ff. 218). Nov. 1938-Feb. 1939.

51183. Vol. CXIII (ff. 232). March-Aug. 1939.

51184. Vol. CXIV (ff. 349). Sept. 1939-Jan. 1940.

51185. Vol. CXV (ff. 295). Feb.-July 1940.

51186. Vol. CXVI (ff. 329). Aug. 1940-Jan. 1941.

51187. Vol. CXVII (ff. 424). Feb.-Aug. 1941.

51188. Vol. CXVIII (ff. 389). Sept. 1941-June 1942.

51189. Vol. CXIX (ff. 287). July 1942-Feb. 1943.

51190. Vol. CXX (ff. 402). March-Dec. 1943.

51191. Vol. CXXI (ff. 325). 1944.

51192. Vol. CXXII (ff. 349). 1945-1953; n.d.

C. LITERARY MANUSCRIPTS, ETC.

51193. CECIL OF CHELWOOD PAPERS. Vol. CXXIII (ff. 314). Miscellaneous correspondence relating to Cecil's writings, speeches, etc.; 1912-1945.

51194-51203. CECIL OF CHELWOOD PAPERS. Vols. CXXIV-CXXXIII. Drafts and copies of articles, etc., together with notes for, and drafts and copies of addresses, speeches and broadcast talks; *circa* 1897-1949. Partly *printed*, many annotated with particulars such as the dates and places of publication or delivery.
Ten volumes.

    51194. Vol. CXXIV (ff. 169). *Circa* 1897-1912.

    51195. Vol. CXXV (ff. 280). 1914-1929.

    51196. Vol. CXXVI (ff. 288). 1930, 1931.

    51197. Vol. CXXVII (ff. 495). 1932-1935.

    51198. Vol. CXXVIII (ff. 336). 1936, 1937.

    51199. Vol. CXXIX (ff. 373). 1938, 1939.

    51200. Vol. CXXX (ff. 418). 1940-1943.

    51201. Vol. CXXXI (ff. 262). 1944, 1945.

    51202. Vol. CXXXII (ff. 290). 1946, 1947.

    51203. Vol. CXXXIII (ff. 301). 1948, 1949.

51204. CECIL OF CHELWOOD PAPERS. Vol. CXXXIV (ff. 69). Miscellaneous extracts and quotations; n.d.

INDEX

Aberconway, *Baron.*
— *v.* M'Laren (Charles Benjamin Bright).

Abraham (*Capt.* G.), *official of the League of Nations.*
— Letter from Lord Cecil to Capt. G. Abraham, 1922. *Copy.* 51095, ff. 97-99.

Abraham (L.), *of the British Red Cross Society.*
— Correspondence between Lord Cecil and L. Abraham, 1943. *Signed.* 51190, ff. 296, 302.

Abrahams (A.), *editor, New Zionist Press.*
— Correspondence between Lord Cecil and A. Abrahams, 1938. *Signed.* 51181, ff. 47, 58.

Abyssinia.
— Notice of protest meeting rel. to Abyssinia, 1938. *Printed.* 51179, f. 199.

Accounts.
— Accounts of Imperial War Relief Fund, 1925. 51164, ff. 120-127v.
— Accounts with Lord Cecil from Harrington, Edwards and Cobban (solicitors), 1925. 51164, ff. 128, 129.
— Auditors' Report on High Commission for Refugees of League of Nations, 1936. 51173, ff. 126-129.
— Donations to and payments by the International Peace Campaign, 1936, 1937. 51177, f. 41.
— Receipt to Lord Cecil from National Joint Committee for Spanish Relief, 1938. 51181, f. 30.
— Note to Lord Cecil rel. to royalties from the Hogarth Press, 1940. 51193, f. 183.
— Note rel. to fee paid to Lord Cecil for published contribution to 'Picture Post', 1940. Partly *printed.* 51193, f. 201.
— Notes to Lord Cecil rel. to fees paid for broadcast speeches from B.B.C, 1940-1941. Partly *printed.* 51193, ff. 163, 229.
— Receipt to Trustees of Cecil Peace Prize from Harrington, Edwards and Cobban (solicitors), 1944. Partly *printed.* 51191, f. 11.

Acland (*Sir* Richard Thomas Dyke), *15th Bart.*
— Correspondence between Lord Cecil and R. T. D. Acland, 1938-1941. *Signed.* 51181, ff. 170, 173, 186; 51182, ff. 4, 15, 97, 104; 51183, ff. 58, 60, 67-71, 85, 100; 51184, ff. 146, 169; 51186, ff. 7, 20; 51187, f. 151.

Acland-Hood (Alexander Fuller-).
— *v.* Fuller-Acland-Hood (Alexander).

Acton.
— Reply by Lord Erne to Parliamentary Question of Lord Cecil rel. to Western Avenue at Acton, 1938. *Signed.* 51180, f. 166.

Adams (Samuel Vyvyan Trerice), *M.P.*
— Correspondence between Lord Cecil and S. V. T. Adams, 1941. 51187, ff. 319, 322.

Addington, *3rd Baron.*
— *v.* Hubbard (John Gellibrand).

Addison (Christopher), *1st Viscount Addison.*
— Correspondence between Lord Cecil and Lord Addison, 1942-1950. *Partly signed.* 51188, ff. 160, 286; 51191, ff. 158, 161; 51192, ff. 218-333 *passim.*

Adie (Leslie), *of the Political Intelligence Dept., Foreign Office.*
— Correspondence between Lord Cecil and L. Adie, 1944. 51191, ff. 184, 249.

Aghnides (Thomassis), *Greek diplomatist at the League of Nations.*
— Memorandum by Lord Cecil rel. to conversation with T. Aghnides, 1931. 51100, f. 101.
— Correspondence between Lord Cecil and T. Aghnides, 1943, 1945. *Signed.* 51190, ff. 357, 366; 51192, f. 123.

Agriculture.
— Minutes of meeting between deputation of National Farmers' Union and D. Lloyd George, 1921. *Copy.* 51162, ff. 142-151.

Agüero y Bethancourt (—), *Cuban representative at the League of Nations.*
— Memorandum by Lord Cecil rel. to conversation with — Agüero y Bethancourt, 1926. *Copy.* 51098, f. 7.

Aguilar (Alberto), *Spanish diplomatist.*
— Memorandum by Lord Cecil rel. to conversation with A. Aguilar, 1923. *Copy.* 51096, f. 1.

Aharonian (Awetis), *Armenian nationalist.*
— Letter to Lord Cecil, 1920. *Signed. Fr.* 51095, f. 7.

Ahlefeldt-Laurvig (*Count* Preben Ferdinand), *Danish diplomatist.*
— Letters to Lord Cecil, 1925, 1930. *Signed.* 51097, f. 147; 51167, f. 41.

Air Ministry.
— Telegrams between Air Vice-Marshal W. F. MacNeece and the Air Ministry, 1927. 51104, ff. 78, 81, 82, 90.

Aitken (William Maxwell), *1st Baron Beaverbrook.*
— Letter to Lord Beaverbrook from the Watching Committee of Parliament, 1941-1942. *Draft. Printed.* 51188, f. 241*.
— Letter to Lord Cecil from Lord Beaverbrook, 1942. *Signed.* 51188, f. 211.

Alderson (*Sir* Edward Hall), *K.C.B.; Clerk of the Parliaments.*
— Letters from Lord Cecil to Sir E. H. Alderson, 1934. *Copies.* 51169, ff. 63, 222.

Alderson (Frederick Cecil), *Rector of Lutterworth.*
— Letter to Lord Cecil, 1906. 51158, f. 53.

INDEX

Alexander (Albert Victor), *Earl Alexander of Hillsborough.*
— Correspondence, partly on his behalf, with Lord Cecil, 1930. 51100, ff. 41-45.

Alexander (Horace Gundry), *author and pacifist.*
— Letter to Lord Cecil, 1941. 51187, f. 332.

Allchurch (Cecil E.), *detainee under Regulation 18B.*
— Correspondence between Lord Cecil and C. E. Allchurch, 1942. *Signed.* 51159, ff. 70-72, 121, 139.

Allen (Charles Peter), *P.C.; M.P.*
— Letter to Lord Cecil, 1913. 51161, f. 26.

Allen (Elisabeth Acland), *of the International Peace Campaign.*
— Letter, etc., to Lord Cecil, 1938. *Signed.* 51179, ff. 120-122.

Allen (G.), *writing from Leyton.*
— Letter to Lord Cecil, 1909. 51159, f. 223.

Allen (George) **and Unwin**, *publishers.*
— Letters, etc., to Lord Cecil, 1940. 51193, ff. 195, 296-312.

Allen (*Sir* John Sandeman), *M.P.*
— Letter from Lord Cecil to Sir J. S. Allen, 1936. *Copy.* 51173, f. 102.

Allen (Philip), *of the Home Office.*
— Letter to A. N. Lancaster from P. Allen on behalf of Miss A. Lenfestey, 1940. *Signed.* 51186, f. 220.

Allen (Reginald Clifford), *Baron Allen of Hurtwood.*
— Correspondence between Lord Cecil and Lord Allen, 1936, 1937. Partly *signed.* 51173, ff. 208-217, 223-228; 51174, ff. 67-69, 104-108, 114, 120, 143; 51177, ff. 172, 175; 51178, ff. 116, 121.

Almazan (*Dr.* Leonides Andreu), *Mexican diplomatist.*
— Correspondence between Lord Cecil and Dr. L. A. Almazan, 1935, 1936. *Signed.* 51171, ff. 221, 227; 51173, ff. 28, 41.

Alvarez del Vayo (Julio), *Spanish diplomatist.*
— Correspondence, including telegram, between Lord Cecil and J. Alvarez del Vayo, 1938. 51179, ff. 84, 119.

American Academy of Political and Social Science.
— *v.* Patterson (Ernest Minor).

American Committee for the Independence of Armenia.
— *v.* Gerard (James W.).

Amery (Leopold Charles Maurice Stennett), *P.C.; statesman.*
— Memorandum to Lord Cecil rel. to the Imperial Fund, 1912. *Copy.* 51160, f. 186.
— Correspondence, partly on his behalf, with Lord Cecil, 1912-1945. 51072, ff. 214-274; 51098, ff. 150, 155.
— Letter to Winston Churchill from L. C. M. S. Amery, 1927. *Copy.* 51072, f. 268.

Ames (*Sir* Herbert Brown), *Lecturer for Carnegie Endowment for International Peace.*
— Correspondence between Lord Cecil and Sir H. B. Ames, 1937. 51178, ff. 8, 24.

Ammon (Charles George), *Baron Ammon.*
— Correspondence between Lord Cecil and Lord Ammon, 1945. *Signed.* 51192, ff. 214, 215.

Anderson (*Sir* Alan Garrett), *G.B.E.*
— Correspondence between Lord Cecil and Sir A. G. Anderson, 1936. *Signed.* 51173, ff. 43, 48.

INDEX

Anderson (*Sir* Francis), *President, League of Nations Union, New South Wales Branch.*
— Letter to Lord Cecil, 1938. *Signed.* 51179, f. 207.

Anderson (John), *1st Viscount Waverley.*
— Letter from Lord Cecil to J. Anderson, 1940. *Copy.* 51185, f. 238.

Andreades (Andrew), *Dean of the Faculty of Law, Athens.*
— Correspondence between Lord Cecil and A. Andreades, 1924. 51164, ff. 7, 15.

Andrew (A. S.), *of Sir Isaac Pitman and Sons.*
— Correspondence, etc., between Lord Cecil and A. S. Andrew, 1937. Partly *printed. Signed.* 51193, ff. 100-104.

Andrews (Wilfred), *Chairman, Rotary International.*
— Correspondence between Lord Cecil and W. Andrews, 1931. *Signed.* 51167, ff. 151, 153.

Angell (*Sir* Norman), *author and journalist.*
— Correspondence between Lord Cecil and Sir N. Angell, 1924-1943. Partly *signed.* 51140, ff. 1-75.

Ansell (F. E.), *of Streetly.*
— Letter to E. P. Beale from F. E. Ansell, 1941. 51187, f. 42.

Apponyi (*Count* Albert), *Hungarian statesman.*
— Statement to Press on revision of Treaty of Versailles, 1931. *Copy.* 51167, f. 85.

Apsley (*Lady* Violet Emily Mildred).
— Correspondence between Lord Cecil and Lady V. E. M. Apsley, 1937. 51136, ff. 131-137.

Archdale (*Mrs* Helen Alexander), *journalist; widow of Maj. T. M. Archdale.*
— Correspondence between Lord Cecil and Mrs H. A. Archdale, 1944, 1945. *Signed.* 51191, ff. 167, 281; 51192, ff. 216, 221.

Argyropoulu (P. A.), *Greek politician.*
— Correspondence between Lord Cecil and P. A. Argyropoulu, 1936-1943. *Signed. Fr.* 51174, f. 220; 51175, f. 2; 51189, ff. 219, 269.

Armitage (John), *of The Fortnightly.*
— Correspondence between Lord Cecil and J. Armitage, 1941. 51193, ff. 232, 234-236, 245, 248-254.

Armstrong (George Gilbert), *author and journalist.*
— Correspondence between Lord Cecil and G. G. Armstrong, 1941. 51187, ff. 86, 163, 217.

Army, *of England.*
— Memorandum by Lord Cecil rel. to treatment of wounded in France, circa 1914-1915. *Copy.* 51162, f. 5.

Arnold (*Miss*—), *of Montague Burton, Ltd.*
— Letter to Miss — Arnold on behalf of the League of Nations Union, 1942. *Copy.* 51188, f. 256.

Arnold (Ralph Crispian Marshall), *of the Royal Institute of International Affairs.*
— Letter to Miss I. M. Butler from R. C. M. Arnold, 1933. *Signed.* 51168, f. 134.
— Letter, etc., to Lord Cecil, 1933. *Signed.* 51168, ff. 150-159.

Arnold-Forster (Katherine), *wife of William Arnold-Forster.*
— Correspondence between Lord Cecil and K. Arnold-Forster, 1936. *Signed.* 51140, ff. 84, 85.

Arnold-Forster (William), *writer on international affairs.*
— Correspondence between Lord Cecil and W. Arnold-Forster, 1930-1948. Partly *signed*. 51140, ff. 76-208v.
— Proposed amendments to League of Nations Union pamphlet, 'The Atlantic Charter', 1942. *Printed.* 51188, ff. 327-328v.
— The British Way and Purpose booklet 18, 'Today and Tomorrow. Britain and the Peace' by W. Arnold-Forster, 1944. *Printed.* 51140, ff. 144-163v.
— Labour Party booklet, 'The United Nations Charter Examined' by W. Arnold-Forster, 1946. *Printed.* 51140, ff. 177-202v.

Art. Miscellaneous.
— List of subscribers to portrait of Lord Cecil, 1931. 51167, ff. 134-146.

Ashby (*Mrs* Margery Corbett), *Chairman, Women's Liberal Federation.*
— Correspondence between Lord Cecil and Mrs M. C. Ashby, 1936-1943. Partly *signed*. 51173, f. 185; 51174, f. 141; 51175, ff. 114, 143; 51176, ff. 26, 30; 51186, f. 165; 51187, ff. 224-226, 304; 51188, ff. 104, 107; 51190, ff. 36, 40.

Ashfield, *Baron.*
— *v.* Stanley (Albert Henry).

Ashforth (George E.), *County Surveyor of Cheshire.*
— Letters, etc., to Lord Cecil, 1936, 1937. *Signed.* 51174, ff. 182-187; 51175, ff. 161-168.

Ashley (Wilfred William), *Baron Mount Temple.*
— Letter to Lord Cecil, 1908. 51158, f. 246.

Ashley-Cooper (Anthony), *9th Earl of Shaftesbury.*
— Letter to Lord Cecil, 1910. 51160, f. 2.

Ashworth (H.), *of Sheffield.*
— Letter to Lord Cecil, 1938. *Copy.* 51179, f. 82.

Asquith, *Baroness.*
— *v.* Carter (Helen Violet Bonham).

Asquith (Betty Constance), *wife of A. M. Asquith.*
— Correspondence, including telegram, between Lord Cecil and B. C. Asquith, 1940. 51186, ff. 136, 137, 235-240v.

Asquith (Emma Alice Margaret), *wife of Herbert, 1st Earl of Oxford and Asquith.*
— Correspondence between Lord Cecil and Lady Oxford and Asquith, 1922-1944. 51073, ff. 40-58.

Asquith (Herbert Henry), *1st Earl of Oxford and Asquith; Prime Minister.*
— Correspondence, partly on his behalf, with Lord Cecil, 1913-1922. 51073, ff. 1-39.
— Letter to H. H. Asquith from Sir A. H. D. R. Steel-Maitland, 1921. *Copy.* 51071, f. 74.
— Letter to G. G. Dawson from J. Ramsay MacDonald, S. Baldwin and Lord Oxford and Asquith, 1924. *Copy.* 51097, f. 83.

Astor (Nancy Witcher), *wife of Waldorf, 2nd Viscount Astor.*
— Letter, etc., on her behalf, to Lord Cecil, 1927. 51165, ff. 123-125.

Astor (Waldorf), *2nd Viscount Astor.*
— Correspondence between Lord Cecil and Lord Astor, 1938-1943. *Signed.* 51182, ff. 118-121, 161, 171; 51190, ff. 371-373, 376.

Atholl, *Duchess of.*
— *v.* Stewart-Murray (Katherine Marjorie).

Atkinson (*Dr.* Henry A.), *Sec., The Church Peace Union, New York.*
— Letter, etc., to Miss I. M. Butler from Dr. H. A. Atkinson, 1937. *Signed.* 51177, f. 152.
— Correspondence, including telegrams, between Lord Cecil and Dr. H. A. Atkinson, 1937-1943. *Signed.* 51177, ff. 189, 192; 51178, ff. 46, 59; 51182, ff. 158, 175; 51189, ff. 177, 251.

Atkinson (Robert d'Escourt), *former Fellow of Hertford College, Oxford.*
— Correspondence between Lord Cecil and R. d'Escourt Atkinson, 1936. 51173, ff. 92, 94.

Atlantic Charter.
— League of Nations Union pamphlet concerning text of and proposed amendments to Atlantic Charter, 1942. 51188, ff. 321-328v, 386-389.

Attlee (Clement Richard), *1st Earl Attlee; Prime Minister.*
— Correspondence between Lord Cecil and C. R. Attlee, 1936-1953. Mostly *signed.* 51174, ff. 109, 125, 130; 51175, ff. 123, 128, 132, 139, 144; 51185, ff. 255, 257; 51192, ff. 239-346 *passim.*

Attolico (Bernardo), *Italian diplomatist.*
— Correspondence between Lord Cecil and B. Attolico, 1918, 1926. *Signed.* 51094, ff. 157, 158; 51098, f. 9.

Auckland, *7th Baron.*
— *v.* Eden (Geoffrey Morton).

Augspurg (Anita), *German emigrant in Zürich.*
— Correspondence between Lord Cecil and A. Augspurg, 1938. *Signed.* 51181, ff. 157, 165, 199; 51182, f. 12.

Avenol (Joseph Louis Anne), *Sec. General of the League of Nations.*
— Memorandum from Lord Cecil to J. L. A. Avenol, 1926. 51098, f. 14.
— Memorandum by Lord Cecil rel. to conversation with J. L. A. Avenol, 1931. 51100, f. 101.

Avon, *1st Earl of.*
— *v.* Eden (Robert Anthony).

Ayala (Ramon Perez de), *Spanish diplomatist.*
— Correspondence between Lord Cecil and R. P. de Ayala, 1933. *Signed.* Partly *Fr.* 51101, ff. 72, 75, 79.

Aydelotte (Frank), *President of Swarthmore College, Pennsylvania.*
— Correspondence, including telegrams, between Lord Cecil and F. Aydelotte, 1938-1944. *Signed.* 51181, f. 192; 51182, f. 32; 51187, f. 339; 51188, f. 18; 51190, ff. 342, 379, 387, 388; 51191, ff. 113, 145, 265, 300.

Azcarate y Florez (Pablo de), *Spanish diplomatist.*
— Letters, etc., to Sir A. Cadogan from P. de Azcarate y Florez, 1924. *Copies.* Partly *Fr.* 51097, ff. 74-78.
— Letter to J. E. Drummond from P. de Azcarate y Florez, 1932. *Signed. Fr.* 51112, ff. 148-153.
— Correspondence, including telegrams, partly on his behalf, with Lord Cecil, 1936-1945. Partly *signed.* Partly *Fr.* 51174, ff. 146-149; 51175, ff. 43, 45; 51182, f. 77; 51185, ff. 67, 78; 51186, ff. 145, 196, 218; 51187, ff. 37, 48; 51189, f. 65; 51191, ff. 202, 247; 51192, ff. 77, 80, 86, 118, 127, 141.

B

Baber (Jocelyn), *of East Grinstead.*
— Letter, etc., to Lord Cecil, 1944. *Signed.* 51191, f. 119.

Bacon (E. Basil), *of Bradford.*
— Correspondence between Lord Cecil and E. B. Bacon, 1940. 51186, ff. 142, 157, 167, 173, 205, 222.

Baddeley (V. C. Clinton-).
— *v.* Clinton-Baddeley (V. C.).

Baddeley (*Sir* Vincent Wilberforce), *K.C.B.*
— Letter to Lord Cecil, 1940. *Signed.* 51186, f. 29.

Badeley (Henry John Fanshawe), *Baron Badeley.*
— Correspondence, partly on his behalf, with Lord Cecil, 1941, 1942. Partly *signed.* 51187, ff. 108-110v, 117, 119, 245, 250-252; 51188, ff. 249-251, 270.

Baden-Powell (Robert Stephenson), *1st Baron Baden-Powell.*
— Letter from Lord Cecil to Lord Baden-Powell, 1936. *Copy.* 51174, f. 229.

Baer (*Gen.* M. de), *Belgian lawyer.*
— Correspondence between Lord Cecil and Gen. M. de Baer, 1942-1945. *Signed.* 51188, f. 288; 51189, ff. 9, 17, 130, 223; 51190, ff. 274-275v, 280, 282; 51192, ff. 13-15.
— Memorandum by Miss E. V. Lazarus rel. to conversation with Gen. M. de Baer, 1945. *Signed.* 51192, f. 18.

Baerlein (*Mrs* Gladys L.), *wife of H. Baerlein; Vice Chairman, The Women's Liberal Federation.*
— Correspondence, partly on her behalf, with Lord Cecil, 1937. *Signed.* 51175, ff. 51, 53, 55.

Bailey (*Sir* Abe), *1st Bart.*
— Correspondence, including telegram, between Lord Cecil and Sir A. Bailey, 1936, 1937. 51173, ff. 68, 107, 112, 125; 51175, f. 201.

Bailey (Gerald), *Sec., National Peace Council.*
— Correspondence, etc., between Lord Cecil and G. Bailey, 1936-1944. *Signed.* Partly *printed.* 51172, ff. 16-23; 51173, ff. 141, 147; 51176, ff. 80, 86; 51178, ff. 141, 153, 160-162; 51179, ff. 223, 224; 51181, ff. 153-156, 164; 51184, ff. 55, 74; 51186, f. 68; 51189, ff. 80, 99; 51191, f. 138.

Bailey (J. James), *of the League of Nations Union, Harrow.*
— Correspondence between Lord Cecil and J. J. Bailey, 1929. *Signed.* 51166, ff. 111-113, 123, 142, 147-150.

Baird (John Lawrence), *1st Viscount Stonehaven.*
— Letter to Lord Stonehaven from Sir H. W. Gepp, 1926. 51072, f. 245.

Baker (Allan), *of Easton-on-the-Hill.*
— Correspondence between Lord Cecil and A. Baker, 1941. 51187, ff. 87, 102.

Baker (James Carthew), *of Taunton.*
— Correspondence between Lord Cecil and J. C. Baker, 1938. 51179, ff. 191, 196.

Baker (Philip John) *afterw.* **Noel-Baker.**
— *v.* Noel-Baker (Philip John).

Bakstansky (Lavy), *General Sec., The Zionist Federation.*
— Correspondence between Lord Cecil and L. Bakstansky, 1941-1946. *Signed.* 51187, ff. 123, 165, 173; 51189, ff. 69, 135, 232, 236; 51190, f. 57; 51192, ff. 7, 11, 224, 227.

Balcarres, *10th Earl of.*
— *v.* Lindsay (David Alexander Edward).

Baldwin (Stanley), *1st Earl Baldwin;* Prime Minister.
— Letter to S. Baldwin from Lord Novar, 1923. *Copy.* 51080, f. 108.
— Correspondence, partly on his behalf, with Lord Cecil, 1923-1939. Partly *signed.* 51080.
— Letter to G. G. Dawson from J. Ramsay MacDonald, S. Baldwin and Lord Oxford and Asquith, 1924. *Copy.* 51097, f. 83.
— Telegrams from Lord Cecil to S. Baldwin, 1927. 51104, ff. 85, 88, 92.
— Telegrams between S. Baldwin and W. C. Bridgeman, 1927. Mostly *printed.* 51104, ff. 153-222 *passim.*

Balfour (Arthur James), *1st Earl of Balfour;* Prime Minister.
— Correspondence, including telegram, partly on his behalf, with Lord Cecil, 1906-1930. Mostly *signed.* Partly *copy.* 51071 A; 51071 B, f. 71; 51104, f. 24.
— Correspondence between A. J. Balfour and S. C. Hunt, 1907. Partly *draft.* 51071 A, ff. 3, 5.
— Letter to A. J. Balfour from M. P. A. Hankey, 1918. *Signed.* 51094, f. 51.
— Correspondence between Lord Cecil and C. H. Tufton, partly on behalf of A. J. Balfour, 1922, 1923. 51071 A, f. 80; 51095, ff. 186, 198.

Balfour (Blanche Elizabeth Campbell) *afterw.* **Dugdale.**
— *v.* Dugdale (Blanche Elizabeth Campbell).

Balfour (Elizabeth Edith), *wife of Gerald, 2nd Earl of Balfour.*
— Correspondence between Lord Cecil and Lady Balfour, 1935, 1940. 51170, ff. 69, 72, 85; 51186, ff. 119-127, 133, 134, 143.

Balfour (*Lady* Frances), *wife of E. J. A. Balfour.*
— Letters to Lord Cecil, 1906, 1912. 51158, f. 49; 51160, f. 122.

Balfour (*Lt.-Col.* Francis Cecil Campbell), *C.B.E.; Sudan Political Service.*
— Correspondence between Lord Cecil and Lt.-Col. F. C. C. Balfour, 1918. 51094, ff. 100, 120-126, 165.

Balfour (Gerald William), *2nd Earl of Balfour.*
— Letter to Lord Cecil, 1941. 51187, f. 369.

Balfour of Burleigh, *6th Baron.*
— *v.* Bruce (Alexander Hugh).

Ball (C. F.), *of Letchworth.*
— Letter to Lord Cecil, 1918. 51162, f. 69.

Balutis (Bronius K.), *Lithuanian diplomatist.*
— Letter from Lord Cecil to B. K. Balutis, 1942. *Copy.* 51188, f. 331.

Banbury (Frederick George), *1st Baron Banbury.*
— Letter to Lord Cecil, 1912. 51160, f. 101.

Barbour (George Freeland), *D. Phil.; author.*
— Correspondence between Lord Cecil and G. F. Barbour, 1937-1945. *Signed.* 51154 B, ff. 20, 21; 51186, ff. 202, 252; 51192, ff. 163, 170.

Barclay (Edwin), *President of Liberia.*
— Telegrams from Lord Cecil to E. Barclay, 1932, 1933. 51101, ff. 11, 60.
— Letter, etc., to E. Barclay from M. D. Mackenzie, 1933. *Copy.* 51101, ff. 86-94.

Bardsley (Cuthbert Killick Norman), *Rector of Woolwich.*
— Letter to Lord Cecil, 1941. *Printed.* 51188, f. 22.

INDEX

Baring (Evelyn), *1st Earl of Cromer.*
— Memorandum rel. to Lord Cromer and the Unionist Free Trade Party, 1908. *Draft.* 51158, ff. 284-288.
— Correspondence between Lord Cecil and Lord Cromer, 1908, 1909. 51072, ff. 1-49.

Baring (Maurice), *author.*
— Correspondence between Lord Cecil and M. Baring, 1935. 51170, ff. 22-26v.

Baring (Rowland Thomas), *2nd Earl of Cromer.*
— Correspondence between Lord Cecil and Lord Cromer as Lord Chamberlain, 1937. 51175, ff. 198, 202.

Barker (Aldred Farrer), *former Professor of Textile Industries, Leeds University.*
— Correspondence between Lord Cecil and A. F. Barker, 1940. *Signed.* 51186, ff. 47-51, 93.

Barker (*Sir* Ernest), *F.B.A.*
— Correspondence between Lord Cecil and Sir E. Barker, 1941, 1944. *Signed.* 51187, ff. 114, 125; 51191, f. 182.

Barker (V. Duckworth), *of the B.B.C.*
— Letter to Miss E. V. Lazarus from V. D. Barker, 1941. *Signed.* 51188, f. 34.

Barling (*Miss* Edith M.), *daughter of Sir H. G. Barling.*
— Correspondence between Lord Cecil and Miss E. M. Barling, 1944. 51191, ff. 280, 286.

Barling (*Sir* Harry Gilbert), *Bart.; surgeon.*
— Letter to Lord Cecil, 1935. 51170, f. 138.

Barlow (*Sir* Clement Anderson Montague-).
— *v.* Montague-Barlow (*Sir* Clement Anderson).

Barlow (*Sir* Thomas), *1st Bart.*
— Correspondence between Lord Cecil and Sir T. Barlow, 1938. *Signed.* 51179, ff. 104-106, 118.

Barnes (Alfred John), *M.P.*
— Letter to Lord Cecil, 1941. *Printed.* 51187, f. 74.

Barnes (George Nicoll), *P.C.*
— Correspondence between Lord Cecil and G. N. Barnes, 1936. *Signed.* 51173, ff. 174, 197, 222.

Barnes (*Maj.* Harry), *M.P.*
— Letter to Sir B. Robertson from Maj. H. Barnes, 1922. *Copy.* 51163, f. 80.

Barnes (James Strachey), *author.*
— Letter to Sir D. Henderson from J. S. Barnes, 1921. *Copy.* 51095, f. 22.
— Letter to P. H. Kerr from J. S. Barnes, 1921. *Copy.* 51095, f. 24.
— Correspondence between Lord Cecil and J. S. Barnes, 1925. Partly *signed.* 51097, ff. 113-117v.

Barrington (Rupert Edward Selborne), *son of Walter, 9th Viscount Barrington.*
— Correspondence between Lord Cecil and R. E. S. Barrington, 1941. Partly *printed* and *signed.* 51187, ff. 175, 176, 191.

Barrington-Ward (Robert M'Gowan), *Editor of The Times.*
— Correspondence between Lord Cecil and R. M'G. Barrington-Ward, 1936, 1942. *Signed.* 51156, f. 34; 51189, ff. 191, 195.

Barrow (Walter), *Pro-Chancellor of the University of Birmingham.*
— Correspondence between Lord Cecil and W. Barrow, 1936, 1938. Partly *signed.* 51173, ff. 230, 235; 51182, ff. 81, 82, 85.

Bartholdy (Albrecht Mendelssohn-).
— *v.* Mendelssohn-Bartholdy (Albrecht).

INDEX

Bartlett (Vernon Oldfield), *author*.
— Correspondence between Lord Cecil and V. O. Bartlett, 1923-1944. *Signed.* 51096, ff. 3, 7, 25; 51099, f. 5; 51181, f. 103; 51182, ff. 9, 16, 23; 51191, f. 243.
— Notes by V. O. Bartlett for speech at Peace Campaign meeting in Leeds, 1938. *Copy.* 51179, f. 109.

Barton (W.), *of the Stockport and District European Famine Relief Committee.*
— Letter to Lord Cecil, 1944. 51191, f. 59.

Bate (Frederick), *of the National Broadcasting Co. of America.*
— Letter to Lord Cecil, 1936. *Signed.* 51193, f. 68.

Bate (Herbert Newell), *Dean of York.*
— Correspondence between Lord Cecil and H. N. Bate, 1935. 51171, ff. 8, 9.

Bates (*Sir* Percy Elly), *4th Bart.*
— Letter from Lord Cecil to Sir P. E. Bates, 1918. *Copy.* 51093, f. 172.

Bathurst (Algernon Harvey), *of The Christian Science Monitor, London.*
— Letter to G. H. Locock from A. H. Bathurst, 1916. *Signed.* 51092, f. 65.
— Letter to J. D. Gregory from A. H. Bathurst, 1916. *Signed.* 51092, f. 75.

Bathurst (Charles), *1st Viscount Bledisloe.*
— Correspondence between Lord Cecil and Lord Bledisloe, 1909-1931. Partly *signed.* 51159, f. 251; 51163, f. 58; 51164, ff. 1-3v, 72, 83-101v, 103; 51167, ff. 63, 68.

Batten (Lauriston Leonard), *K.C.*
— Letter to Lord Cecil, 1909. 51159, f. 128.

Batterbee (*Sir* Harry Fagg), *G.C.M.G.*
— Correspondence between Lord Cecil and Sir H. F. Batterbee, 1930. *Signed.* 51100, ff. 1, 2.

Battley (H. A.), *Sec., World Brotherhood Federation.*
— Letter, etc., to Lord Cecil, 1940. *Signed.* 51186, ff. 56-59.

Baxendale (Arthur Salisbury), *author.*
— Correspondence between Lord Cecil and A. S. Baxendale, 1939. 51183, ff. 2, 13.

Baxter (Charles William), *C.M.G.; of the Foreign Office.*
— Letter to S. A. Heald from C. W. Baxter, 1934. *Signed.* 51082, ff. 228-231.

Bazley-White (John), *M.P.*
— Letter to Lord Cecil, 1912. 51160, f. 89.

Beach (Michael Edward Hicks-).
— *v.* Hicks-Beach (Michael Edward).

Beaconsfield, *Earl of.*
— *v.* Disraeli (Benjamin).

Beale (A. Lucy), *wife of E. P. Beale.*
— Correspondence between Lord Cecil and A. L. Beale on behalf of her husband, 1941. 51187, ff. 7, 29, 40.

Beale (Edmund Phipson), *Pro-Chancellor of Birmingham University.*
— Letter to E. P. Beale from F. E. Ansell, 1941. 51187, f. 42.
— Correspondence, partly on his behalf, with Lord Cecil, 1941-1945. Mostly *signed.* 51187, ff. 7, 29, 40, 314; 51188, ff. 303, 311; 51189, f. 99; 51190, ff. 101, 112, 168, 386; 51191, ff. 4-322v *passim*; 51192, ff. 17, 19, 194, 201.

Beamish (Margaret Antonia), *wife of Rear-Adm. T. P. H. Beamish.*
— Letters to Lord Cecil, 1941, 1944. 51187, f. 79; 51191, f. 244.

Beamish (*Rear-Adm.* Tufton Percy Hamilton), *M.P.*

— Correspondence between Lord Cecil and Rear-Adm. T. P. H. Beamish, 1944. 51191, ff. 14, 90, 93.

Beauchamp, *7th Earl.*

— *v.* Lygon (William).

Beaufort-Palmer (Francis), *Sec., Abyssinia Association.*

— Correspondence between Lord Cecil and F. Beaufort-Palmer, 1938. *Signed.* 51179, ff. 198, 200, 217, 219; 51181, ff. 128, 147; 51182, f. 11.

Beaumont (Hubert), *M.P.*

— Correspondence between Lord Cecil and H. Beaumont, 1939. *Signed.* 51182, f. 218; 51183, ff. 1, 19.

Beaverbrook, *Baron.*

— *v.* Aitken (William Maxwell).

Beazley (*Sir* Charles Raymond).

— Correspondence between Lord Cecil and Sir C. R. Beazley, 1936. 51172, ff. 189, 197, 205; 51173, ff. 59, 74.

Bedford, *12th Duke of.*

— *v.* Russell (Hastings William Sackville).

Beecroft (Edward R.), *of Tunbridge Wells.*

— Correspondence between Lord Cecil and E. R. Beecroft, 1938. *Signed.* 51182, ff. 45, 57.

Behrens (Beatrice Mary), *wife of Sir L. F. Behrens.*

— Letter to Lord Cecil, 1941. 51186, f. 263.

Behrens (*Sir* Leonard Frederick).

— Correspondence, etc., between Lord Cecil and Sir L. F. Behrens, 1935-1948. *Signed.* 51171, f. 45; 51179, f. 97; 51184, ff. 2, 9; 51185, ff. 195, 203, 253-254, 256; 51186, ff. 85, 86, 264, 273; 51187, ff. 88, 101, 283-285, 306; 51186, ff. 85, 86, 264, 273; 51187, ff. 88, 101, 283-285, 306; 51191, ff. 308-309v, 311; 51192, ff. 291, 297.

— Letter, etc., to Sir L. F. Behrens from I. R. Ewing, 1941. *Signed.* 51186, f. 258.

— Speech by Sir L. F. Behrens to the National League of Young Liberals at Bradford, 1941. *Printed.* 51187, f. 284.

Belisha (Leslie Hore-), *Baron Hore-Belisha.*

— *v.* Hore-Belisha (Leslie).

Bell (*Sir* Francis Henry Dillon), *G.C.M.G.*

— Correspondence between Lord Cecil and Sir F. H. D. Bell, 1926. 51098, ff. 101-103.

Bell (George Kennedy Allen), *Bishop of Chichester.*

— Correspondence between Lord Cecil and Bishop of Chichester, 1931-1944. Partly *signed.* 51154 B, ff. 82-179.

— Memorandum by Bishop of Chichester rel. to interview with Sir S. J. G. Hoare, 1938. *Copy.* 51154 B, f. 100.

Bell (Gertrude Margaret Lowthian), *Oriental Sec. to the Civil Commissioner of Iraq.*

— Correspondence between Lord Cecil and G. M. L. Bell, 1921-1924. 51162, f. 160; 51163, ff. 1, 167, 187; 51164, f. 9.

Bell (*Sir* Hugh), *2nd Bart.*

— Correspondence between Lord Cecil and Sir H. Bell, 1928. *Signed.* 51166, ff. 33-37.

Bell (Nancy E.), *Sec., British National Committee, International Peace Campaign.*
— Correspondence between Lord Cecil and N. E. Bell, 1936-1938. *Signed.* 51143, f. 100; 51174, f. 165; 51179, f. 4; 51181, f. 32.
— Report, 1937. *Copy.* 51175, ff. 89-92.
— Correspondence between N. E. Bell and Miss I. M. Butler, 1938, 1939. 51180, f. 45; 51181, ff. 32, 50; 51182, ff. 153, 193, 202-206.

Bellairs (Carlyon), *M.P.*
— Letter to Lord Cecil, *circa* 1912-1922. 51163, f. 90.

Bellman (*Sir* Harold), *Chairman, National Association of Building Societies.*
— Correspondence between Lord Cecil and Sir H. Bellman, 1934. *Signed.* 51169, ff. 226, 228, 230.

Belshaw ([T?]), *writing from Cricklewood, London.*
— Letters to Lord Cecil, 1909. 51159, ff. 8, 112.

Benavente (Jacinto), *Spanish dramatist and poet.*
— Telegram to Lord Cecil, 1938. *Copy.* 51179, f. 86.

Beneš (Eduard), *President of Czechoslovakia.*
— Memoranda rel. to interviews with E. Beneš, 1923-1931. 51096, ff. 41, 137; 51100, f. 143.
— Correspondence between Lord Cecil and E. Beneš, 1923-1944. *Signed.* Partly *printed.* Partly *Fr.* 51095, f. 152; 51169, f. 192; 51170, f. 231; 51171, f. 99; 51172, ff. 8, 37; 51177, f. 203; 51181, f. 166; 51182, f. 8; 51183, ff. 209, 210; 51185, ff. 233, 277, 290; 51186, f. 90; 51187, ff. 32, 342, 354; 51189, f. 188; 51190, ff. 126, 136; 51191, ff. 192, 236; 51193, f. 184.
— Letter to Sir J. Stavridi from E. Beneš, 1932. *Signed.* 51101, f. 37.
— Letter to President Beneš from Quo Tai-chi, 1934. *Copy.* 51101, f. 153.
— Letter to E. Beneš from H. G. Wells, 1938. *Copy.* 51181, f. 166.
— Memorandum rel. to proposed Nobel Prize for E. Beneš, 1939. 51182, f. 42.

Beneš (Hana), *wife of President E. Beneš.*
— Letter and telegram to Lord Cecil from H. Beneš, 1940, 1943. Partly *signed.* 51186, f. 100; 51190, f. 128.

Benn (William Wedgwood), *1st Viscount Stansgate.*
— Correspondence between Lord Cecil and Lord Stansgate, 1931-1945. Partly *signed.* 51100, f. 130; 51188, f. 151; 51192, ff. 154-156, 193.

Bennett (Andrew), *Sec. and Registrar, University of St. Andrews.*
— Letter to Lord Cecil, 1926. *Signed.* 51164, f. 146.

Bennett (*Sir* John Wheeler Wheeler-).
— *v.* Wheeler-Bennett (*Sir* John Wheeler).

Bennett (*Sir* Reginald), *Vice-Chancellor, The Primrose League.*
— Letter to Lord Cecil, 1913. *Signed.* 51161, f. 28.

Bentinck (*Lord* Henry Cavendish), *M.P.*
— Correspondence between Lord Cecil and Lord H. C. Bentinck, 1908-1913. 51158, ff. 167-169v, 171-172v; 51160, ff. 209, 213, 234; 51161, f. 42.

Bentinck (Victor Frederick William Cavendish-).
— *v.* Cavendish-Bentinck (Victor Frederick William).

Bentwich (Norman), *Professor of International Relations, Jerusalem.*
— Letter to Miss I. M. Butler from N. Bentwich, 1934. *Signed.* 51145, f. 33.

Beresford (*Adm.* Charles William de la Poer), *Baron Beresford.*
— Letter to Lord Cecil, 1912. 51160, f. 134.

Berkeley (*Capt.* Reginald Cheyne), *of the League of Nations Union.*
— Correspondence between Lord Cecil and Capt. R. C. Berkeley, 1921, 1922. Partly *signed.* 51162, f. 126; 51163, ff. 86-89.

Bernstein (Herman), *U.S. author and diplomatist.*
— Correspondence between Lord Cecil and H. Bernstein, 1926. *Signed.* 51164, ff. 172-174.

Bernstorff (*Count* Johann Heinrich Andreas Hermann), *German diplomatist.*
— Memorandum by Lord Cecil rel. to conversation with Count J. H. A. H. Bernstorff, 1931. 51100, f. 99.

Bertie (Francis Leveson), *1st Viscount Bertie of Thame.*
— Letter to G. B. Clemenceau from Lord Bertie, 1918. *Copy. Fr.* 51093, f. 88.

Bertram (Henry), *of the Junior Carlton Club.*
— Letters to Lord Cecil, 1909, 1913. 51159, f. 5; 51161, f. 40.

Bessborough, *9th Earl of.*
— *v.* Ponsonby (Vere Brabazon).

Bethancourt (— Agüero y).
— *v.* Agüero y Bethancourt (—).

Bethlen (*Count* Stephen), *Hungarian statesman.*
— Statement to Press on revision of Treaty of Versailles, 1931. *Copy.* 51167, f. 88.

Beveridge (William Henry), *Baron Beveridge.*
— Correspondence on his behalf with Lord Cecil, 1935. 51170, ff. 110, 114.

— Letter, etc., to G. G. A. Murray from W. H. Beveridge, 1939. *Signed.* 51133, ff. 122-125.

Bevin (Ernest), *M.P.; P.C.; statesman.*
— Correspondence, partly on his behalf, with Lord Cecil, 1945-1948. Mostly *signed.* 51192, ff. 133-302 *passim.*

Bevir (*Sir* Anthony), *K.C.V.O.*
— Correspondence between E. C. Henty and Sir A. Bevir, 1926. *Signed.* 51098, ff. 86, 87.

Biddulph (*Col.* W. H.), *of the League of Nations Union, Warwickshire and Birmingham Federal Council.*
— Correspondence between Lord Cecil and Col. W. H. Biddulph, 1940. 51186, ff. 98, 99.

Bienstock (V. M.), *of the Jewish Telegraphic Agency.*
— Correspondence between Lord Cecil and V. M. Bienstock, 1936. *Signed.* 51173, ff. 229, 240.

Bigot (A. L. Th. L.), *of Amsterdam.*
— Correspondence between Lord Cecil and A. L. Th. L. Bigot, 1940. *Signed.* 51184, ff. 306, 307, 327.

Bigwood (Edouard Jean), *of the Belgian Commission for the Study of Post-War Problems, London.*
— Correspondence between Lord Cecil and E. J. Bigwood, 1942. *Signed.* 51189, ff. 77, 81.

Bingham (George Charles), *5th Earl of Lucan.*
— Reply by Lord Lucan to Parliamentary Question of Lord Cecil rel. to German refugees, 1933. *Signed.* 51168, f. 87.
— Correspondence between Lord Cecil and Lord Lucan, 1938, 1939. Partly *signed.* 51180, ff. 77-82v; 51183, ff. 43-44v.

Binns (R.), *correspondence editor, The Daily Telegraph.*
— Letter, etc., to Lord Cecil from R. Binns, 1937. *Signed.* 51177, f. 88.

Birkeland (Peter Hersleb), *Norwegian diplomatist.*
— Letters to Lord Cecil from P. H. Birkeland, 1925. *Signed.* 51097, ff. 143, 150.

Birkenhead, *1st Earl of.*
— *v.* Smith (Frederick Edwin).

Bismarck (*Count* Otto von), *German diplomatist.*
— Correspondence between Lord Cecil and Count O. von Bismarck, 1935. *Signed.* 51171, ff. 112, 121.

Bisonieks (George W.) *al.* **Bisseneek.**
— *v.* Bisseneek (George W.).

Bisseneek (George W.) *al.* **Bisonieks**, *Latvian banker and diplomatist.*
— Letter, etc., to Lord Cecil from G. W. Bisseneek, 1923. *Signed.* 51096, ff. 123-126.

Black (James Macdougall), *D.D.; Moderator of the General Assembly of the Church of Scotland.*
— Letter to Lord Cecil from J. M. Black, 1939. *Signed.* 51184, f. 83.

Black (John Bennett), *Professor of History at Aberdeen.*
— Correspondence between Lord Cecil and J. B. Black, 1940. *Signed.* 51184, ff. 334, 336.

Blackpool.
— Message from Lord Cecil for Peace Week at Blackpool, 1937. *Draft.* 51176, f. 3.

Blackwood (A. G.), *of Dundee.*
— Letter to Lord Cecil from A. G. Blackwood, 1942. *Signed.* 51188, f. 316.

Blackwood (Basil Sheridan Hamilton-Temple-).
— *v.* Hamilton-Temple-Blackwood (Basil Sheridan).

Blair-Fish (Wallace Wilfrid), *playwright and editor.*
— Correspondence between Lord Cecil and W. W. Blair-Fish, 1938. *Signed.* 51180, ff. 163, 170.

Bland (C. P.), *of Debden Manor, Saffron Walden.*
— Correspondence between Lord Cecil and C. P. Bland, 1942. 51188, ff. 292, 301, 312.

Blankenburg (*Sir* Reginald Andrew), *K.B.E.; Official Sec., Office of the High Commissioner for S. Africa, London.*
— Letter to Lord Cecil on behalf of J. C. Smuts, 1921. *Signed.* 51076, f. 99.

Bledisloe, *1st Viscount.*
— *v.* Bathurst (Charles).

Blevin (John), *writing from Haulfryn, N. Wales.*
— Letter to Lord Cecil from J. Blevin, 1909. 51159, f. 114.

Block (*Sir* Adam Samuel James), *K.C.M.G.*
— Correspondence between Sir A. S. J. Block and W. Spens, 1918. 51093, ff. 174-176.

Blofeld (*Miss* Mildred), *of Christchurch, co. Hants.*
— Correspondence between Lord Cecil and Miss M. Blofeld, 1937. 51176, ff. 19, 28, 44.

Blum (Léon), *French statesman.*
— Correspondence between Lord Cecil and L. Blum, 1938-1945. Partly *Fr.* 51179, ff. 30, 239, 247; 51181, ff. 34, 38-40; 51183, f. 130; 51192, ff. 88, 99.

Blundel (Muriel A.), *Sec., Abyssinia Association.*
— Letters, etc., to Lord Cecil from M. A. Blundel, 1940, 1941. *Signed.* 51186, f. 46; 51187, f. 408.

Bodisco (Arvid de), *Sec. General, L'Entente Européenne, Paris.*
— Letters to Lord Cecil from A. de Bodisco, 1936. *Fr.* 51773, ff. 66, 119.

INDEX

Boissier (Leopold), *Sec. General, Union Interparlementaire.*
— Correspondence between Lord Cecil and L. Boissier, 1936. *Signed.* 51173, ff. 131, 137.

Bolton Peace Week Committee.
— List of affiliated organisations, 1936. 51174, f. 3.

Bonar Law (Andrew).
— *v.* Law (Andrew Bonar).

Boncour (Joseph Paul-).
— *v.* Paul-Boncour (Joseph).

Bonham Carter (Helen Violet), *Baroness Asquith.*
— *v.* Carter (Helen Violet Bonham).

Bonham-Carter (*Sir* Maurice), *K.C.B.*
— Letter to Lord Cecil on behalf of H. H. Asquith, 1915. 51073, f. 8.

Bonin-Longare (*Count* —).
— Letter to Count — Bonin-Longare from Lord Parmoor, 1924. *Copy.* 51096, f. 153.

Bonser (Wilfrid), *Librarian, University of Birmingham.*
— Letters to Lord Cecil from W. Bonser, 1941. *Signed.* Partly *printed.* 51187, f. 231; 51188, f. 11.

Boon (*Rev.* John), *formerly Sec., League of Nations Union, Lewisham Branch.*
— Letter to Lord Cecil from Rev. J. Boon, 1940. *Signed.* 51185, f. 265.

Bootle.
— Message from Lord Cecil for Peace Week at Bootle, 1937. 51177, f. 44.

Borden (*Sir* Robert Laird), *G.C.M.G.; Canadian Prime Minister.*
— Correspondence between Lord Cecil and Sir R. L. Borden, 1912, 1923. *Signed.* 51096, ff. 54, 80, 86, 92; 51160, f. 173.

Borel (Emile), *Président, Fédération des Associations Françaises pour la Société des Nations.*
— Correspondence between Lord Cecil and E. Borel, 1944. *Signed.* Partly *Fr.* 51191, ff. 165, 252.

Borriello (*Signor* —), *Vice-President, Italian Chamber of Commerce.*
— Memorandum by Lord Cecil rel. to interview with Signor — Borriello, 1931. 51100, f. 129.

Borriello (Biagio), *of Naples.*
— Letter to Lord Cecil, 1934. *Signed.* 51169, f. 202.

Boswell (Ronald), *of the B.B.C.*
— Letters to Lord Cecil, 1936-1941. Partly *printed. Signed.* 51193, ff. 63, 113, 158, 159, 165, 166, 199, 227.

Boulnois (Edmund), *M.P.*
— Letters to Lord Cecil from E. Boulnois, 1904, 1906. 51158, ff. 1, 41-44v.

Bourgeois (Léon Victor Auguste), *French statesman.*
— Letter from Lord Cecil to L. V. A. Bourgeois, 1922. *Copy.* 51095, f. 57.

Bowden (*Sir* Harold), *2nd Bart.; President, Raleigh Industries Ltd.*
— Speech by Sir H. Bowden to the Labour Co-Partnership Association, 1927. *Draft.* 51165, ff. 102-112.

Bowers (William), *of Gorton, Manchester.*
— Correspondence between Lord Cecil and W. Bowers, 1938. 51181, ff. 184, 193.

Bowles (George Frederick Stewart), *M.P.*
— Letters to Lord Cecil from G. F. S. Bowles, 1906-1909. 51072, ff. 109-158v.

Bowles (Thomas Gibson), *M.P.*
— Letters to Lord Cecil from T. G. Bowles, 1907, 1919. Partly *signed.* 51158, f. 122; 51162, f. 90.

Boyle (*Sir* Edward), *2nd Bart.*
— Correspondence between Lord Cecil and Sir E. Boyle, 1940, 1941. *Signed.* 51186, ff. 185, 198, 250, 297.

Brabazon (John Theodore Cuthbert Moore-).
— *v.* Moore-Brabazon (John Theodore Cuthbert).

Brabazon of Tara, *1st Baron.*
— *v.* Moore-Brabazon (John Theodore Cuthbert).

Bracewell (W. Hartley), *of Blackpool.*
— Letter to Lord Cecil from W. H. Bracewell, 1940. 51186, f. 117.

Bracey (Bertha L.), *Sec., German Emergency Committee, Society of Friends.*
— Letter to Lord Cecil from B. L. Bracey, 1938. *Signed.* 51180, f. 32.

Bracken (Brendan), *Viscount Bracken.*
— Correspondence between Lord Cecil and B. Bracken, 1942, 1943. 51189, ff. 165, 171; 51190, ff. 343, 347.

Bradbury (John Swanwick), *1st Baron Bradbury.*
— Correspondence between Lord Cecil and J. S. Bradbury, 1923. *Signed.* 51080, ff. 102-107; 51096, ff. 104-106.

Bradby (Edward), *General Sec., International Student Service.*
— Letters to Lord Cecil from E. Bradby, 1937. Partly *signed.* 51178, ff. 39, 47, 58.

Braden (R.), *of London, N 11.*
— Letter from Lord Cecil to R. Braden, 1935. *Copy.* 51170, f. 160.

Braden (Ronald), *of World Press Features Ltd.*
— Letter to Lord Cecil from R. Braden, 1937. *Signed.* 51177, f. 94.

— Letters, etc., to R. Braden from Miss I. M. Butler, 1937. 51177, ff. 144-150.

Bradley (Wesley H.), *Sec., National Committee of the Canadian Student Peace Movement.*
— Correspondence between Lord Cecil and W. H. Bradley, 1936. *Signed.* 51174, ff. 51, 64.

Brander (William Browne), *Sec., Universities Bureau of the British Empire.*
— Letters to Lord Cecil from W. B. Brander, 1940-1944. *Signed.* 51184, f. 326; 51187, f. 9; 51188, ff. 170-172, 204; 51189, ff. 271, 276; 51191, f. 18.

Brantom (Joseph H.), *writer on agriculture.*
— Letters to Lord Cecil, 1941. 51188, ff. 101, 127.

Braun-Stammfest (*Dr.* —), *Viennese lawyer.*
— Letter from Lord Cecil to Dr. — Braun-Stammfest, 1938. *Copy.* 51182, f. 83.

Brémond (Émile), *Editor, La Revue des Vivants, Paris.*
— Correspondence between Lord Cecil and É. Brémond, 1935. *Signed.* Partly *Fr.* 51171, ff. 168, 179, 201.

Brenier (Henri), *of Marseilles.*
— Correspondence between Lord Cecil and H. Brenier, 1935. 51171, ff. 216, 223, 231, 234.

Brentford, *1st Viscount.*
— *v.* Joynson-Hicks (William).

Briand (Aristide), *French statesman.*
— Memorandum by Lord Cecil rel. to conversation with A. Briand, 1926. 51098, f. 9.

Bridgeman (William Clive), *1st Viscount Bridgeman.*
— Correspondence between Lord Cecil and Lord Bridgeman, 1904-1935. Partly *signed.* 51095, ff. 136, 152; 51097, ff. 132-137, 139-142v, 204; 51098, ff. 31, 62-69, 173, 175; 51099, ff. 1, 76, 80-82, 99-105, 114-124v; 51158, f. 11; 51164, ff. 42, 45; 51170, ff. 235-238.
— Telegram to Lord Cecil from W. C. Bridgeman, 1927. 51104, f. 116.
— Telegrams between S. Baldwin and W. C. Bridgeman, 1927. Mostly *printed.* 51104, ff. 153-222 *passim.*

Bristol, *Bishop of.*
— *v.* Woodward (Clifford Salisbury).

British Broadcasting Corporation.
— Notes to Lord Cecil rel. to fees paid for broadcast speeches, 1940-1941. Partly *printed.* 51193, ff. 163, 229.
— *v. also* Barker (V. Duckworth).
— *v. also* Boswell (Ronald).
— *v. also* Dawney (*Col.* Alan Geoffrey Charles).
— *v. also* De Lotbinière (S. J.).
— *v. also* Freeston (B. D.).
— *v. also* Maconachie (*Sir* Richard Roy).
— *v. also* Montgomery (Peter).
— *v. also* Murray (William Ewart Gladstone).
— *v. also* Ogilvie (*Sir* Frederick Wolff).
— *v. also* Olsson (H. William).
— *v. also* Tallents (*Sir* Stephen).
— *v. also* Walford (R. G.).
— *v. also* Winther (H. D.).

Broadbent (Benjamin), *J.P.; woollen merchant, of Huddersfield.*
— Letters to Lord Cecil from B. Broadbent, 1907. 51158, ff. 96-107v, 126-132.

Broadhurst (*Sir* Edward Talbot), *Bart.*
— Telegram to Lord Cecil from Sir E. T. Broadhurst, 1908. 51158, f. 227.

Broadhurst (*Sir* Edward Tootal), *Bart.*
— Letters to Lord Cecil from E. T. Broadhurst, 1908, 1909. Partly *signed.* 51158, ff. 229, 238, 243v, 248v; 51159, ff. 105, 132, 174, 261.

Broadhurst (Mary Adelaide), *Hon. President and Organising Sec., National Political League.*
— Letter, on her behalf, to Lord Cecil, 1914. 51161, f. 105.

Brodetsky (Selig), *Professor of Mathematics at Leeds University.*
— Correspondence between Lord Cecil and S. Brodetsky, 1939-1944. *Signed.* 51184, ff. 60, 73; 51186, ff. 74-80, 92; 51187, ff. 223, 228; 51189, ff. 132, 158; 51190, ff. 281, 283, 284; 51191, ff. 168, 223.

Brodrick (William St. John Fremantle), *1st Earl of Midleton.*
— Correspondence between Lord Cecil and Lord Midleton, 1905, 1908. 51158, ff. 32, 35, 190.

Brooke (Loombe [Cullum?]), *churchwarden, St. Marylebone Church.*
— Letter to Lord Cecil from L. [C?] Brooke, 1909. 51159, f. 168.

Brooks (N. D.), *Chairman, Midland Conservative Club.*
— Letter to Lord Cecil from N. D. Brooks, 1914. *Signed.* 51161, f. 79.

Brooks (W. H.), *journalist.*
— Letter to Lord Cecil, 1944. 51191, f. 228.

Brotherton (Edward Allen), *Baron Brotherton.*
— Letters to Lord Cecil from E. A. Brotherton, 1909. 51159, ff. 118, 131.

Brotman (A. G.), *Sec., Board of Deputies of British Jews.*
— Correspondence between Lord Cecil and A. G. Brotman, partly on behalf of N. J. Laski, 1935-1944. *Signed.* 51171, ff. 113-117, 120, 133; 51189, f. 144; 51191, f. 178.

Brouckière (Louis de), *Belgian politician and representative at the League of Nations.*
— Correspondence between Lord Cecil and L. de Brouckière, 1932, 1942. *Signed. Partly Fr.* 51100, ff. 172, 177; 51187, f. 67; 51188, ff. 180, 187, 195.
— Memorandum rel. to 'World Settlement after the War', 1941. *Copy. Fr.* 51186, ff. 308-326.

Brougham (Victor Henry Peter), *4th Baron Brougham and Vaux.*
— Correspondence between Lord Cecil and Lord Brougham and Vaux, 1934. *Signed.* 51169, ff. 19, 32, 53.

Brougham and Vaux, *4th Baron.*
— *v.* Brougham (Victor Henry Peter).

Brown (Alfred Barratt), *Principal of Ruskin College, Oxford.*
— Correspondence, etc., between Lord Cecil and A. B. Brown, 1934, 1937. *Signed.* 51169, ff. 13-17, 31, 116-121, 130, 143, 148; 51176, ff. 31-34.

Brown (James E.), *U.S. diplomatist.*
— Letter to Lord Cecil on behalf of J. G. Winant, 1941. *Signed.* 51187, f. 282.

Browne (Nancy), *Sec., The Peace Pledge Union.*
— Correspondence between Lord Cecil and N. Browne, 1938. *Signed.* 51178, ff. 157, 163.

Bruce (Alexander Hugh), *6th Baron Balfour of Burleigh.*
— Correspondence between Lord Cecil and Lord Balfour, 1906-1928. Partly *signed.* 51158, f. 75; 51159, ff. 39, 55, 72, 76, 211v; 51160, ff. 10-12, 49, 143; 51162, ff. 94-96v; 51165, ff. 154, 165; 51166, ff. 1, 27, 29.
— Letter to E. G. Brunker from Lord Balfour, 1909. *Copy.* 51072, f. 208.

Bruce (D. J.), *Organising Sec., The International Good-Fellowship Organisation.*
— Letter to Lord Cecil from D. J. Bruce, 1940. *Signed.* 51185, f. 112.

Bruce (Edward James), *10th Earl of Elgin.*
— Correspondence between Lord Cecil and Lord Elgin, 1942. Partly *signed.* 51189, ff. 63, 66, 126, 202, 217.

Bruce (Herbert Alexander), *Lt.-Governor of Ontario.*
— Letter to Lord Cecil from H. A. Bruce, 1937. *Signed.* 51177, f. 200.

Bruce (Nigel Henry Clarence), *son of Clarence, 3rd Baron Aberdare.*
— Correspondence between Lord Cecil and N. H. C. Bruce, 1942. 51185, ff. 205, 210, 240.

Bruce (Stanley Melbourne), *Viscount Bruce.*
— Correspondence between Lord Cecil and S. M. Bruce, 1926. *Signed.* 51098, ff. 113, 120, 122.

Brunel (Christopher), *member of the League of Nations Union.*
— Letter to Lord Cecil from C. Brunel, 1938. *Signed.* 51180, f. 92.

Brunet (Jules), *of the Belgian Ministry for Foreign Affairs.*
— Memorandum by Lord Cecil rel. to conversation with J. Brunet, 1918. 51094, f. 106.

Brunet (Jules), *of the Belgian Ministry for Foreign Affairs*.
continuation
— Visiting card, 1918. *Printed. Fr.* 51094, f. 107.

Brüning (Heinrich), *German statesman*.
— Memorandum by Lord Cecil rel. to conversation with H. Brüning, 1931. 51100, f. 121.

Brunker (Edward George), *Sec., afterw. Director, Free Trade Union*.
— Letters to Lord Cecil from E. G. Brunker, 1908, 1909. 51072, ff. 159-213v.
— Letter to E. G. Brunker from Lord Balfour, 1909. *Copy.* 51072, f. 208.

Bruun (Urban Malthe-).
— *v.* Malthe-Bruun (Urban).

Buchan (John), *1st Baron Tweedsmuir*.
— Letters to Lord Cecil from Lord Tweedsmuir, 1908-1940. Partly *signed.* 51158, f. 204; 51092, f. 271; 51184, f. 338.

Buchan (Susan Charlotte), *widow of John, 1st Baron Tweedsmuir*.
— Telegram from Lord Cecil to Dowager Lady Tweedsmuir, 1940. *Copy.* 51185, f. 24.

Buckland (Walter Basil), *Vicar of St. Peter's, Battersea*.
— Letter to Lord Cecil, 1941. *Printed. Signed.* 51188, f. 20.

Buell (Raymond Leslie), *President, Foreign Policy Association, U.S.A.*
— Correspondence between Lord Cecil and R. L. Buell, 1928-1944. *Signed.* 51166, ff. 55-59; 51168, ff. 101, 113; 51181, ff. 63, 160; 51182, f. 44; 51191, ff. 26, 60, 266, 285.

Bülow (Fritz Wilhelm von), *of the International Labour Office*.
— Letter to Miss I. M. Butler from F. W. von Bülow, 1938. *Signed.* 51180, f. 157.

Bulwer-Lytton (*Lady* Constance Georgina), *daughter of Edward, 1st Earl of Lytton*.
— Correspondence between Lord Cecil and Lady C. G. Bulwer-Lytton, 1921. 51163, ff. 30-33.

Bulwer-Lytton (Pamela), *wife of Victor, 2nd Earl of Lytton*.
— Letter from Lord Cecil to Lady Lytton, 1932. *Copy.* 51139, f. 93.

Bulwer-Lytton (Victor Alexander George Robert), *2nd Earl of Lytton*.
— Correspondence between Lord Cecil and Lord Lytton, 1922-1946. Partly *signed.* 51139, ff. 84-226v; 51188, ff. 31-33.
— Letter to Miss I. M. Butler from Lord Lytton, 1938. *Signed.* 51139, f. 138.
— Memorial Address by Lord Lytton for Maj. A. J. C. Freshwater, 1943. *Copy.* 51139, f. 186.
— Letter to C. W. Judd from Lord Lytton, 1944. *Copy.* 51139, f. 218.

Bunbury (*Brig.-Gen.* Vesey Thomas).
— Letter to Lord Cecil from Brig.-Gen. V. T. Bunbury, 1914. 51161, f. 187.

Bunnelle (Robert), *journalist*.
— Correspondence between Lord Cecil and R. Bunnelle, 1940, 1945. *Signed.* 51185, ff. 289, 292-295; 51191, ff. 28, 35; 51192, f. 110.

Burge (Milward Rodon Kennedy), *of the International Labour Office*.
— Correspondence with Lord Cecil on behalf of E. J. Phelan, 1936. 51173, ff. 75, 97.

Burns (Cecil Delisle), *author and university lecturer*.
— Correspondence between Lord Cecil and C. D. Burns, 1924. 51164, ff. 41, 43.

Burns (John Elliott), *P.C.; M.P.*
— Letter to J. E. Burns from C. F. Fenton, 1909. *Copy.* 51159, f. 11.

Burris (Fred M.), *of Westbury-on-Trym.*
— Correspondence between Lord Cecil and F. M. Burris, 1942. Partly *signed*. 51188, ff. 213, 218-221, 235, 236.

Burrows ([Arthur Richard?]), *Sec. General, Union Internationale de Radiophone.*
— Letters to Lord Cecil from [A. R?] Burrows, 1925, 1926. *Signed*. 51098, f. 183; 51164, f. 175.

Burton (C. G.), *Sec., University of Birmingham.*
— Correspondence between Lord Cecil and C. G. Burton, 1941-1943. *Signed*. 51188, ff. 122, 200, 342, 343, 346; 51190, ff. 115, 146-148.

Burton (*Sir* Montague), *Chairman, Montague Burton Ltd.*
— Correspondence between Lord Cecil and Sir M. Burton, 1942, 1944. *Signed*. 51188, ff. 254, 268; 51190, ff. 201-206, 210, 236, 240, 243; 51191, f. 177.

Bush (*Miss* Irene N.), *Sec., League of Nations Union, Essex Branch.*
— Correspondence between Lord Cecil and Miss I. N. Bush, 1938. 51182, ff. 5, 10.

Butchart (*Lt.-Col.* Henry Jackson), *Sec. to Aberdeen University.*
— Letter to Lord Cecil from Lt.-Col. H. J. Butchart, 1928. *Signed*. 51166, f. 30.

Butcher (*Sir* John George), *Bart.*
— Correspondence between Lord Cecil and J. G. Butcher, 1918. 51094, ff. 9, 50.

Butler (*Sir* Harold Beresford), *K.C.M.G.*
— Correspondence between Lord Cecil and Sir H. B. Butler, 1927-1942. *Signed*. 51099, f. 89; 51165, f. 167; 51183, ff. 28-42, 53, 59, 62, 193, 201; 51187, f. 303; 51188, f. 197; 51189, f. 181.

— Memorandum by Lord Cecil rel. to conversation with Sir H. B. Butler, 1931. 51100, f. 103.

Butler (*Miss* Irene M.), *Sec. to Lord Cecil.*
— Letter, etc., to Miss I. M. Butler from Sir A. W. Flux, 1928. *Signed*. 51166, ff. 13-18.
— Correspondence between Rev. E. N. P. Goff and Miss I. M. Butler, 1931. *Signed*. 51167, f. 58.
— Letters to Miss I. M. Butler from M. Fanshawe, 1931, 1942. 51167, f. 100; 51189, f. 233.
— Letter to Miss I. M. Butler from R. C. M. Arnold, 1933. *Signed*. 51168, f. 134.
— Letters to Miss I. M. Butler from Mrs M. Ormerod, 1933, 1938. Partly *signed*. 51168, f. 97; 51180, f. 44.
— Correspondence between Lord Cecil and Miss I. M. Butler, 1933-1942. Partly *signed*. 51168, f. 63; 51170, f. 248; 51173, f. 239; 51174, f. 109; 51178, f. 147; 51181, ff. 24, 37; 51182, f. 76; 51183, ff. 11, 114, 127, 196; 51184, ff. 102, 344; 51185, ff. 25, 41, 83, 281; 51188, ff. 120, 129, 157, 186, 378; 51189, ff. 226, 233; 51193, ff. 157, 207.
— Letter to Miss I. M. Butler from N. Bentwich, 1934. *Signed*. 51145, f. 33.
— Correspondence between C. W. Judd and Miss I. M. Butler, 1934. 51169, ff. 145, 176.
— Letter to Miss I. M. Butler from K. S. Macgregor, 1934. *Signed*. 51193, f. 14.
— Letter to Miss I. M. Butler from M. S. Jameson, 1934. *Signed*. 51193, f. 19.
— Letter to Miss I. M. Butler from N. B. Foot, 1935. *Signed*. 51138, f. 38.
— Correspondence between V. C. Duffy and Miss I. M. Butler, 1935. 51171, ff. 33, 34.

Butler (*Miss* Irene M.), *Sec. to Lord Cecil. continuation*
— Letter to Miss I. M. Butler from J. W. Ferguson, 1935. *Signed.* 51171, f. 35.
— Correspondence between Col. H. F. T. Fisher and Miss I. M. Butler, 1935. 51171, ff. 146, 169.
— Correspondence between Dr. E. Künstler and Miss I. M. Butler, 1935, 1936. Mostly *signed.* 51145, ff. 81-118 *passim.*
— Correspondence between J. Eppstein and Miss I. M. Butler, 1935, 1936. 51171, f. 16; 51172, ff. 39, 98.
— Correspondence between Vice-Adm. S. R. Drury-Lowe and Miss I. M. Butler on behalf of Lord Cecil, 1935-1939. 51171, ff. 43, 58, 84, 88, 90; 51178, ff. 131-133v; 51180, ff. 102, 113; 51181, ff. 82, 85; 51184, ff. 51, 67.
— Correspondence between R. H. Lucas and Miss I. M. Butler, 1936. *Signed.* 51172, ff. 71, 80, 96.
— Letter to Miss I. M. Butler from Geneva Press Service, 1936. *Germ.* 51172, f. 193.
— Letter to C. E. Clift from Miss I. M. Butler, 1936. *Copy.* 51172, f. 207.
— Letter to Miss I. M. Butler from A. Hamrin, 1936. *Signed.* 51173, f. 70.
— Letter, etc., to Miss I. M. Butler from R. M. Makins, 1936. 51173, ff. 77-89.
— Letter to Miss I. M. Butler from W. A. Selby, 1936. *Signed.* 51173, f. 124.
— Correspondence between Miss I. M. Butler and P. Matthews, 1936. 51174, ff. 5, 44.
— Letter to Miss I. M. Butler from J. Leftwich, 1936. 51174, f. 71.
— Letter to Miss I. M. Butler from C. Ogilvy, 1936. *Signed.* 51174, f. 163.
— Correspondence between Maj. A. J. C. Freshwater and Miss I. M. Butler, 1936-1939. 51136, ff. 126-162 *passim*; 51181, f. 178.
— Letters, etc., to R. Braden from Miss I. M. Butler, 1937. 51177, ff. 144-150.
— Letter, etc., to Miss I. M. Butler from Dr. H. A. Atkinson, 1937. *Signed.* 51177, f. 152.
— Letter to Miss I. M. Butler from W. Gottleib, 1937. 51178, f. 104.
— Correspondence between Miss I. M. Butler and C. A. C. J. Hendriks on behalf of Lord Halifax, 1938. *Signed.* 51084, ff. 121-123.
— Letter to Miss I. M. Butler from Lord Lytton, 1938. *Signed.* 51139, f. 138.
— Correspondence between W. A. Jones and Miss I. M. Butler, 1938. *Signed.* 51179, ff. 143, 168, 179, 202-205.
— Correspondence between J. B. Childs and Miss I. M. Butler, 1938. 51179, ff. 212-216; 51180, ff. 20, 54.
— Letter to Miss I. M. Butler from R. Cecil, 1938. 51180, f. 83.
— Letter to Miss I. M. Butler from F. W. von Bülow, 1938. *Signed.* 51180, f. 157.
— Letter to H. W. Le Prevost from Miss I. M. Butler, 1938. *Signed.* 51181, f. 49.
— Correspondence between [M. J?] Frischauer and Miss I. M. Butler, 1938. *Signed.* 51181, ff. 150, 198; 51182, f. 84.
— Letter to Miss I. M. Butler from A. Koestler, 1938. *Signed.* 51181, f. 194.
— Correspondence between Dr. E. Müller-Sturmheim and Miss I. M. Butler, 1938, 1939. *Signed.* 51145, ff. 131-169 *passim.*

Butler (*Miss* Irene M.), *Sec. to Lord Cecil. continuation*
— Correspondence between N. E. Bell and Miss I. M. Butler, 1938, 1939. 51180, f. 45; 51181, ff. 32, 50; 51182, ff. 153, 193, 202-206.
— Correspondence between A. Reeve and Miss I. M. Butler, 1939. 51182, ff. 178, 183.
— Memoranda, partly by Miss I. M. Butler, rel. to Dr. V. Matejka, 1939. 51183, ff. 17, 127.
— Letter to Miss I. M. Butler from V. Chapin, 1939. *Signed.* 51183, f. 45.
— Letter to Miss I. M. Butler from A. Macnair, 1939. *Signed.* 51183, f. 79.
— Letter to W. I. Mallet from Miss I. M. Butler, 1939. *Copy.* 51183, f. 99.
— Letter to Miss I. M. Butler from F. de Rose, 1939. *Signed.* 51183, f. 119.
— Correspondence between Dr. F. Wolff and Miss I. M. Butler, 1939. *Signed.* 51184, ff. 1, 13, 21.
— Letter to Miss I. M. Butler from Miss N. S. Parnell, 1940. *Signed.* 51184, f. 314.
— Memorandum by Miss I. M. Butler rel. to conversation with S. Gascoyne-Cecil, 1940. 51185, f. 281.
— Letter to S. Gascoyne-Cecil from Miss I. M. Butler, 1940. *Copy.* 51185, f. 282.
— Correspondence between S. Zavalani and Miss I. M. Butler, 1940. *Fr.* 51186, ff. 15, 21.
— Correspondence between Miss I. M. Butler and D. Wickings, 1940. 51186, ff. 219, 223, 255.
— Letter to Miss I. M. Butler from R. G. Walford, 1940. 51193, f. 167.
— Correspondence between I. R. Ewing and Miss I. M. Butler, 1941. *Signed.* 51186, ff. 296, 302; 51187, ff. 44, 83, 165.
— Correspondence between Dr. F. Epstein and Miss I. M. Butler, 1941. 51187, ff. 81, 120, 152, 166, 186.
— Letters to Miss I. M. Butler from G. W. Howard, 1941. *Signed.* 51187, ff. 84, 111.
— Correspondence between Miss L. M. Livingstone and Miss I. M. Butler, 1941. *Signed.* 51187, ff. 115, 116, 126, 210.
— Correspondence between Miss I. M. Butler and her cousin V. Butler, 1941. Partly *signed.* 51187, ff. 129-131v, 146.
— Letter to Miss I. M. Butler from T. Hole, 1941. *Signed.* 51187, f. 183.
— Correspondence between P. P. Howe and Miss I. M. Butler, 1941. *Signed.* 51193, ff. 213-215, 221, 223-225.
— Letters, etc., to Miss I. M. Butler from P. H. Edwards, 1941, 1942. *Signed.* 51187, f. 13; 51188, f. 201; 51189, ff. 175, 176, 192.
— Correspondence between Chai Feng-yang and Miss I. M. Butler, 1941, 1942. *Signed.* 51188, ff. 131, 146, 162, 168.
— Correspondence between P. Montgomery and Miss I. M. Butler, 1942. *Signed.* 51188, ff. 166-167v, 177.
— Correspondence between T. L. [Dylan?] and Miss I. M. Butler, 1942. *Signed.* 51188, ff. 247, 335.
— Letter to Miss I. M. Butler from P. N. Loxley, 1942. *Signed.* 51189, f. 166.
— Letter to A. W. Peterson from Miss I. M. Butler, 1942. *Copy.* 51189, f. 228.
— Letter to Miss I. M. Butler from H. A. Strutt, 1942. *Signed.* 51189, f. 230.
— Correspondence between H. R. Pelletier and Miss I. M. Butler, 1942. *Signed.* 51193, ff. 267-270.

INDEX

Butler (K. M.), *of Cheam.*
— Correspondence between Lord Cecil and K. M. Butler, 1943. *Signed.* 51190, ff. 22, 28.

Butler (*Sir* Nevile Montagu), *K.C.M.G.*
— Letter, etc., to A. G. M. Cadogan from Sir N. M. Butler, 1923. 51096, ff. 109-122.

Butler (Nicholas Murray), *President of Columbia University.*
— Correspondence between Lord Cecil and N. M. Butler, 1925-1945. *Signed.* Partly *printed.* 51071, f. 98; 51144, ff. 133-205; 51182, f. 199.

Butler (Richard Austen), *Baron Butler.*
— Correspondence between Lord Cecil and R. A. Butler, 1939-1941. *Signed.* 51184, ff. 14, 47, 244, 300; 51185, ff. 70-76; 51186, ff. 243, 244, 283, 284.

Butler (Victor), *of the Oil Control Board.*
— Correspondence between Miss I. M. Butler and her cousin V. Butler, 1941. Partly *signed.* 51187, ff. 129-131v, 146.

Butterworth (*Sir* Alexander Kaye).
— Correspondence between Lord Cecil and Sir A. K. Butterworth, 1932, 1943. Partly *signed.* 51168, f. 3; 51190, ff. 98, 104, 154, 159, 169, 175, 177.

Butterworth (Thornton) **Ltd.**, *publishers.*
— Correspondence with Lord Cecil, 1939. 51193, ff. 118, 119, 135, 136.
— *v. also* Lever (*Sir* Tresham Joseph Philip).

Buxton (Alfred Barclay), *missionary in the Congo and Abyssinia.*
— Correspondence between Lord Cecil and A. B. Buxton, 1937. 51177, ff. 129, 139, 168.

Buxton (*Maj.* Anthony), *of the League of Nations Secretariate.*
— Correspondence between Lord Cecil and Maj. A. Buxton, 1923-1944. 51113, ff. 115-157v.

Buxton (Charles Roden), *M.P.*
— Correspondence between Lord Cecil and C. R. Buxton, 1938. *Signed.* 51178, ff. 117-182; 51179, ff. 2, 22, 28.

Buxton (Dorothy Frances), *wife of C. R. Buxton, M.P.*
— Correspondence between Lord Cecil and D. F. Buxton, 1929-1939. Partly *signed.* 51100, ff. 178-183; 51183, ff. 81-83, 97, 105, 108; 51193, ff. 6-13.

Buxton (Noel Edmund) *afterw.* **Noel-Buxton.**
— *v.* Noel-Buxton (Noel Edmund).

Buysman (*Miss* H. C.), *Headmistress, Priory Grove Senior Girls' School, Wandsworth.*
— Correspondence between Lord Cecil and Miss H. C. Buysman, 1934. 51169, ff. 165, 168, 169.

C

Cadbury (Laurence John), *Director, Daily News Ltd.; Chairman, British Cocoa and Chocolate Co. Ltd.*
— Correspondence between Lord Cecil and L. J. Cadbury, 1928. *Signed.* 51166, ff. 49-51.

Cadogan (*Sir* Alexander George Montagu), *G.C.M.G.*
— Letter, etc., to A. G. M. Cadogan from Sir N. M. Butler, 1923. 51096, ff. 109-122.

Cadogan (*Sir* Alexander George Montagu), *G.C.M.G.*
continuation
— Correspondence between Lord Cecil and Sir A. G. M. Cadogan, partly on behalf of Lord Halifax, 1923-1944. Partly *signed*. 51084, ff. 159, 192-194; 51089; 51096, ff. 109-122; 51097, ff. 74-78; 51098, f. 42.
— Letter to Lord Parmoor from Sir A. G. M. Cadogan, 1924. *Copy*. 51096, f. 154.
— Letter to Lord Phillimore from Sir A. G. M. Cadogan, 1924. *Copy*. 51096, f. 155.
— Letters, etc., to Sir A. Cadogan from P. de Azcarate y Florez, 1924. *Copies. Partly Fr*. 51097, ff. 74-78.
— Memorandum to Sir A. G. M. Cadogan (?) from W. St. C. H. Roberts, 1926. *Copy*. 51098, f. 42.
— Signature, 1927. 51099, f. 24.
— Letter to Lord Cecil from Sir G. J. V. Thomas on behalf of Sir A. G. M. Cadogan, 1940. *Signed*. 51089, f. 161.

Caine (*Sir* Hall), *K.B.E.; author and dramatist*.
— Correspondence between Lord Cecil and Sir H. Caine, 1922, 1925. 51163, f. 65; 51164, ff. 106, 114.

Caldecote, *1st Viscount*.
— *v*. Inskip (Thomas Walker Hobart).

Cale (M. L.), *Sec., Association of Post Office Women Clerks*.
— Letter to Lord Cecil from M. L. Cale, 1911. 51160, f. 43.

Campbell (Robert), *of Glasgow*.
— Correspondence between Lord Cecil and R. Campbell, 1940. 51185, ff. 87, 130, 160, 178.

Campbell (Ronald I.), *C.M.G.; of the Foreign Office*.
— Correspondence between Lord Cecil and R. I. Campbell, 1936. *Signed*. 51172, f. 171; 51173, ff. 14, 19.

Canadian League of Nations Society.
— Correspondence, including telegram, between Lord Cecil and Canadian League of Nations Society, 1943. 51190, ff. 67, 76.

Canney (Leigh), *of Bexhill*.
— Correspondence between Lord Cecil and L. Canney, 1940. 51185, ff. 110, 139, 162, 177.

Canning-Freeman (Edward), *of the Sussex Society for Polish Relief*.
— Letters to Lord Cecil from E. Canning-Freeman, 1940. Partly *signed*. 51185, ff. 143, 153.

Cannock (Raymond P.), *Treasurer of the Henleaze and Westbury Youth Group of the League of Nations Union, Bristol*.
— Correspondence between Lord Cecil and R. P. Cannock, 1936. 51173, ff. 25, 37.

Canterbury, *Archbishop of*.
— *v*. Davidson (Randall Thomas).
— *v*. Fisher (Geoffrey Francis).
— *v*. Lang (Cosmo Gordon).
— *v*. Temple (William).

Canton, *in China*.
— Telegram to Lord Cecil from the presidents and professors of universities at Canton, 1938. 51180, f. 41.

Canton Committee for Justice.
— Telegram to Lord Cecil from the Canton Committee for Justice, 1938. 51179, f. 252.

Cape (Herbert Jonathan), *publisher*.
— Correspondence between Lord Cecil and H. J. Cape, 1939. Partly *extract*. 51184, f. 41; 51193, ff. 143-147.

Cape (Jonathan) **Ltd.**, *publishers*.
— Contract for publication of Lord Cecil's autobiography, 1939. *Draft*. 51193, ff. 120v-133.

Capel (Arthur), *British expert on coal, reporting from France*.
— Letters, etc., to Lord Cecil from A.

Capel, 1918. *Signed.* 51093, ff. 97-100, 116-118, 127-129, 134-146, 157.

Cardiff, *co. Glam.*
— Election address by Maj. H. L. Nathan in Cardiff, 1935. *Printed.* 51171, f. 166.

Carlebach (Alexander), *Rabbi.*
— Correspondence between Lord Cecil and A. Carlebach, 1941. *Signed.* 51187, ff. 365, 387.

Carlisle, *League of Nations Union Branch.*
— Message from Lord Cecil to League of Nations Union Branch, Carlisle, 1938. *Copy.* 51182, f. 36.

Carlow (Charles Augustus), *of the Fife Coal Company.*
— Correspondence between Lord Cecil and C. A. Carlow, 1943. *Signed.* 51190, ff. 289, 301, 308.

Carnac (Wilfrid Theodore Rivett-).
— *v.* Rivett-Carnac (Wilfrid Theodore).

Carnegie Endowment for International Peace.
— *v.* Ames (*Sir* Herbert Brown).
— *v.* Gott (Florence).
— *v.* Haskell (Henry S.).
— *v.* Jones (Amy Heminway).
— *v.* Shotwell (James Thomson).

Carnevali (*Dr.* Don Atilano), *Venezuelan diplomatist.*
— Correspondence between Lord Cecil and Dr. D. A. Carnevali, 1942. *Signed.* 51189, ff. 133, 141.

Carney (Mina), *friend of Dr. V. Matejka.*
— Correspondence between Lord Cecil and M. Carney, 1938. *Signed.* 51179, ff. 92, 93.

Carpenter (George Kingsford), *Vicar of Crosthwaite.*
— Correspondence between Lord Cecil and Rev. G. K. Carpenter, 1941. *Signed.* 51186, ff. 5, 22.

Carpenter (George Lyndon), *General, Salvation Army.*
— Correspondence between Lord Cecil and G. L. Carpenter, 1943, 1944. *Signed.* 51190, ff. 365, 377; 51191, f. 196.

Carr (Edward Hallett), *of the Foreign Office; afterw. Professor of International Politics, University of Wales.*
— Letter to Lord Cecil, 1936. *Signed.* 51172, f. 97.

Carr-Saunders (*Sir* Alexander Morris), *Director, London School of Economics.*
— Letter to Lord Cecil from Sir A. M. Carr-Saunders, 1940. *Signed.* 51185, f. 81.

Carson (Edward Henry), *Baron Carson.*
— Letter to Lord Cecil from Lord Carson, 1917. 51162, f. 12.

Carter (G. P.), *of London, SW 19.*
— Letter from Lord Cecil to G. P. Carter, 1940. 51185, ff. 113, 134.

Carter (George Wallace), *of the Free Trade Union.*
— Letters from Lord Cecil to G. W. Carter, 1908. *Partly signed.* 51158, ff. 189-193, 200, 215-219, 222.

Carter (Helen Violet Bonham), *Baroness Asquith.*
— Correspondence between Lord Cecil and H. V. Bonham Carter, 1940, 1941. 51186, ff. 131, 135; 51187, ff. 181, 200, 204, 211.

Carter (*Rev.* Henry), *C.B.E.; General Sec., the Social Welfare Dept. of the Methodist Church.*
— Correspondence between Lord Cecil and Rev. H. Carter, 1935, 1937. *Signed.* 51170, ff. 104-107; 51176, f. 153.

Carter (*Sir* Maurice Bonham).
— *v.* Bonham-Carter (*Sir* Maurice).

Carter (Reginald Carlyle), *barrister.*
— Correspondence between Lord Cecil and R. C. Carter, 1943. 51190, ff. 32, 34.

Carter (William Horsfall), *Editor, The Fortnightly.*
— Correspondence between Lord Cecil and W. H. Carter, 1938. *Signed.* 51179, ff. 113-117, 124.

Cartier de Marchienne (*Baron* Emile Ernest), *Belgian diplomatist.*
— Memorandum by Lord Cecil rel. to interview with Baron E. E. Cartier de Marchienne, 1938. *Copy.* 51180, f. 129.

Cassin (Renée), *French jurist.*
— Correspondence between Lord Cecil and R. Cassin, 1934-1941. *Signed.* Partly *Fr.* 51169, ff. 107, 112; 51172, ff. 124-131, 139; 51185, ff. 275, 280; 51187, f. 286.

Castle (E. C.), *journalist.*
— Letter to Lord Cecil, 1944. *Signed.* 51191, f. 278.

Catchpool (Thomas Corder Pettifor), *pacifist.*
— Correspondence between Lord Cecil and T. C. P. Catchpool, 1941. *Signed.* 51188, ff. 119, 126, 128.

Catt (Carrie Chapman), *widow of G. W. Catt; Chairman, National Committee on the Cause and Cure of War, U.S.A.*
— Telegram to Lord Cecil from C. C. Catt, 1930. 51167, f. 21.

Cavan, *10th Earl of.*
— *v.* Lambart (*Field-Marshal* Frederic Rudolph).

Cavendish (Edward William Spencer), *Marquess of Hartington; 10th Duke of Devonshire, 1938.*
— Correspondence between Lord Cecil and Lord Hartington, 1921-1938. Partly *signed.* 51163, ff. 23, 75; 51164, ff. 65, 77-99v; 51165, ff. 65, 77; 51181, ff. 91, 95, 172, 185.
— Letter to — Fletcher from Lord Hartington, 1922. *Copy.* 51163, f. 72.

Cavendish (*Lady* Moyra de Vere), *wife of Lord Richard Cavendish.*
— Letters from Lord Cecil to Lady M. de Vere Cavendish, 1924, 1937. *Copies.* 51164, ff. 4, 50; 51178, f. 102.

Cavendish (*Col.* Reginald R. [T?]).
— Correspondence between Lord Cecil and Col. R. R. [T?] Cavendish, 1936, 1937. 51173, f. 62; 51177, ff. 30-32, 70-74, 82.

Cavendish (Spencer Compton), *8th Duke of Devonshire.*
— Letters to Lord Cecil from the Duke of Devonshire, 1906. 51158, ff. 70, 73.

Cavendish (Victor Christian William), *9th Duke of Devonshire.*
— Letter to Lord Cecil from E. H. Marsh on behalf of the Duke of Devonshire, 1923. *Signed.* 51096, f. 91.
— Correspondence between Lord Cecil and the Duke of Devonshire, 1923, 1935. 51096, f. 91; 51171, f. 89.

Cavendish-Bentinck (Victor Frederick William), *9th Duke of Portland.*
— Correspondence between E. C. Henty and V. F. W. Cavendish-Bentinck, 1926. *Signed.* 51098, ff. 19-29, 32-38.
— Letters, etc., to Lord Cecil, 1926, 1935. *Signed.* 51098, ff. 19-29, 32; 51171, ff. 21, 89.

Cecil (Algernon), *author.*
— Correspondence between Lord Cecil and A. Cecil, 1922-1941. 51163, ff. 56, 137, 142, 145; 51165, ff. 10-16v, 114, 117; 51166, ff. 61-63v, 87; 51187, ff. 169, 190.

Cecil (Evelyn), *1st Baron Rockley.*
— Letter to Lord Cecil from E. Cecil, 1905. 51158, f. 83.

Cecil (Robert), *of the Foreign Office.*
— Letter to Lord Cecil from R. Cecil, 1938. 51179, f. 9.
— Letter to Miss I. M. Butler from R. Cecil, 1938. 51180, f. 83.

INDEX

Cecil (William Thomas Brownlow), *6th Marquess of Exeter.*
— Letter to Lord Cecil from W. T. B. Cecil, 1913. 51071, f. 82.

Cecil, Gascoyne-, *family.*
— *v.* Gascoyne-Cecil.

Cecil of Chelwood, *Viscount.*
— *v.* Gascoyne-Cecil (Edgar Algernon Robert).

Cecil Peace Prize.
— Memoranda rel. to its award, [1940?]. 51186, ff. 241, 242.
— Receipt to Trustees of Cecil Peace Prize from Harrington, Edwards and Cobban (solicitors), 1944. Partly *printed.* 51191, f. 11.

Central News Agency of China.
— *v.* Liem (H. D.).

Černy (Vilém), *Czech diplomatist.*
— Letter to Lord Cecil from V. Černy, 1930. *Signed.* 51100, f. 6.

Chai Feng-yang, *Chinese diplomatist.*
— Correspondence between Chai Feng-yang and Miss I. M. Butler, 1941, 1942. *Signed.* 51188, ff. 131, 146, 162, 168.

Chalk (George Brisbane), *solicitor.*
— Correspondence between Lord Cecil and G. B. Chalk, 1939. *Signed.* 51184, ff. 90, 106, 186, 202-204.

Chamberlain (Arthur Neville), *Prime Minister.*
— Correspondence between Lord Cecil and A. N. Chamberlain, 1937-1939. *Signed.* 51087, ff. 178-266.
— Letter to A. N. Chamberlain from R. Lutyens, 1939. *Printed.* 51182, f. 37.
— Letter to A. N. Chamberlain from G. W. Rushton, 1939. *Draft.* 51184, f. 24.

Chamberlain (Joseph), *statesman.*
— Letter to Sir F. Trippel from J. Chamberlain, 1912. *Copy.* 51160, f. 187.

Chamberlain (*Sir* Joseph Austen), K.G.
— Letter to Sir F. Trippel from Sir J. A. Chamberlain, 1912. *Copy.* 51160, f. 182.
— Note, 1913. 51161, f. 38.
— Correspondence between Lord Cecil and Sir J. A. Chamberlain, 1918-1936. Partly *signed.* 51078; 51079.

Chamberlain (Mary Endicott), *wife of J. Chamberlain.*
— Letter to Lord Cecil from M. E. Chamberlain, 1909. 51159, f. 266.

Chance (*Sir* William), *2nd Bart.; High Sheriff of Surrey.*
— Letters to Lord Cecil from Sir W. Chance, 1907-1914. 51158, f. 91; 51159, f. 58; 51160, ff. 39, 47; 51161, ff. 130, 138-142v.
— Letter to Sir W. Chance from Lord Aberconway, 1914. *Signed.* 51161, f. 140.

Chang Po-ling, *of the People's Political Council, Chung King.*
— Telegram to Lord Cecil from Chang Po-ling, 1940. 51186, f. 84.

Chapin (Vinton), *U.S. diplomatist.*
— Letter to Miss I. M. Butler from V. Chapin, 1939. *Signed.* 51183, f. 45.

Chaplin (Henry), *1st Viscount Chaplin.*
— Letters to Lord Cecil from Lord Chaplin, 1915. 51161, ff. 208, 212-219v.

Chapman (Sydney), F.R.S.
— Correspondence between Lord Cecil and S. Chapman, 1938. 51181, ff. 142, 201.

Charap (Leon), *foreign correspondent in London.*
— Letter to Lord Cecil from L. Charap, 1937. *Signed.* 51175, f. 179.

INDEX

Charles (*Lt.-Gen. Sir* James Ronald Edmondston), *K.C.B.*
— Letter, etc., to Lord Cecil from Lt.-Gen. Sir J. R. E. Charles, 1926. *Signed.* 51098, f. 49.

Chase (Lawrence), *of Boston, Massachusetts.*
— Correspondence between Lord Cecil and L. Chase, 1941. *Signed.* 51187, ff. 288, 355.

Chayla (— du), *independent representative of the Soviet Union in Geneva.*
— Memorandum by Lord Cecil rel. to conversation with — du Chayla, 1924. 51097, f. 23.

Cheng Ming-shu, *General; of the Chinese People's Foreign Relations Association.*
— Letter to Lord Cecil from Cheng Ming-shu, 1939. *Signed.* 51184, f. 263.

Cheng Yin-fu, *Executive Sec., China Branch, International Peace Campaign.*
— Letter to International Peace Campaign (International Secretariate) from Cheng Yin-fu, 1940. *Copy.* 51184, f. 345.

Chesney (*Lt.-Col.* Clement Hope Rawdon), *D.S.O.*
— Letter, etc., to Lord Cecil from Lt.-Col. C. H. R. Chesney, 1940. 51185, ff. 151, 166.

Chester, *Bishop of.*
— *v.* Fisher (Geoffrey Francis).

Chesterfield, *co. Derby.*
— Message from Lord Cecil for Peace Week at Chesterfield, 1938. *Copy.* 51180, f. 40.

Chiang Kai-shek, *President of the Republic of China.*
— Telegram to Lord Cecil from Chiang Kai-shek, 1938. 51180, f. 119.
— Farewell message to the people of India from Chiang Kai-shek, 1942. *Printed.* 51188, f. 216.

Chichester, *Bishop of.*
— *v.* Bell (George Kennedy Allen).

Chichester (Arthur Claud Spencer), *4th Baron Templemore.*
— Correspondence between Lord Cecil and Lord Templemore, 1941-1943. 51187, ff. 18, 34; 51188, ff. 352, 372; 51190, f. 30.

Chien Tuam-sheng, *Dean of Peking University.*
— Letters to Lord Cecil from Chien Tuam-sheng, 1938-1943. *Signed.* 51181, f. 29; 51183, f. 72; 51186, ff. 147, 275; 51188, ff. 73, 145, 252, 333; 51189, f. 200; 51190, f. 18.

Childs (James B.), *Chief of the Division of Documents, Library of Congress, Washington.*
— Correspondence, partly on his behalf, with Lord Cecil, 1938. *Signed.* 51179, ff. 150, 212-216; 51180, ff. 20, 54, 114.

China.
— Message from Lord Cecil to the people of China, 1942. *Draft.* 51189, f. 6.

China Campaign Committee.
— *v.* Clegg (Arthur D.).
— *v.* Timperly (Harold John).
— *v.* Woodman (*Miss* Dorothy).

Chinda (*Count* Sutemi), *Japanese diplomatist.*
— Memoranda by Lord Cecil rel. to meetings with Count S. Chinda, 1918. *Copies.* 51093, ff. 202, 207; 51094, f. 94.

Chinese People's Foreign Relations Association.
— *v.* Cheng Ming-shu.
— *v.* Wang (*Prof.* Shelley).

Chingford, *co. Essex.*
— Message from Lord Cecil for Peace Week at Chingford, 1938. *Copy.* 51179, f. 101.

INDEX

Chipman (Warwick Fielding), *Canadian diplomatist.*
— Letter, etc., to Lord Cecil from W. F. Chipman, 1940, 1942. Partly *signed.* 51185, ff. 51v-61, 164, 206, 227; 51187, ff. 123, 186.

Chown (Alice A.), *President, Women's League of Nations Association, Canada.*
— Correspondence between Lord Cecil and A. A. Chown, 1933. *Signed.* 51168, ff. 107, 128.

Christian Council for Refugees from Germany and Central Europe.
— *v.* Wickings (Dorothy).

Chu Chia-hua, *Chinese politician.*
— Telegrams to Lord Cecil, 1938, 1940. 51181, f. 78; 51185, f. 266.
— Letter to League of Nations from Chu Chia-hua, 1943. *Signed.* 51190, f. 333.

Chung king, *in China.*
— Telegram and letter to Lord Cecil, etc., on behalf of People's Political Council at Chung king, 1940. Partly *signed.* Partly *Chinese.* 51186, ff. 84, 107.

Churchill (Clementine Ogilvy), *wife of Sir Winston Churchill; Baroness Spencer-Churchill, 1965.*
— Telegram to Lord Cecil from Lady Spencer-Churchill, 1943. 51073, f. 183.

Churchill (Frank Spooner), *physician, of Cape Cod, Massachusetts.*
— Letter, etc., to Lord Cecil, 1943. Partly *printed. Signed.* 51190, ff. 194-199v, 245.
— Article, "The Children of Germany and Permanent Peace", by F. S. Churchill, reprinted from 'Cape Cod Standard-Times', 1943. *Printed.* 51190, ff. 195-199v.

Churchill (*Lord* Ivor Charles Spencer).
— Letter to Lord Cecil from Lord Churchill, 1939. *Signed.* 51183, f. 152.

Churchill (*Sir* Winston Leonard Spencer), *K.G.; Prime Minister.*
— Correspondence between Lord Cecil and Winston Churchill, 1910-1952. Partly *signed.* 51073, ff. 97-195.
— Letter to Winston Churchill from Sir C. E. Ellis, 1918. *Signed.* 51093, f. 152.
— Letter to Winston Churchill from L. C. M. S. Amery, 1927. *Copy.* 51072, f. 268.

Chuter-Ede (James), *Baron Chuter-Ede.*
— *v.* Ede (James Chuter).

Citrine (Walter MacLennan), *1st Baron Citrine.*
— Correspondence between Lord Cecil and W. MacL. Citrine, 1936, 1939. *Signed.* 51174, ff. 133, 134; 51184, ff. 114, 135.

Clarke (Charles William Arden), *former missionary in India.*
— Correspondence between Lord Cecil and C. W. A. Clarke, 1937. 51175, f. 212; 51176, f. 11.

Clarke (*Sir* Edward George), *M.P.*
— Correspondence between Lord Cecil and Sir E. G. Clarke, 1906. 51158, ff. 68, 78.

Classen (A. J.), *Luxembourg diplomatist.*
— Letters to Lord Cecil, 1943. *Signed.* 51190, ff. 209, 248.

Clay (*Sir* Charles Travis), *Librarian of the House of Lords.*
— Letters to Lord Cecil from Sir C. T. Clay, 1941. 51187, ff. 54, 118.

Clayton (R.), *of Bournemouth.*
— Correspondence between Lord Cecil and R. Clayton, 1940. 51185, ff. 105, 132, 141.

Cleeve (*Miss* Margaret), *Acting Sec., Royal Institute of International Affairs.*
— Correspondence between Lord Cecil and Miss M. Cleeve, 1938-1944. Partly *printed. Signed.* 51182, ff. 49, 55, 60, 63; 51191, ff. 289, 292-296; 51193, ff. 194, 196.

Clegg (Arthur D.), *National Organiser, China Campaign Committee.*
— Correspondence between Lord Cecil and A. D. Clegg, 1938. *Signed.* 51180, f. 21; 51181, ff. 28, 33.

Clemenceau (Georges Benjamin), *French statesman.*
— Letter from Lord Cecil to G. B. Clemenceau, 1918. *Copy.* 51093, f. 86.
— Letter to G. B. Clemenceau from Lord Bertie, 1918. *Copy. Fr.* 51093, f. 88.
— Memorandum by Lord Cecil rel. to conversation with G. B. Clemenceau, 1929. 51099, f. 146.

Clemens (Cyril), *President, International Mark Twain Society.*
— Correspondence, etc., between Lord Cecil and C. Clemens, 1937-1940. Partly *printed.* 51176, ff. 23, 75; 51177, ff. 18, 42, 85, 87; 51182, f. 197; 51183, f. 63; 51185, f. 267; 51186, f. 38.

Clémentel (Étienne), *French statesman and economist.*
— Letter from Lord Cecil to É. Clémentel, 1918. *Copy.* 51093, f. 160.

Clerk (*Sir* George Russell), *G.C.M.G.; diplomatist.*
— Letter to Lord Cecil from Sir G. R. Clerk, 1935. *Signed.* 51170, f. 233.

Clift (C. E.), *Sec., League of Nations Union, Manchester.*
— Letter to C. E. Clift from Miss I. M. Butler, 1936. *Copy.* 51172, f. 207.

— Correspondence with and on behalf of Lord Cecil, 1936, 1938. Partly *printed.* 51136, ff. 158-160; 51174, f. 150; 51175, ff. 36-40; 51176, ff. 65, 101-106.

Clinton-Baddeley (V. C.), *of the Joint Broadcasting Committee.*
— Correspondence between Lord Cecil and V. C. Clinton-Baddeley, 1941. *Signed.* 51154 A, f. 115; 51187, ff. 68, 72.

Clynes (John Robert), *M.P.*
— Letter to J. R. Clynes from R. G. Vansittart on behalf of J. Ramsay MacDonald, 1929. *Signed.* 51099, f. 199.
— Letter from Lord Cecil to J. R. Clynes, 1929. 51162, f. 117.

Cofinas (George Nicolas), *Greek economist and statesman.*
— Letter to M. C. Norman from G. N. Cofinas, 1923. *Copy.* 51096, f. 97.
— Correspondence between G. N. Cofinas and H. Morgenthau, 1923. *Copies.* 51096, ff. 100, 101.

Cohen-Stuart (A. B.), *President, Netherlands Committee, International Peace Campaign.*
— Correspondence between Lord Cecil and A. B. Cohen-Stuart, 1940. *Signed.* 51184, ff. 265, 316.

Colban (Erik), *of the League of Nations Secretariate; Norwegian diplomatist.*
— Correspondence, mostly on behalf of Lord Cecil, between P. J. Noel-Baker and E. Colban, 1922-1924. 51115, ff. 3-189 *passim.*
— Correspondence between Lord Cecil and E. Colban, 1922-1943. *Signed.* Partly *Fr.* 51115 *passim.*
— Letter to C. H. Tufton from E. Colban, 1923. *Signed.* 51115, f. 25.

INDEX

Colby (Everett), *U.S. lawyer and politician.*
— Correspondence between Lord Cecil and E. Colby, 1932, 1933. 51168, ff. 12, 13.

Cole (Lowry Arthur Casamaijor), *grandson of William, 3rd Earl of Enniskillen.*
— Correspondence between Lord Cecil and L. A. C. Cole, 1936. 51174, ff. 87, 91.

Collas (Constantin), *Greek diplomatist.*
— Letter to Lord Cecil from C. Collas, 1923. *Signed.* 51096, f. 88.

Collier (Charles St. John), *Comptroller and Auditor General to the Ethiopian Government.*
— Correspondence, etc., between Lord Cecil and C. St.J. Collier, 1937. *Signed.* 51177, ff. 47, 51-57v, 65-67.

Collings (Jesse), *P.C.; M.P.*
— Letter, etc., to Lord Cecil from J. Collings, 1914. *Signed.* 51161, ff. 131-137v.

Colomb (*Mme* Honorine), *retired French servant from Lord Cecil's household.*
— Letter to Lord Cecil, 1944. 51191, f. 287.

Comert (Pierre), *of the League of Nations.*
— Correspondence between Lord Cecil and P. Comert, 1923-1945. Partly *signed.* Partly *Fr.* 51095, ff. 143, 144; 51101, f. 12; 51167, ff. 191-195; 51184, ff. 181, 190, 206, 236, 251; 51191, ff. 171, 324; 51192, f. 10; 51193, ff. 271-273.

Commercial Union Assurance Co. Ltd.
— Letter to Lord Cecil, 1939. 51182, f. 191.

Committee for Development of Refugee Industries.
— Minutes, 1940. *Printed.* 51185, ff. 196-200.

Comyn-Platt (*Sir* Thomas).
— *v.* Platt (*Sir* Thomas).

Consett (*Rear-Adm.* Montagu William Warcop Peter), *C.M.G.*
— Correspondence between Lord Cecil and Rear-Adm. M. W. W. P. Consett, 1918. *Signed.* 51093, ff. 163, 165.

Conwell-Evans (Thomas P.), *author.*
— Correspondence between Lord Cecil and T. P. Conwell-Evans, 1934, 1937. 51169, ff. 232-238v, 247; 51175, ff. 65, 68, 74.

Cook (*Sir* Basil Alfred Kemball-).
— *v.* Kemball-Cook (*Sir* Basil Alfred).

Cook (David), *civil engineer.*
— Letter to Lord Crawford from D. Cook, 1913. *Signed.* 51160, f. 267.

Cooper (Alfred Duff), *1st Viscount Norwich.*
— Correspondence between Lord Cecil and A. Duff Cooper, 1922, 1939. *Signed.* 51095, ff. 66-67v; 51184, f. 149.

Cooper (E. M.), *of the Home Office Aliens Department.*
— Correspondence between Lord Cecil and E. M. Cooper, 1938, 1939. 51182, ff. 90, 115, 134; 51183, ff. 46-51, 57.

Cooper (Wibrahim Villiers), *journalist and author.*
— Correspondence between Lord Cecil and W. V. Cooper, 1940. 51185, ff. 187, 190.

Cope (Fred S.), *President, Rotary Club of Erith.*
— Correspondence between Lord Cecil and F. S. Cope, 1934, 1935. *Signed.* 51169, ff. 224, 229, 231; 51170, ff. 99, 100.

Corbin (Charles), *French diplomatist.*
— Letter from Lord Cecil to C. Corbin, 1935. *Copy.* 51171, f. 123.

Corcoran (Judith V.), *of the League of Nations Union.*
— Correspondence between Lord Cecil and J. V. Corcoran, 1938-1944. *Signed.* 51179, ff. 72-75, 78, 80, 126; 51180, f. 53; 51183, f. 156; 51184, ff. 147, 148; 51193, ff. 137-142.

Corkey (*Rev.* Robert), *Professor of Ethics and Practical Theology, Presbyterian College, Belfast.*
— Correspondence between Lord Cecil and Rev. R. Corkey, 1939. *Signed.* 51193, ff. 148-154.

Cornish (Philip Gordon Pym), *Vicar of Dane Hill.*
— Correspondence between Lord Cecil and P. G. P. Cornish, 1944, 1945. 51191, ff. 87-89, 272; 51192, f. 92.

Cot (Pierre), *French statesman.*
— Correspondence, including telegram, between Lord Cecil and P. Cot, 1932-1943. Partly *signed* and *printed.* Partly *Fr.* 51143, ff. 1-83v; 51101, f. 23.
— Memorandum by Lord Cecil rel. to P. Cot, 1940. Partly *signed* and *printed.* 51186, ff. 39-41.

Courtenay (James M.), *writing from Stevenage.*
— Letter to Lord Cecil from J. M. Courtenay, 1912. 51160, f. 138.

Courtney (Catherine), *widow of Leonard, Baron Courtney of Penwith.*
— Correspondence between Lord Cecil and Dowager Lady Courtney, 1925. 51164, ff. 107-110, 116.

Courtney (*Dame* Kathleen D'Olier), *D.B.E.*
— Correspondence, etc., between Lord Cecil and Dame K. D'O. Courtney, 1930-1946. Mostly *signed.* 51141, ff. 1-261; 51188, f. 164.
— Letter to Dame K. D'O. Courtney from C. W. Judd, 1941. *Signed.* 51141, f. 160.

Cove (Ernest G.), *Organising Sec., Committee for Development of Refugee Industries.*
— Correspondence, etc., partly on his behalf, with Lord Cecil, 1940-1942. *Signed.* 51185, ff. 30-39, 45, 219, 224, 243; 51186, f. 19; 51187, ff. 56-62; 51188, ff. 337, 345.

Cowdray, *1st Viscount.*
— *v.* Pearson (Weetman Dickinson).

Cox (Harold), *M.P.*
— Letters to Lord Cecil from H. Cox, 1909, 1915. Partly *signed,* partly *copy.* 51159, ff. 31, 34, 57; 51161, f. 248.

Craig (James), *Director, Empire Co-operative Industries, Morecambe.*
— Letter to Lord Cecil from J. Craig, 1912. 51160, f. 83.

Craigie (*Sir* Robert Leslie), *P.C.; G.C.M.G.*
— Letter, etc., to Lord Cecil from Sir R. L. Craigie, 1933. *Signed.* 51101, ff. 64-68.

Cranborne, *Viscount.*
— *v.* Gascoyne-Cecil (Robert Arthur James).

Crawford, *27th Earl of.*
— *v.* Lindsay (David Alexander Edward).

Creedy (*Sir* Herbert James), *G.C.B.*
— Correspondence between Sir H. J. Creedy and W. H. M. Selby, 1918. 51090, ff. 53-54v.

Crees (*Miss* Mary E.), *Hon. Sec., Letchworth Vigilance Association.*
— Letter to Lord Cecil from Miss M. E. Crees, 1918. 51162, f. 68.

Crewe-Milnes (Robert Offley Ashburton) *formerly* **Milnes,** *Marquess of Crewe.*
— Correspondence between Lord Cecil and Lord Crewe, 1923-1943. *Signed.* 51096, ff. 45, 52; 51184, f. 158; 51189, f. 281.

INDEX

Crichton (John Henry George), *5th Earl of Erne.*
— Letter to Lord Cecil from Lord Erne, 1938. 51180, f. 165.
— Reply by Lord Erne to Parliamentary Question of Lord Cecil rel. to Western Avenue at Acton, 1938. *Signed.* 51180, f. 166.

Cripps (Charles Alfred), *1st Baron Parmoor.*
— Letter to J. Ramsay MacDonald from Lord Parmoor, 1924. *Signed.* 51081, f. 27.
— Memorandum by Lord Parmoor rel. to conversation with Sir W. G. Max-Muller, 1924. 51096, f. 144.
— Letter to H. A. L. Fisher from Lord Parmoor, 1924. *Copy.* 51096, f. 148.
— Letter to E. F. L. Wood from Lord Parmoor, 1924. *Copy.* 51096, f. 149.
— Letter to Count — Bonin-Longare from Lord Parmoor, 1924. *Copy.* 51096, f. 153.
— Letter to Lord Parmoor from Sir A. G. M. Cadogan, 1924. *Copy.* 51096, f. 154.
— Memorandum, etc., by Lord Parmoor rel. to conversation with R. Donald, 1924. 51096, f. 162.
— Memorandum by Lord Parmoor rel. to conversation with C. Skirmunt, 1924. 51096, ff. 167, 168.
— Letter to Lord Parmoor from L. M. de Sousa Dantas, 1924. *Signed. Fr.* 51097, f. 4.
— Letter to Lord Phillimore from Lord Parmoor, 1924. *Copy.* 51097, f. 16.
— Letter, etc., to Lord Parmoor from J. Eppstein, 1924. *Signed.* Partly *printed.* 51097, ff. 27-45.
— Letter to Dame R. E. Crowdy from Lord Parmoor, 1924. *Copy.* 51097, f. 46.
— Letter to G. Hanotaux from Lord Parmoor, 1924. *Copy.* 51097, f. 50.
— Letter to F. Sthamer from Lord Parmoor, 1924. *Copy.* 51097, f. 59.
— Correspondence between Lord Parmoor and Sir W. G. Max-Muller, 1924. 51097, ff. 61, 65.
— Letter to Lord Parmoor from A. Dufour-Feronce, 1924. *Signed.* 51097, f. 64.
— Correspondence between Lord Parmoor and J. E. Drummond, 1924. *Copies.* 51110, ff. 104-119.
— Correspondence, partly on his behalf, with Lord Cecil, 1924-1939. Partly *signed.* 51096, f. 157; 51097, ff. 27-45; 51110, ff. 104-119; 51165, ff. 157, 164, 176-178; 51166, ff. 79, 85; 51173, ff. 15, 18; 51174, ff. 156, 157v, 181; 51176, ff. 89, 95, 107; 51179, ff. 221, 227; 51180, f. 100; 51182, ff. 62, 73, 133.
— Memorandum by Lord Cecil rel. to conversation with Lord Parmoor, 1929. ; 51099, f. 170.

Cripps (Isobel), *wife of Sir R. S. Cripps.*
— Correspondence between Lord Cecil and Lady Cripps, 1942. *Signed.* 51189, ff. 11, 21, 28.

Cripps (*Sir* Richard Stafford), *politician.*
— Letter to Lord Cecil on behalf of Sir R. S. Cripps, 1943. 51190, f. 353.

Croft (Henry Page), *1st Baron Croft.*
— Correspondence, including telegrams, between Lord Cecil and Lord Croft, 1935-1945. *Signed.* 51171, ff. 188, 189, 194, 197; 51188, ff. 347, 356; 51190, ff. 310, 312, 344, 355; 51191, ff. 277, 284, 318, 320; 51192, ff. 47, 48, 50, 53.

Cromer, *1st Earl of.*
— *v.* Baring (Evelyn).

Cromer, *2nd Earl of.*
— *v.* Baring (Rowland Thomas).

Cross (*Professor* Ephraim), *of New York.*
— Correspondence between Lord Cecil and Professor E. Cross, 1938. *Signed.* 51180, ff. 160, 172.

Cross (*Sir* Ronald Hibbert), *Bart.*
— Correspondence between Lord Cecil and R. H. Cross, 1939, 1940. *Signed.* 51184, ff. 207, 213, 243, 249, 309; 51185, ff. 136, 155.

Crossley (Anthony Crommelin), *M.P.*
— Correspondence between Lord Cecil and A. C. Crossley, 1937. 51176, ff. 77, 79, 82-85.

Crowdy (*Dame* Rachel Eleanor) afterw. **Thornhill**, *D.B.E.*
— Correspondence between P. J. Noel-Baker and Dame R. E. Crowdy, 1923. *Signed.* 51106, ff. 120-122.
— Letter to Dame R. E. Crowdy from Lord Parmoor, 1924. *Copy.* 51097, f. 46.

Crowe (*Sir* Eyre), *G.C.B.*
— Correspondence between Lord Cecil and Sir E. Crowe, 1923, 1925. 51095, ff. 180, 190; 51097, ff. 120-121v.

Crozier (*Brig.-Gen.* Frank Percy).
— Correspondence between Lord Cecil and Brig.-Gen. F. P. Crozier, 1937. 51175, ff. 157, 170, 173.

Crozier (William Percival), *Editor of The Manchester Guardian.*
— Correspondence, including telegram, between Lord Cecil and W. P. Crozier, 1940-1943. *Partly printed. Signed.* 51185, ff. 66, 77; 51189, ff. 64, 67, 98, 100, 107, 123, 131; 51190, ff. 8, 27, 30.

Cummings (H. R.), *formerly of the League of Nations staff.*
— Correspondence between Lord Cecil and H. R. Cummings, 1939. 51183, ff. 124, 125.

Cunliffe-Lister (Philip), *Earl of Swinton.*
— Correspondence, etc., partly on his behalf, with Lord Cecil, 1925-1938. Partly *signed.* 51098, ff. 3, 6; 51164, f. 142; 51174, f. 230; 51181, ff. 116, 133, 143.
— Reply by Lord Swinton to Parliamentary Question of Lord Cecil rel. to Royal Commission under presidency of Sir J. E. Banks, 1936. *Signed.* 51174, f. 231.

Cunningham (Alfred G.), *Commissioner, Salvation Army.*
— Letter to Lord Cecil from A. G. Cunningham, 1943. *Signed.* 51190, f. 123.

Currey (Muriel [Innes?]), *[author?].*
— Correspondence between Lord Cecil and M. [I?] Currey, 1941. *Signed.* 51187, f. 424; 51188, f. 9.

Curtis (John), *Prime Minister of Australia.*
— Correspondence between Lord Cecil and J. Curtis, 1944. *Signed.* 51191, ff. 96, 102, 105, 106.

Curtis (Lionel George), *writer.*
— Speech by L. G. Curtis to the Conference of the Institute of Pacific Relations, Shanghai, 1931. *Printed.* 51167, ff. 170-184.
— Correspondence between Lord Cecil and L. G. Curtis, 1932. *Signed.* 51167, ff. 169-185.

Curtius (Julius), *German statesman.*
— Memorandum by Lord Cecil rel. to conversation with J. Curtius, 1931. 51100, f. 121.

Curzon (George Nathanial), *Marquess Curzon of Kedleston.*
— Correspondence, partly on his behalf, with Lord Cecil, 1910-1925. Partly *signed.* 51077, ff. 1-305; 51080, ff. 4-10, 31-38.
— Letter to N. Titulescu, 1923. *Copy.* 51096, f. 12.
— Letter to Sir W. G. Max-Muller from E. Ovey on behalf of Lord Curzon, 1923. *Copy.* 51096, f. 17.

INDEX

Curzon (George Nathanial), *Marquess Curzon of Kedleston.* continuation
— Correspondence between L. Wolf and Lord Curzon, 1923, 1927. Mostly *signed.* 51096, f. 8; 51099, ff. 88, 95.
— Letters to Lord Curzon from E. N. L. Sturt, 1942. *Signed.* 51189, ff. 128, 230.

Cushendun, *Baron.*
— *v.* MacNeill (Ronald John).

Cushman (Ralph Spaulding), *Methodist bishop in Denver, Colorado.*
— Telegram to Lord Cecil from R. S. Cushman, 1939. 51182, f. 155.

Czechlin (*Dr.* —), *of the German Ministry of Foreign Affairs.*
— Letter from Lord Cecil to Dr. — Czechlin, 1923. *Copy.* 51096, f. 129.
— Memorandum by Lord Cecil rel. to conversation with Dr. — Czechlin, 1924. 51097, ff. 66-69.

Czechoslovakia.
— Message from Lord Cecil, etc., to the Republic of Czechoslovakia, 1938. *Copy.* 51181, f. 191.

D

D'Abernon, *Viscount.*
— *v.* Vincent (Edgar).

Dafoe (J. W.), *President, Winnipeg Free Press Company.*
— Correspondence between Lord Cecil and J. W. Dafoe, 1941, 1942. *Signed.* 51187, f. 410; 51188, f. 24; 51189, ff. 170, 185.

Dale (Anthony), *League of Nations Union, Brighton Branch.*
— Correspondence between Lord Cecil and A. Dale, 1944. 51191, ff. 313, 317.

Dalton (Edward Hugh John Neale), *Baron Dalton.*
— Correspondence between Lord Cecil and E. H. J. N. Dalton, 1930-1942. Partly *signed.* 51100, ff. 25, 35-39, 51-56, 63-68, 109; 51174, ff. 132, 135, 136; 51175, ff. 12, 29, 130, 133, 141; 51185, ff. 171-176, 179; 51188, ff. 175, 192.
— Memorandum by E. H. J. N. Dalton rel. to D. M. Foot's conversation on his behalf with Lord Cecil, 1942. *Copy.* 51188, f. 161.

Danckwerts (William Otto Adolph Julius), *K.C.*
— Legal opinion, 1908. *Copy.* 51074, ff. 164-166v.
— Correspondence between Lord Cecil and W. O. A. J. Danckwerts, 1911. 51160, ff. 13-18.

Dantas (L. M. de Sousa).
— *v.* Sousa Dantas (L. M. de).

Dartmouth, *6th Earl of.*
— *v.* Legge (William Heneage).

Darwin (*Maj.* Leonard), *M.P.*
— Letters to Lord Cecil from Maj. L. Darwin, 1906-1938. Partly *signed.* 51158, ff. 63, 141, 176-179v, 182, 208, 211-214, 223, 282; 51159, ff. 85, 108-111; 51170, ff. 39, 49; 51179, f. 11.

Davidson (John Colin Campbell), *1st Viscount Davidson.*
— Correspondence between Lord Cecil and J. C. C. Davidson, 1923, 1927. Partly *signed.* 51080, ff. 66-72v, 92, 232; 51165, ff. 193, 197-201.

Davidson (*Mrs* R.).
— Message to Mrs R. Davidson etc., from King George and Queen Mary, 1920. *Copy.* 51162, f. 107.

Davidson (Randall Thomas), *Archbishop of Canterbury; Baron Davidson of Lambeth, 1928.*
— Memorandum rel. to his interview with the Archbishop of York and the Bishop of St. Asaph, 1915. *Copy.* 51161, ff. 237-242.
— Letters to Lord Cecil from Archbishop of Canterbury, 1915, 1923. Partly *signed.* 51161, f. 205; 51163, ff. 151, 173.

Davies (D. Edward), *writing from Hampstead Garden Suburb.*
— Letter to Lord Cecil from D. E. Davies, 1912. *Signed.* 51160, f. 84.

Davies (David), *1st Baron Davies; President, Welsh Council, League of Nations Union.*
— Correspondence between Lord Cecil and Lord Davies, 1923-1943. Mostly *signed.* 51138.
— Memoranda rel. to visits by Lord Davies to Paris and Switzerland, 1939. *Copies.* 51184, ff. 217-228, 229-233.

Davies (*Rev.* Gwilym), *of the League of Nations Union, Welsh National Council.*
— Correspondence between Lord Cecil and Rev. G. Davies, 1945. 51192, ff. 192, 204.

Davies (W. Robert), *Sec., Liberal Party Organisation.*
— Letters to Lord Cecil from W. R. Davies, 1938, 1940. *Signed.* 51179, f. 50; 51181, f. 161; 51185, f. 262.

Davies (*Sir* William), *Editor of The Western Mail, Cardiff.*
— Letters, etc., to Lord Cecil from Sir W. Davies, 1908. 51074, ff. 172-179.

Davis (John William), *U.S. lawyer and diplomatist.*
— Telegram to Lord Cecil from J. W. Davis, 1923. 51095, f. 133.

Davis (Malcolm W.), *Director, Geneva Research Center.*
— Correspondence between Lord Cecil and M. W. Davis, 1934. 51169, ff. 86, 89-91, 132-134, 136, 156.

Davis (Norman H.), *U.S. diplomatist.*
— Correspondence between Lord Cecil and N. H. Davis, 1925, 1938. Partly *signed.* 51164, ff. 59-61; 51180, f. 122.
— Memoranda by Lord Cecil rel. to conversation with N. H. Davis, 1933. 51101, f. 76.

Dawes (Charles Gates), *U.S. banker and diplomatist.*
— Letter, etc., to Lord Cecil from C. G. Dawes, 1929. *Signed.* 51099, f. 200.

Dawney (*Col.* Alan Geoffrey Charles), *of the B.B.C.; afterw. of the War Office.*
— Correspondence between Lord Cecil and Col. A. G. C. Dawney, 1935. *Signed.* 51170, f. 244; 51171, ff. 1, 25.

Dawson (Geoffrey George) *formerly Robinson, Editor of The Times.*
— Correspondence between Lord Cecil and G. G. Dawson, 1923-1940. *Signed.* 51156, ff. 1-38.
— Letter to G. G. Dawson from J. Ramsay MacDonald, S. Baldwin and Lord Oxford and Asquith, 1924. *Copy.* 51097, f. 83.

De Lotbinière (S. J.), *of the B.B.C.*
— Letter to Lord Cecil, 1935. Partly *printed. Signed.* 51193, f. 34.

De Rayne (Adela Bowly), *wife of F. De Rayne.*
— Correspondence on her behalf with Lord Cecil, 1940, 1941. 51186, ff. 168, 192, 293.

De Rayne (Francis), *of St. Albans.*
— Correspondence between Lord Cecil and F. De Rayne, 1940, 1941. 51186, ff. 168, 192, 293.

Dean (J. S.), *of the Pedestrians' Association.*
— Correspondence between Lord Cecil and J. S. Dean, 1937. *Signed.* 51175, ff. 117-122; 124.

Deas (*Miss* Margaret), *of the Liberal Party Organisation, London.*
— Correspondence between Lord Cecil and Miss M. Deas, 1938. *Signed.* 51181, ff. 4, 10.

Deedes (*Brig.-Gen. Sir* Wyndham).
— Letter, etc., to Lord Cecil from Brig.-Gen. Sir W. Deedes, 1943. *Signed.* 51190, ff. 91-94.

Degerman (Allan), *of the International Peace Campaign, Swedish Committee.*
— Correspondence, including telegram, between Lord Cecil and A. Degerman, 1942. 51188, ff. 140, 154.

d'Egville (*Sir* Howard), *K.B.E.*
— Correspondence between Lord Cecil and Sir H. d'Egville, 1933. *Signed.* 51168, ff. 109, 112, 116, 119-124, 139, 147.

Delevingne (*Sir* Malcolm), *K.C.B.*
— Correspondence, etc., between Lord Cecil and Sir M. Delevingne, 1923-1926. *Signed.* 51096, f. 107; 51098, ff. 12, 52-61, 127, 139-144, 149.

Dell (Robert).
— Correspondence between Lord Cecil and R. Dell, 1922. *Signed.* 51095, ff. 121, 124.

Deloitte, Plender, Griffiths & Co., *accountants.*
— Report on accounts of League of Nations High Commission for Refugees, 1936. 51173, ff. 126-129.

Delvima (Hikmet), *Albanian statesman.*
— Telegram to Lord Cecil from H. Delvima, 1941. *Fr.* 51187, f. 389.

Denton-Thompson (Merrick Arnold Bardsley), *Vice-Consul in Brussels.*
— Letter to Lord Cecil from M. A. B. Denton-Thompson, 1924. 51096, f. 136.

Derby, *17th Earl of.*
— *v.* Stanley (Edward George Villiers).

Dernburg (*Dr.* B[ernhard?]), *writer on international affairs.*
— Correspondence, etc., between Lord Cecil and Dr. B. Dernburg, 1922. Partly *printed.* 51095, ff. 110-119.

Desborough, *Baron.*
— *v.* Grenfell (William Henry).

Deutsch (Julia) *née* **Ward,** *wife of Dr. G. F. Deutsch.*
— Correspondence between Lord Cecil and J. Deutsch, 1941. 51187, ff. 380, 419.

Deuxième Congrès Mondial de la Jeunesse, Paris.
— *v.* Wallace (Michael).

Devonshire, *8th Duke of.*
— *v.* Cavendish (Spencer Compton).

Devonshire, *9th Duke of.*
— *v.* Cavendish (Victor Christian William).

Devonshire, *10th Duke of.*
— *v.* Cavendish (Edward William Spencer).

Diamond (Charles), *M.P.*
— Correspondence between Lord Cecil and C. Diamond, 1912. *Signed.* 51160, ff. 66, 69-73.

Diaries and Memoranda.
— Lord Cecil: Accounts of visits and tours abroad, 1917-1937. Mostly *copies;* partly *printed.* 51131; 51169, f. 54; 51171, f. 229; 51177, ff. 75, 76, 154; 51178, ff. 14-20.

Diaries and Memoranda.
continuation
— Lord Cecil: biographical summary prepared for 'Revue des Deux Mondes', 1932. *Copy.* 51167, f. 192.
— Memoranda rel. to visits by Lord Davies to Paris and Switzerland, 1939. *Copies.* 51184, ff. 217-228, 229-233.

Dickinson (Willoughby Hyett), *1st Baron Dickinson.*
— Correspondence between Lord Cecil and Lord Dickinson, 1918-1936. *Signed.* 51162, ff. 30-36; 51171, ff. 69-78; 51174, f. 154.

Dickson (*Maj.* Dhannuil Gordon), *of the International Peace Campaign.*
— Letter to Lord Cecil, 1937. *Signed.* 51177, f. 63.

Disraeli (Benjamin), *Earl of Beaconsfield; Prime Minister.*
— Speech by B. Disraeli on installation as Lord Rector of Glasgow University, 1873. *Copy,* 20th cent. 51174, ff. 25-37.

Dixon (Frederick), *Editor of The Christian Science Monitor, Boston, Massachusetts.*
— Telegrams between F. P. Leay and G. H. Locock on behalf of F. Dixon, 1915-1917. Partly *draft.* Partly *signed.* 51092, ff. 23-288 *passim.*
— Correspondence, partly on his behalf, between F. Dixon and Lord Cecil, 1915-1923. Partly *signed.* 51092, ff. 1-316 *passim.*
— Letter to Lord Grey from F. Dixon, 1916. 51092, f. 115.

Dixon (Pierson John), *of the Foreign Office.*
— Correspondence between Lord Cecil and P. J. Dixon, 1946. *Signed.* 51192, ff. 233, 236.

Dobbs (*Sir* Henry Robert Conway), *G.B.E.*
— Memorandum by Lord Cecil rel. to conversation with Sir H. R. C. Dobbs, 1931. 51100, f. 85.

Docherty (Frank), *Press Sec., Peace and Empire Congress, Glasgow.*
— Correspondence between Lord Cecil and F. Docherty, 1938. *Signed.* 51181, ff. 41-46; 51199, ff. 216-230.

Docker (*Col.* P.), *Chairman, League of Nations Union, Olton Branch.*
— Correspondence between Lord Cecil and Col. P. Docker, 1934. *Signed.* 51169, ff. 43, 47, 67, 68, 87.
— Letter, etc., to Col. P. Docker from Capt. E. G. W. Vaughan, 1934. *Signed.* 51169, f. 84.

Dodd (William Edward), *U.S. diplomatist.*
— Correspondence between Lord Cecil and W. E. Dodd, 1936, 1937. Partly *signed.* 51174, ff. 75, 85, 110, 216; 51175, ff. 150, 156, 183, 207.

Dodson (John William), *2nd Baron Monk Bretton.*
— Letter to Lord Cecil from Lord Monk Bretton, 1909. 51159, f. 195.

Dolivet (Louis), *Sec., International Peace Campaign.*
— Letters to P. J. Noel-Baker from L. Dolivet, 1936-1941. *Signed.* Partly *copy.* Mostly *Fr.* 51143, ff. 93, 175, 180.
— Correspondence, including telegram, partly on his behalf, with Lord Cecil, 1936-1944. Partly *signed.* Partly *Fr.* 51143, ff. 84-192v; 51180, f. 37.
— Telegram to L. Dolivet from Tseng Yang-Fu, 1938. *Copy.* 51180, f. 37.

Dollfuss (Engelbert), *Federal Chancellor of Austria.*
— Letter to Lord Cecil from E. Dollfuss, 1934. *Signed. Fr.* 51169, ff. 105, 155.

Dollfuss (*Col.* R.), *of Château de Kietsen, Berne, Switzerland.*
— Correspondence between Lord Cecil and Col. R. Dollfuss, 1941. *Signed.* 51187, f. 415; 51188, ff. 42-44, 94.

Don (*Sir* Alan Campbell), *K.C.V.O; Chaplain and Sec. to the Archbishop of Canterbury.*
— Correspondence with Lord Cecil on the Archbishop's behalf, 1936-1945. *Signed.* 51154 A, ff. 64, 79, 80, 117; 51172, f. 139; 51193, ff. 293-295, 313, 314.

Donald (Robert).
— Memorandum, etc., by Lord Parmoor rel. to conversation with R. Donald, 1924. 51096, f. 162.

Donnet (William), *of the Junior Conservative Club.*
— Letters to Lord Cecil from W. Donnet, 1913. 51160, ff. 225, 228.

Donville-Maillefeu, *Vicomte de.*
— Correspondence between Lord Cecil and Vicomte de Donville-Maillefeu, 1936. *Fr.* 51172, ff. 141, 150.

Dormer (*Sir* Cecil Francis Joseph), *K.C.M.G.*
— Letters to Lord Cecil from Sir C. F. J. Dormer, 1937, 1938. 51178, f. 117; 51179, f. 245.

Douglas (D. S.), *writing from East Road, London, N.*
— Letter to Lord Cecil, 1907. 51158, f. 108.

Douglas (*Canon* John Albert), *Vicar of St. Luke's, Camberwell.*
— Letter to Lord Cecil from Canon J. A. Douglas, 1925. *Signed.* 51097, f. 159.

Douglas (Margaret), *Sec., Insurance Tax Registers' Defence Association.*
— Letters to Lord Cecil from M. Douglas, 1915. Partly *signed.* 51160, f. 273; 51161, ff. 224, 232, 236.

Drage (Geoffrey), *author.*
— Correspondence between Lord Cecil and G. Drage, 1941. 51187, ff. 15, 20.

Drake (*Sir* Eugen John Henry Vanderstegen Millington-).
— *v.* Millington-Drake (*Sir* Eugen John Henry Vanderstegen).

Dreyer (*Adm. Sir* Frederic Charles), *G.B.E.*
— Correspondence between Lord Cecil and Adm. Sir F. C. Dreyer, 1931. *Signed.* 51100, ff. 114-116.

Dreyse (Fritz), *German economist and banker.*
— Memorandum by J. G. McDonald rel. to conversation with F. Dreyse, 1934. 51101, f. 189.

Drummond (Angela), *wife of James, 16th Earl of Perth.*
— Letter to Lord Cecil from A. Drummond, 1927. 51111, f. 98.

Drummond (E).
— Letter to E. Drummond from E. S. Montagu, 1916. *Signed.* 51093, f. 9.

Drummond (James Eric), *16th Earl of Perth; Sec.-General of the League of Nations.*
— Correspondence between Lord Cecil and Lord Perth, 1921-1948. Mostly *signed.* Partly *Fr.* 51110-51112.
— Letters to J. E. Drummond from F. P. Walters, 1923, 1930. *Signed.* 51110, f. 50; 51112, f. 26.
— Letter to P. J. Noel-Baker from J. E. Drummond, 1924. *Signed.* 51106, f. 206.

Drummond (James Eric), *16th Earl of Perth; Sec.-General of the League of Nations. continuation*
— Correspondence between Lord Parmoor and J. E. Drummond, 1924. *Copies.* 51110, ff. 104-119.
— Letter to J. E. Drummond from P. de Azcarate y Florez, 1932. *Signed. Fr.* 51112, ff. 148-153.
— Letters and telegrams to the Sec.-General, League of Nations from S. Nabwe on behalf of Chief Nimley, 1934. *Copies.* 51101, ff. 121-129, 131, 133.

Drummond (Lindsay), *publisher.*
— Letter to Lord Cecil, 1943. *Signed.* 51190, f. 221.

Drury-Lowe (*Vice-Adm.* Sidney Robert).
— Correspondence between Vice-Adm. S. R. Drury-Lowe and Miss I. M. Butler on behalf of Lord Cecil, 1935-1939. 51171, ff. 43, 58, 84, 88, 90; 51178, ff. 131-133v; 51180, ff. 102, 113; 51181, ff. 82, 85; 51184, ff. 51, 67.

Dufferin and Ava, *4th Marquess of.*
— *v.* Hamilton-Temple-Blackwood (Basil Sheridan).

Duffy (V. C.), *Official Sec., Australian High Commission, London.*
— Correspondence between V. C. Duffy and Miss I. M. Butler, 1935. 51171, ff. 33, 34.

Dufour-Feronce (Albert), *German diplomatist.*
— Letter, etc., to Lord Cecil from A. Dufour-Feronce, 1923. *Signed.* 51096, ff. 32-36, 44.
— Letter to Lord Parmoor from A. Dufour-Feronce, 1924. *Signed.* 51097, f. 64.
— Memorandum by Lord Cecil rel. to conversation with A. Dufour-Feronce, [1926?]. 51098, f. 84.

Dugdale (Blanche Elizabeth Campbell) née **Balfour**, *wife of E. T. S. Dugdale; of the League of Nations Union.*
— Correspondence between Lord Cecil and his cousin B. E. C. Dugdale, 1921-1946. Partly *signed.* 51157, ff. 231-316v.
— Memorandum by Lord Cecil rel. to conversation with B. E. C. Dugdale, 1930. 51100, f. 61.
— Letter to B. E. C. Dugdale from the Dean of Chichester, 1941. *Signed.* 51157, f. 279.
— Letter to B. E. C. Dugdale from L. Herrman, 1945. *Signed.* 51157, f. 302.

Dumont (*Lt.-Col.* J.), *of Comité de Secours aux Prisonniers, in Paris.*
— Letter, etc., to Lord Cecil from Lt.-Col. Dumont, 1938. *Signed. Fr.* 51182, ff. 107-112.

Dunbar (Robert Haig), *Editor of Derbyshire Printing Co.'s papers.*
— Letter to Lord Cecil from R. H. Dunbar, 1914. 51161, f. 123v.

Duncan-Jones (Arthur Stuart), *Dean of Chichester.*
— Letter to B. E. C. Dugdale from the Dean of Chichester, 1941. *Signed.* 51157, f. 279.
— Correspondence between Lord Cecil and Dean of Chichester, 1941-1944. Partly *signed.* 51186, ff. 245, 261, 292, 301; 51187, f. 5; 51190, ff. 12, 16, 19, 38; 51191, f. 160.

Duncan-Jones (Vincent), *Sec., The Peace Penny Fund.*
— Correspondence between Lord Cecil and V. Duncan-Jones, 1938, 1939. Mostly *signed.* 51137, ff. 176-224.

Dundas (Lawrence John Lumley), *Earl of Ronaldshay; Marquess of Zetland, 1929.*
— Correspondence between Lord Cecil and Lord Ronaldshay, 1928. 51166, ff. 68-70v.

INDEX

Dunrossil, *1st Viscount.*
— *v.* Morrison (William Shepherd).
Durham, *3rd Earl of.*
— *v.* Lambton (John George).
Durham, *4th Earl of.*
— *v.* Lambton (Frederick William).
Durham, *Bishop of.*
— *v.* Henson (Herbert Hensley).
— *v.* Williams (Alwyn Terrell Petre).
Durham (*Miss* M. Edith), *writing from London NW 3.*
— Letter to Lord Cecil, 1944. *Signed.* 51191, f. 206.
Dutton (*Sir* Ernest Rowe-).
— *v.* Rowe-Dutton (*Sir* Ernest).
Duxbury (Richard Cobden), *Sec., League of Nations Union, Carlisle Branch.*
— Correspondence between Lord Cecil and R. C. Duxbury, 1936-1938. *Signed.* 51174, ff. 66, 70; 51181, ff. 171, 174, 181, 190, 196; 51182, f. 100.
Dwyer-Gray (Edmund), *Australian politician.*
— Correspondence between Lord Cecil and E. Dwyer-Gray, 1945. *Signed.* 51192, ff. 3, 114-117, 160, 162, 165-169, 175.
[Dylan?] (T. L.), *Editor, Pictorial Press.*
— Correspondence between T. L. [Dylan?] and Miss I. M. Butler, 1942. *Signed.* 51188, ff. 247, 335.
— Correspondence between Lord Cecil and T. L. [Dylan?], 1942. *Signed.* 51188, f. 339.

E

Eaves (Harry), *Secretary, League of Nations Union, Nelson Branch.*
— Letter to Lord Cecil, 1944. *Signed.* 51191, f. 282.
Eberlin (A.), *Chairman, League of Nations Union, Nottingham branch.*
— Correspondence between Lord Cecil and A. Eberlin, 1923. 51163, ff. 127-130v, 185, 188.
Ebury, *2nd Baron.*
— *v.* Grosvenor (Robert Wellesley).
Eddison (Eric Rucker), *of the Board of Trade; author.*
— Correspondence with Lord Cecil on behalf of Sir A. H. Stanley, 1918. *Signed.* 51094, f. 139.
Ede (James Chuter) *afterw.* **Chuter-Ede,** *Baron Chuter-Ede.*
— Correspondence, partly on his behalf, with Lord Cecil, 1946-1949. *Signed.* 51192, ff. 251, 257, 268, 269, 314, 315.
Edelman (Maurice), *author and journalist; afterwards M.P.*
— Correspondence between Lord Cecil and M. Edelman, 1944, 1945. *Signed.* 51191, ff. 312, 316; 51192, f. 69.
Eden (Geoffrey Morton), *7th Baron Auckland.*
— Letter to Lord Cecil from Lord Auckland, 1943. *Signed.* 51190, f. 131.
Eden (George Rodney), *Bishop of Wakefield.*
— Letter to Lord Cecil from Bishop of Wakefield, 1912. *Signed.* 51160, f. 64.
Eden (Robert Anthony), *1st Earl of Avon.*
— Correspondence, partly on his behalf, with Lord Cecil, 1932-1945. Mostly *signed.* 51083, ff. 48-196.

INDEX

Edinburgh, *League of Nations Union Branch.*
— Telegram to Lord Cecil, 1944. 51191, f. 173.

Edwards (Alfred George), *Bishop of St. Asaph; Archbishop of Wales, 1920.*
— Memorandum rel. to his interview with the Archbishops of Canterbury and York, 1915. *Copy.* 51161, ff. 237-242.

Edwards (Edward), *Vice-Principal, University College of Wales, Aberystwyth.*
— Correspondence between Lord Cecil and E. Edwards, 1926. *Signed.* 51165, ff. 17, 18.

Edwards (Patrick Harrington), *solicitor.*
— Correspondence between Lord Cecil and P. H. Edwards, 1908-1943. Partly *printed.* Mostly *signed.* 51158, f. 198v; 51164, ff. 23-156 *passim;* 51165, ff. 22-33, 35-64v; 51184, f. 189; 51185, f. 204; 51186, ff. 139, 144, 149, 300; 51187, f. 63; 51188, ff. 63, 95, 179; 51189, ff. 142, 175, 176, 235; 51190, ff. 20, 23, 49, 133, 137, 162; 51190, ff. 285, 291, 294, 316, 319, 324, 383.
— Letters, etc., to Miss I. M. Butler from P. H. Edwards, 1941, 1942. *Signed.* 51187, f. 13; 51188, f. 201; 51189, ff. 175, 176, 192.
— Correspondence between P. H. Edwards and Miss E. V. Lazarus, 1943. *Signed.* 51189, f. 263; 51190, ff. 319, 320.

Egerton (*Rear-Adm.* Wilfrid Allan), *C.M.G.*
— Correspondence between Lord Cecil and Rear-Adm. W. A. Egerton, 1927. 51165, ff. 151, 161.

Eichelberger (Clark Mel), *Director, League of Nations Association Inc., New York.*
— Correspondence, including telegrams, between Lord Cecil and C. M. Eichelberger, 1937-1945. *Signed.* 51143, f. 185; 51178, f. 9; 51183, f. 131; 51184, f. 325; 51189, ff. 160-163, 193; 51192, ff. 12, 16.

Eisendrath (Maurice Nathan), *Rabbi, of Toronto.*
— Letter to Lord Cecil from Rabbi M. N. Eisendrath, 1936. *Signed.* 51173, f. 177.

Elections, *Parliamentary.*
— Addresses, etc., by Lord Cecil to the electors of North Herts, 1918, 1923. Partly *printed.* 51162, ff. 72-76v; 51163, f. 175.
— Advice to electors, by Lord Cecil, 1929. Partly *draft* and *printed.* 51166, ff. 103-107.
— Election address by Maj. H. L. Nathan in Cardiff, 1935. *Printed.* 51171, f. 166.
— Memorandum by Lord Cecil rel. to Parliamentary elections, 1938. *Copy.* 51182, f. 47.

Elfterwalde (T.), *of Prague.*
— Correspondence between Lord Cecil and T. Elfterwalde, 1935. *Signed.* Partly *Germ.* 51170, ff. 139, 170, 179, 180.

Elgin, *10th Earl of.*
— *v.* Bruce (Edward James).

Elibank, *2nd Viscount.*
— *v.* Murray (Gideon).

Elliot (Arthur Ralph Douglas), *M.P.*
— Letters to Lord Cecil from A. R. D. Elliot, 1905, 1908. 51158, ff. 17-27v, 242.

Elliot (Walter Elliot), *P.C.; M.P.*
— Correspondence between Lord Cecil and W. E. Elliot, 1935. *Signed.* 51170, ff. 119, 126, 134.

Elliott (Sydney Robert), *Managing Editor, Reynolds News.*
— Letter to Lord Cecil from S. R. Elliott, 1940. *Signed.* 51186, f. 162.

Ellis (*Sir* Charles Edward), *G.B.E.*
— Letter to Winston Churchill from Sir C. E. Ellis, 1918. *Signed.* 51093, f. 152.

Ellis (*Sir* Charles Henry Brabazon Heaton-).
— *v.* Heaton-Ellis (*Sir* Charles Henry Brabazon).

Ellis (*Miss* Edith), *Sec., League of Nations Union, Scarborough.*
— Correspondence between Lord Cecil and Miss E. Ellis, 1935-1945. 51142, ff. 93-151v.

Ellis (*Sir* Robert Geoffrey), *Bart.*
— Memorandum to members of the Watching Committee, 1942. *Printed.* 51188, ff. 158-159v.

Eltisley, *Baron.*
— *v.* Newton (George Douglas Cochrane).

Elton (Godfrey), *1st Baron Elton.*
— Correspondence between Lord Cecil and Lord Elton, 1936. Mostly *signed.* 51174, ff. 11, 14, 17, 24, 78, 81.

Emile-Weil (Alain), *of Endsleigh Gardens, London.*
— Visiting card, 1939. *Printed.* 51183, f. 153.

Emmott (Alfred), *Baron Emmott.*
— Letter to Lord Cecil from Lord Emmott, 1918. *Copy.* 51093, f. 64.

Empson (William), *poet.*
— Correspondence between Lord Cecil and W. Empson, 1942. 51193, ff. 260-262.

Emrys-Evans (Paul Vychan), *M.P.*
— Correspondence between Lord Cecil and P. V. Emrys-Evans, 1940, 1941. 51186, ff. 24, 30, 37, 106, 117; 51187, ff. 41, 324, 325.

ENGLAND. SOVEREIGNS OF, *and transactions in particular reigns. GEORGE V.*
— Message to Mrs R. Davidson etc., from King George and Queen Mary, 1920. *Copy.* 51162, f. 107.
— Memorandum by Lord Cecil on the political situation, 1921. *Copy.* 51163, ff. 36-40.
— General Full Power for Lord Cecil at the League of Nations, 1923. *Signed.* Seal *en placard.* 51077, f. 202.

ENGLAND. SOVEREIGNS OF, *and transactions in particular reigns. EDWARD VIII.*
— Letter to Lord Cecil from H. L. Thomas, on behalf of Edward VIII as Prince of Wales, 1932. 51168, f. 1.

ENGLAND. SOVEREIGNS OF, *and transactions in particular reigns. ELIZABETH II.* Philip, *Duke of Edinburgh; consort of Queen Elizabeth.*
— Letter from Lord Cecil to Duke of Edinburgh, 1949. *Draft.* 51192, f. 322.

Eppstein (John), *author; of the League of Nations Union Secretariate.*
— Correspondence, partly on his behalf, with Lord Cecil, 1923-1937. Partly *signed.* 51096, f. 48; 51170, f. 130; 51171, ff. 47-52; 51172, f. 111; 51173, f. 172; 51174, f. 92; 51175, f. 134; 51178, f. 122; 51179, ff. 243-244.
— Letter, etc., to Lord Parmoor from J. Eppstein, 1924. *Signed.* Partly *printed.* 51097, ff. 27-45.
— Memorandum, etc., rel. to the Holy See and the League of Nations, 1924. *Signed.* Mostly *printed.* 51097, ff. 29-45.
— Memorandum by J. Eppstein rel. to interview with Sir R. W. A. Leeper, 1935. *Copy.* 51171, ff. 94-98.

Eppstein (John), *author; of the League of Nations Union Secretariate.* continuation
— Correspondence between J. Eppstein and Miss I. M. Butler, 1935, 1936. 51171, f. 16; 51172, ff. 39, 98.

Epstein (*Dr.* Felix), *Czech chemical engineer.*
— Correspondence between Dr. F. Epstein and Miss I. M. Butler, 1941. 51187, ff. 81, 120, 152, 166, 186.

Erich (Rafael Waldemar), *Finnish diplomatist.*
— Correspondence between Lord Cecil and R. W. Erich, 1926, 1929. *Signed.* Partly *Fr.* 51098, ff. 133-138; 51099, ff. 65-68, 193.

Erlebach (Elsworth), *of Woodford House School, Birchington.*
— Correspondence between Lord Cecil and E. Erlebach, 1942. 51188, ff. 260, 265.

Erne, *5th Earl of.*
— *v.* Crichton (John Henry George).

Ernle, *Baron.*
— *v.* Prothero (Rowland Edmund).

Essayan (Ohannes), *representative of Armenian refugees at the League of Nations.*
— Correspondence between Lord Cecil and O. Essayan, 1937. *Signed.* 51176, f. 159; 51177, f. 26.

Essendon (Frederick William Lewis), *1st Baron Essendon.*
— Letter to Lord Cecil on behalf of the King George's Fund for Sailors, 1935. *Signed.* 51171, f. 235.

Esslemont (Peter), *publisher.*
— Letter from Lord Cecil to P. Esslemont, 1942. 51188, f. 230.

ETHIOPIA.
— Map of Ethiopia, 1935. *Printed* with MS. annotations. *Fr.* and *Ital.* 51177, f. 56v.

ETHIOPIA. SOVEREIGNS OF, *and transactions in particular reigns. HAILE SELASSIE I.*
— Correspondence between Haile Selassie as heir to the throne of Ethiopia and C. F. W. Russell, 1923. *Copies.* 51096, ff. 78, 79.
— Correspondence between Lord Cecil and Emperor Haile Selassie, 1936-1938. *Amharic*, with *Engl. transl.* 51174, ff. 210, 211, 226; 51178, ff. 119, 120, 137; 51182, ff. 113, 114.

Evang (Karl), *of the Norwegian Ministry of Social Welfare in London.*
— Letter, etc., to Lord Cecil from K. Evang, 1941. *Signed.* 51188, ff. 108-112.

Evans (Ifor Leslie), *Principal, University College of Wales, Aberystwyth.*
— Letter to G. G. A. Murray from I. L. Evans, 1941. *Signed.* 51133, f. 223.

Evans (*Sir* Laming Worthington-).
— *v.* Worthington-Evans (*Sir* Laming).

Evans (Paul Vychan Emrys-).
— *v.* Emrys-Evans (Paul Vychan).

Evans (Thomas P. Conwell-).
— *v.* Conwell-Evans (Thomas P.).

Eversley, *Baron.*
— *v.* Shaw-Lefevre (George John).

Ewing (Irene Rosetta), *1st wife of Sir A. W. G. Ewing; of the University of Manchester.*
— Letter, etc., to Sir L. F. Behrens from I. R. Ewing, 1941. *Signed.* 51186, f. 258.
— Correspondence between I. R. Ewing and Miss I. M. Butler, 1941. *Signed.* 51186, ff. 296, 302; 51187, ff. 44, 83, 165.
— Correspondence between Lord Cecil and I. R. Ewing, 1941. *Signed.* 51187, ff. 353, 356, 360, 397.

Ewing (*Sir* James Alfred), *K.C.B.*
— Letters to Lord Cecil from Sir J. A. Ewing, 1921. 51162, ff. 140, 167.

Ewing (*Rev.* John William), *President, National Free Church Council.*
— Letter to Lord Cecil from Rev. J. W. Ewing, 1939. 51184, ff. 118, 164.

Ewins (M. A.), *Sec., League of Nations Union, Coventry District Committee.*
— Correspondence between Lord Cecil and M. A. Ewins, 1937. *Signed.* 51176, ff. 112, 126.

Exeter, *6th Marquess of.*
— *v.* Cecil (William Thomas Brownlow).

Exeter, *Bishop of.*
— *v.* Gascoyne-Cecil (*Lord* William).

Eysinga (*Dr.* Willem Jan Mari van), *Dutch lawyer and diplomatist.*
— Correspondence between Lord Cecil and Dr. W. J. M. van Eysinga, 1923. 51096, ff. 73, 84.

F

Faber (George Denison), *M.P.; barrister.*
— Letter to Lord Cecil from G. D. Faber, 1914. 51161, f. 114.

Falconer (James), *M.P.*
— Correspondence between Lord Cecil and J. Falconer, 1913. *Signed.* 51160, ff. 243, 271.

Fanshawe (Maurice), *author and official of the League of Nations Union.*
— Letters to Miss I. M. Butler from M. Fanshawe, 1931, 1942. 51167, f. 100; 51189, f. 233.
— Correspondence between Lord Cecil and M. Fanshawe, 1940, 1941. 51185, ff. 228, 229, 239; 51186, f. 44; 51187, ff. 16, 33.

Farquhar (Horace Brand), *Earl Farquhar.*

— Letter to Lord Cecil from Lord Farquhar, 1909. *Signed.* 51159, f. 158.

Farquharson (Arthur Spenser Loat), *C.B.E.; Vice-Master of University College, Oxford.*
— Letter to G. H. Locock from A. S. L. Farquharson, 1916. *Signed.* 51093, f. 11.

Farr (A. E.), *of Barnwell, co. Northt.*
— Letter on behalf of Lord Cecil to A. E. Farr, 1940. *Copy.* 51185, f. 285.

Fawcett (*Dame* Millicent Garrett), *G.B.E.*
— Correspondence between Lord Cecil and M. G. Fawcett, 1922. 51163, ff. 96-103.

Federal Union.
— Memoranda rel. to Federal Union, 1939. *Printed.* 51184, ff. 272-290, 291-297.

Feierabend (*Dr.* Ladislav), *President, Czechoslovak League of Nations Union.*
— Letters to Lord Cecil from Dr. L. Feierabend, 1943, 1944. *Signed.* 51190, f. 187; 51191, ff. 269, 273.

Felkin (Arthur Elliott), *of the League of Nations Secretariate.*
— Correspondence between Lord Cecil and A. E. Felkin, 1937. 51176, ff. 16-18, 27.

Felstead (E. A.), *writing from Nottingham.*
— Letter to Lord Cecil from E. A. Felstead, 1912. 51160, f. 110.

Fenby (Charles), *of Picture Post.*
— Letter to Lord Cecil from C. Fenby, 1944. *Signed.* 51191, f. 108.

Fenn (Eric Alfred Humphrey), *of the Student Christian Movement; author.*
— Correspondence between Lord Cecil and E. A. H. Fenn, 1940. Partly *signed.* 51185, ff. 95, 103.

Fenton (C. F.), *Medical Officer of Health, Barking.*
— Letter to J. E. Burns from C. F. Fenton, 1909. *Copy.* 51159, f. 11.

Ferguson (George Howard), *High Commissioner for Canada in London.*
— Correspondence between Lord Cecil and G. H. Ferguson, 1933. *Signed.* 51168, ff. 92, 100.

Ferguson (J. W.), *representative of the Government of New South Wales in London.*
— Letter to Miss I. M. Butler from J. W. Ferguson, 1935. *Signed.* 51171, f. 35.

Ferguson (Ronald Crauford Munro-), *1st Viscount Novar.*
— *v.* Munro-Ferguson (Ronald Crauford).

Fermor-Hesketh (Thomas), *1st Baron Hesketh.*
— Letter from Lord Cecil to Lord Hesketh, 1936. *Copy.* 51172, f. 163.

Feronce (Albert Dufour-).
— *v.* Dufour-Feronce (Albert).

Figgures (F. E.), *of the League of Nations Union Secretariate.*
— Memorandum by Lord Cecil rel. to interview with F. E. Figgures, 1938. *Signed.* 51180, f. 131.
— Correspondence between Lord Cecil and F. E. Figgures, 1938, 1939. *Signed.* 51178, ff. 147-148v; 51179, ff. 24, 52; 51184, ff. 10, 53.

Filipowicz (Tytus), *Polish author.*
— Correspondence between Lord Cecil and T. Filipowicz, 1942. *Signed.* 51189, ff. 31, 55.

Findlay (*Sir* Mansfeldt de Cardonnel), *G.B.E.*

— Correspondence between Lord Cecil and Sir M. de Cardonnel Findlay, 1918. *Signed.* 51091, ff. 145-211.
— Telegrams to Lord Cecil from Sir M. de Cardonnel Findlay, 1918. 51104, ff. 1-4, 6-10.

Findlay (Ranald M.), *General Sec., Scottish Liberal Federation.*
— Correspondence between Lord Cecil and R. M. Findlay, 1939. *Signed.* 51183, ff. 18, 21, 64.

Fink (— von Renthe-).
— *v.* Renthe-Fink (— von).

Finlay (Robert Bannatyne), *1st Viscount Finlay.*
— Letter, etc., to Lord Cecil from R. B. Finlay, 1913. 51161, ff. 65-69.

Finlay (William), *2nd Viscount Finlay.*
— Letter to Lord Cecil from W. Finlay, 1906. 51158, f. 66.

Finney (Victor H.), *General Sec., Council of Action for Peace and Reconstruction.*
— Correspondence between Lord Cecil and V. H. Finney, 1939. *Signed.* 51183, ff. 65, 80, 88, 101.

Fischer (*Dr.* I.), *Austrian refugee in London.*
— Letters, etc., to Lord Cecil from Dr. I. Fischer, 1940, 1941. *Signed.* 51186, ff. 113-116, 256.

Fish (Wallace Wilfrid Blair-).
— *v.* Blair-Fish (Wallace Wilfrid).

Fisher (Geoffrey Francis), *Bishop of Chester and (1945) Archbishop of Canterbury; Baron Fisher 1961.*
— Correspondence between Lord Cecil and G. F. Fisher, 1939, 1949. *Signed.* 51184, f. 143; 51192, f. 324.

Fisher (*Col.* H. Frank T.), *former Sec. General, League of Nations Union.*

INDEX

— Correspondence between Lord Cecil and Col. H. F. T. Fisher, 1930. Partly *signed*. 51167, ff. 32-40.

— Correspondence between Col. H. F. T. Fisher and Miss I. M. Butler, 1935. 51171, ff. 146, 169.

Fisher (Herbert Albert Laurens), *O.M.; F.R.S.*

— Correspondence between Lord Cecil and H. A. L. Fisher, 1921. 51095, ff. 31-35.

— Letter to H. A. L. Fisher from Lord Parmoor, 1924. *Copy*. 51096, f. 148.

Fisher (*Sir* Norman Fenwick Warren), *G.C.B.*

— Correspondence between Lord Cecil and Sir N. F. W. Fisher, 1923, 1930. *Signed.* 51096, ff. 26, 37; 51100, f. 40.

Fitch (Bennett), *writing from Ealing.*

— Letter, etc., to G. Wootton from B. Fitch, 1909. 51159, f. 61.

Fitzalan-Howard (Edmund Bernard), *1st Viscount Fitzalan of Derwent.*

— Correspondence between Lord Cecil and Lord Fitzalan, 1913-1921. Partly *signed*. 51099, f. 90v; 51161, ff. 36, 55, 169, 176; 51162, ff. 100, 101, 135-137.

— Letter to her brother Lord Fitzalan from Lady P. Stewart, 1919. 51162, f. 97.

Fitzalan of Derwent, *1st Viscount.*

— *v.* Fitzalan-Howard (Edmund Bernard).

FitzClarence (Geoffrey William Richard Hugh), *5th Earl of Munster.*

— Reply by Lord Munster to Parliamentary Question of Lord Cecil rel. to refugees, 1938. *Signed.* 51182, f. 117.

— Correspondence between Lord Cecil and Lord Munster, 1938-1944. *Signed.* 51182, ff. 138, 170; 51183, ff. 3, 9, 14; 51191, f. 135.

FitzMaurice (Henry Charles Keith Petty-).

— *v.* Petty-FitzMaurice (Henry Charles Keith).

Fitzroy (*Sir* Almeric William), *K.C.B.; Clerk of the Privy Council.*

— Record of Lord Cecil's swearing in and admission as Privy Counsellor, 1915. *Signed.* 51161, f. 251.

Fletcher (—).

— Letter to — Fletcher from Lord Hartington, 1922. *Copy.* 51163, f. 72.

Fleuriau (Aimé Joseph de), *French diplomatist.*

— Memorandum by Lord Cecil rel. to conversation with A. J. de Fleuriau, 1918. 51094, f. 135.

— Correspondence between Lord Cecil and A. J. de Fleuriau, 1918, 1926. 51093, ff. 83, 184; 51094, ff. 10, 13, 14, 110; 51098, ff. 131, 132, 146.

Flexner (Abraham), *U.S. educational reformer.*

— Memorandum by Lord Cecil rel. to conversation with A. Flexner, 1928. 51099, f. 133.

Flood (Bernard), *President, British Universities League of Nations Society.*

— Memorandum rel. to the Canadian visit of B. Flood, 1937. *Copy.* 51177, ff. 204-214.

Florez (Pablo de Azcarate y).

— *v.* Azcarate y Florez (Pablo de).

Flux (*Sir* Alfred William), *economist.*

— Letter, etc., to Miss I. M. Butler from Sir A. W. Flux, 1928. *Signed.* 51166, ff. 13-18.

Foley (Thomas C.), *Sec., Pedestrians' Association.*
— Correspondence between Lord Cecil and T. C. Foley, 1929-1945. *Signed.* 51152.
— Letter to Lady Salisbury from T. C. Foley, 1943. *Copy.* 51190, f. 325.

Follette (Phillip F. La).
— *v.* La Follette (Philip F.).

Foot (*Sir* Dingle Mackintosh), *P.C.; Q.C.*
— Letter to G. G. A. Murray from D. M. Foot, 1941. *Signed.* 51188, f. 69.
— Memorandum by E. H. J. N. Dalton rel. to D. M. Foot's conversation on his behalf with Lord Cecil, 1942. *Copy.* 51188, f. 161.
— Letters to Lord Cecil from D. M. Foot, 1942, 1943. *Signed.* 51188, f. 185; 51190, ff. 179, 189-190v, 207.

Foot (N. B.), *General Sec., The New Commonwealth.*
— Letter to Miss I. M. Butler from N. B. Foot, 1935. *Signed.* 51138, f. 38.
— Letter, etc., to Lord Cecil from N. B. Foot, 1939. *Signed.* 51184, ff. 258-262.

'Forbát, Sandor'.
— *v.* Forbath (*Dr.* Alex).

Forbath (*Dr.* Alex), *al. 'Sandor Forbát', Hungarian author.*
— Correspondence between Lord Cecil and Dr. A. Forbath, 1937. *Signed.* 51178, ff. 49, 107.

Forbes-Sempill (William Francis), *19th Baron Sempill.*
— Letters to Lord Cecil from Lord Sempill, 1943. Partly *signed.* 51189, ff. 270, 275.

Ford (A. L.), *of Sutton, co. Surr.*
— Correspondence between Lord Cecil and A. L. Ford, 1936. 51173, ff. 42, 47.

Ford (G.), *of Sutton, co. Surr.*
— Correspondence between Lord Cecil and G. Ford, 1936. 51173, ff. 42, 47.

Fordham (*Sir* Herbert George), *writer on cartography.*
— Correspondence between Lord Cecil and Sir H. G. Fordham, 1927. 51165, ff. 159, 169.

Foreign Office.
— Telegrams between Lord Cecil, etc., and the Foreign Office, 1918-1930. Mostly *printed copies* for official circulation. 51104.
— Memorandum, 'The Foreign Policy of His Majesty's Government in the United Kingdom' by the Foreign Office, 1931. *Printed.* 51089, ff. 58-82.
— *v. also* Adie (Leslie).
— *v. also* Baxter (Charles William).
— *v. also* Campbell (Ronald I.).
— *v. also* Carr (Edward Hallett).
— *v. also* Cecil (Robert).
— *v. also* Dixon (Pierson John).
— *v. also* Lawford (V. G.).
— *v. also* Locock (*Sir* Guy Harold).
— *v. also* Loxley (P. N.).
— *v. also* Makins (Roger Mellor).
— *v. also* Mallet (William Ivo).
— *v. also* Smith (Charles Howard).
— *v. also* Spens (*Sir* Will).
— *v. also* Tufton (Charles Henry).
— *v. also* Warner (G.).
— *v. also* Wellesley (*Sir* Victor Alexander Augustus Henry).
— *v. also* Wigram (Ralph Follet).

Forell (*Dr.* Birger), *Swedish pastor in Berlin.*
— Memorandum by Lord Cecil rel. to conversation with Dr. B. Forell, 1935. 51170, ff. 172-174.

Forester (Orlando St. Maur Weld), *Vicar of Battersea.*
— Letter to Lord Cecil from O. St.M. W. Forester, 1941. *Printed. Signed.* 51188, f. 20.

INDEX

Forster (Henry William), *Baron Forster.*
— Correspondence between Lord Cecil and H. W. Forster, 1909, 1914. 51159, ff. 268-270v; 51161, f. 104.

Forster (Katherine Arnold-).
— *v.* Arnold-Forster (Katherine).

Forster (William Arnold-).
— *v.* Arnold-Forster (William).

Fortescue (Hugh), *4th Earl Fortescue.*
— Letter to Lord Cecil from Lord Fortescue, 1909. 51159, f. 253.

Fosdick (Raymond Blaine), *President of the Rockefeller Foundation, New York.*
— Correspondence between Lord Cecil and R. B. Fosdick, partly on behalf of J. D. Rockefeller, 1936-1938. *Signed.* 51173, f. 21; 51174, ff. 113, 166; 51175, f. 35; 51178, ff. 184-203.

Foster (Henry Read), *Vicar of Great Wymondley with St. Ippolyts.*
— Correspondence between Lord Cecil and H. R. Foster, 1922. 51163, ff. 69-71.

Foster (*Air Vice-Marshal* William MacNeece) *formerly* **MacNeece.**
— *v.* MacNeece (*Air Vice-Marshal* William).

FRANCE.
— Memorandum by Maj.-Gen. P. A. M. Nash rel. to coal supply for France and Italy, 1918. *Signed.* 51093, ff. 92-96.

Franco (Afranio de Mello-).
— *v.* Mello-Franco (Afranio de).

Frankenstein (Georg), *Austrian diplomatist.*
— Correspondence between Lord Cecil and G. Frankenstein, 1922. *Signed.* 51095, ff. 126-128.

Franklin (Henrietta), *Honorary Sec., Parents' National Educational Union; wife of E. L. Franklin.*
— Letter to Lord Cecil from H. Franklin, 1941. 51187, f. 73.

Fraser (*Sir* John Malcolm), *1st Bart.*
— Letters to Lord Cecil from J. M. Fraser, 1913, 1914. *Signed.* 61161, ff. 30, 87.

Fraser (Peter), *Prime Minister of New Zealand.*
— Correspondence, partly on his behalf, with Lord Cecil, 1944. 51191, ff. 97, 99.
— Memorandum by Lord Cecil rel. to interview with P. Fraser, 1945. *Copy.* 51192, f. 91.

Frazier (Arthur Hugh), *U.S. diplomatist.*
— Correspondence between Lord Cecil and A. H. Frazier, 1935, 1942. *Signed.* 51170, ff. 250, 252; 51187, ff. 31, 104; 51188, ff. 102, 141.

Free Albania Committee in the U.S.A.
— *v.* Zavalani (Trajar).

Free German Youth in Great Britain.
— *v.* Loerken (*Miss* Edith).

Freeland (Edward Lionel Thornton Stilwell), *solicitor.*
— Correspondence between Lord Cecil and E. L. T. S. Freeland, 1934. 51169, ff. 50, 52.

Freeman (Arnold), *Warden, the Sheffield Educational Settlement.*
— Correspondence between Lord Cecil and A. Freeman, 1936. *Signed.* 51172, ff. 75, 108.

Freeman (Edward Canning-).
— *v.* Canning-Freeman (Edward).

Freeman (*Sapper* Richard), *R.E.*
— Correspondence between Lord Cecil and Sapper R. Freeman, 1941. 51187, ff. 35, 50.

Freeman (*Mrs* Violet A. L.), *mother of Sapper R. Freeman.*
— Letter to Lord Cecil from Mrs V. A. L. Freeman, 1941. 51187, f. 30.

Freeston (B. D.), *of the B.B.C.*
— Letters to Lord Cecil, 1934. Partly *printed. Signed.* 51193, ff. 33, 44.

Fremantle (*Sir* Francis Edward), *M.P.*
— Correspondence between Lord Cecil and Sir F. E. Fremantle, 1931, 1935. *Signed.* 51167, ff. 96, 101; 51170, ff. 191, 193.

Freshwater (*Maj.* A. J. C.), *M.C.; T.D.; Sec., League of Nations Union.*
— Correspondence between Lord Cecil and Maj. A. J. C. Freshwater, 1935-1943. Mostly *signed.* 51136, ff. 126-235.
— Correspondence between Maj. A. J. C. Freshwater and Miss I. M. Butler, 1936-1939. 51136, ff. 126-162 *passim*; 51181, f. 178.
— Correspondence between Col. G. N. Wyatt and Maj. A. J. C. Freshwater, 1936, 1940. 51136, f. 138; 51184, f. 328.
— Memorial Address by Lord Lytton for Maj. A. J. C. Freshwater, 1943. *Copy.* 51139, f. 186.

Freudenberg (*Princess* Elisabeth Zu Löwenstein-Wertheim-) *afterw.* **Merton.**
— *v.* Merton (Elisabeth).

Frischauer ([Monica J?]), *of Die Zukunft.*
— Correspondence between [M. J?] Frischauer and Miss I. M. Butler, 1938. *Signed.* 51181, ff. 150, 198; 51182, f. 84.
— Letter to — from [M. J?] Frischauer, 1938. *Signed.* 51181, f. 158.

Fry (Anna Ruth), *Quaker relief worker and publicist.*
— Correspondence between Lord Cecil and A. R. Fry, 1930-1942. Partly *signed.* 51167, ff. 4-6; 51187, f. 122; 51188, ff. 143, 147, 155.

Fry (*Sir* Geoffrey Storrs), *Bart.*
— Correspondence between Lord Cecil and Sir G. S. Fry on behalf of S. Baldwin, 1934. *Signed.* 51080, ff. 256-260.

Fuller-Acland-Hood (Alexander), *1st Baron St. Audries.*
— Correspondence between Lord Cecil and A. Fuller-Acland-Hood, 1908. 51158, ff. 270-280.

Fussinger (Raymond), *son of C. Fussinger, a Swiss interned in the Isle of Man.*
— Letters to Lord Cecil from R. Fussinger, 1940, 1941. 51186, ff. 111, 159, 163, 262.

Fyfe (*Sir* David Patrick Maxwell), *Earl Kilmuir.*
— Correspondence between Lord Cecil and Sir D. P. M. Fyfe, 1943, 1952. *Signed.* 51190, f. 348; 51192, f. 344.

G

Gage (Henry Rainald), *6th Viscount Gage.*
— Correspondence between Lord Cecil and Lord Gage, 1931, 1934. *Signed.* 51167, ff. 71-75, 95; 51169, ff. 256-259, 262, 265.

Gainsborough, *co. Linc.*
— Message from Lord Cecil for Peace Week at Gainsborough, 1938. *Copy.* 51181, f. 55.

Gale (Marguerite R.), *Sec., National Union of Students.*
— Correspondence between Lord Cecil and M. R. Gale, 1943, 1944. *Signed.* 51190, f. 378; 51191, ff. 9, 10.
— Letter to Miss E. V. Lazarus from M. R. Gale, 1944. *Signed.* 51191, f. 22.

INDEX

Garbett (Cyril Forster), *Bishop of Winchester; afterw. Archbishop of York.*
— Correspondence between Lord Cecil and Bishop of Winchester, 1934-1937. *Signed.* 51169, ff. 220, 225; 51171, f. 108; 51178, ff. 68, 100.

Gardiner (Margaret), *Sec., For Intellectual Liberty.*
— Correspondence between Lord Cecil and M. Gardiner, 1938. *Signed.* 51179, ff. 225, 232, 235, 237, 238.

Gardy (Frédéric), *director of Municipal Library, Geneva.*
— Correspondence between Lord Cecil and F. Gardy, 1923. *Signed. Partly Fr.* 51163, ff. 164-166v.

Garner (Percy W.), *of the League of Nations Union, Harrow Branch.*
— Correspondence between Lord Cecil and P. W. Garner, 1937. 51177, ff. 92, 93.

Garnett (James Clerk Maxwell), *C.B.E.; Sec., League of Nations Union.*
— Correspondence between Lord Cecil and J. C. M. Garnett, 1923-1945. Mostly *signed.* 51136, ff. 1-125v.

Garnett (Rebecca), *widow of W. Garnett.*
— Letter to Lord Cecil from R. Garnett, 1938. 51178, f. 142.

Garnsey (*Canon* Arthur H.), *President, International Peace Campaign, New South Wales.*
— Letter to Lord Cecil from Canon Garnsey, 1938. *Signed.* 51179, f. 208.

Garratt (Geoffrey Theodore), *of the National Joint Committee for Spanish Relief.*
— Memorandum rel. to the administration of Spanish relief, 1938. *Printed.* 51179, f. 70.

Garrett (W. B.), *of Rugby.*
— Correspondence between Lord Cecil and W. B. Garrett, 1936. 51173, ff. 156-161, 170.

Garvin (James Louis), *Editor of The Observer.*
— Correspondence between Lord Cecil and J. L. Garvin, 1929-1931. *Signed.* 51166, ff. 143-146, 151-156; 51167, ff. 7-12, 154-159.

Gascoyne-Cecil (Cecily Alice), *wife of James, 4th Marquess of Salisbury.*
— Correspondence, partly on her behalf, with her brother-in-law, Lord Cecil, 1928-1944, n.d. Partly *signed.* 51086, f. 229; 51166, f. 64; 51187, f. 312; 51189, f. 167; 51191, ff. 30, 33, 94, 98; 51192, ff. 347-348v.
— Letter to Lady Salisbury from T. C. Foley, 1943. *Copy.* 51190, f. 325.

Gascoyne-Cecil (Edgar Algernon Robert), *Viscount Cecil of Chelwood; d.1958.*
— Correspondence and papers, 1893-1953, n.d. 51071-51204.

Gascoyne-Cecil (*Lord* Edward Herbert), *Financial Adviser to the Government of Egypt.*
— Letter to Lord Cecil from his brother, Lord E. H. Gascoyne-Cecil, 1912. *Signed.* 51160, f. 207.

Gascoyne-Cecil (Eleanor), *wife of Lord Cecil of Chelwood.*
— Letter to Lady Cecil from J. D. Rockefeller, 1925. 51164, f. 65.
— Letters to Lady Cecil from Col. E. D. Mackenzie, 1937. Partly *copy.* 51177, ff. 43, 118.

Gascoyne-Cecil (Gwendolin), *daughter of Robert, 3rd Marquess of Salisbury.*
— Correspondence between Lord Cecil and his sister, G. Gascoyne-Cecil, 1906-1941. 51158, f. 45; 51165, f. 144; 51166, ff. 24-26; 51180, ff. 33, 48; 51182, ff. 163, 188, 195; 51187, f. 76.

Gascoyne-Cecil (Hugh Richard Heathcote), *Baron Quickswood.*
— Correspondence between Lord Cecil and his brother Lord Quickswood, 1908-1944. Partly *signed.* 51157, ff. 1-65v.
— Letter to H. R. H. Gascoyne-Cecil from A. Mendelssohn-Bartholdy, 1910. 51157, ff. 10-13.

Gascoyne-Cecil (James Edward Hubert), *4th Marquess of Salisbury.*
— Correspondence between Lord Cecil and his brother, Lord Salisbury, 1906-1945. Partly *signed.* 51085, 51086.
— Letter to Lord Salisbury on behalf of Sir A. H. D. R. Steel-Maitland, 1926. *Copy.* 51085, f. 180.
— Telegrams between Lord Cecil and his brother Lord Salisbury, 1927. 51104, ff. 97-253 *passim.*

Gascoyne-Cecil (Robert Arthur James), *Viscount Cranborne; 5th Marquess of Salisbury.*
— Correspondence between Lord Cecil and his nephew Viscount Cranborne, 1922-1945. Partly *signed.* 51087, ff. 1-177.

Gascoyne-Cecil (Stella), *wife of V. A. Gascoyne-Cecil.*
— Memorandum by Miss I. M. Butler rel. to conversation with S. Gascoyne-Cecil, 1940. 51185, f. 281.
— Letter to S. Gascoyne-Cecil from Miss I. M. Butler, 1940. *Copy.* 51185, f. 282.
— Letter from Lord Cecil to S. Gascoyne-Cecil, 1940. *Copy.* 51185, f. 282.

Gascoyne-Cecil (Victor Alexander), *son of Lord William Gascoyne-Cecil.*
— Correspondence between Lord Cecil and his nephew, V. A. Gascoyne-Cecil, 1915-1918, 1934, 1935. Mostly *signed.* 51162, f. 24; 51169, ff. 239, 248, 252-255, 260; 51170, ff. 27-37, 50.

Gascoyne-Cecil (*Lord* William), *Bishop of Exeter.*
— Letter to Lord Cecil from his brother, the Bishop of Exeter, 1912. 51160, f. 154.
— Memorandum rel. to the Welsh Church Disestablishment Bill, 1914. *Draft.* 51161, ff. 177-180.

Gaselee (*Sir* Stephen), *K.C.M.G.*
— Correspondence between Lord Cecil and Sir S. Gaselee, 1924, 1937. *Signed.* 51097, ff. 85-87; 51175, ff. 159, 169.

Gaulle (*Général* Charles André Joseph Marie de), *President of France.*
— Correspondence between Lord Cecil and Général C. A. J. M. de Gaulle, 1940. *Signed. Fr.* 51186, ff. 70, 71.

Gauntlett (G. Raymond), *Chairman, National Youth Committee of the League of Nations Union.*
— Correspondence between Lord Cecil and G. R. Gauntlett, 1938-1941. Partly *signed.* 51180, ff. 50, 55, 89, 94; 51183, ff. 211, 212, 225; 51187, ff. 12-417 *passim.*

Gauntlett (Helen Parkins), *wife of G. R. Gauntlett; Sec., Committee to Defend America by Aiding the Allies.*
— Correspondence between Lord Cecil and H. P. Gauntlett, 1940. *Signed.* 51186, ff. 1, 36, 215.

Geddes (Auckland Campbell), *1st Baron Geddes.*
— Correspondence, including telegram, between Lord Cecil and A. C. Geddes, 1923. 51104, f. 25; 51095, f. 141.

Geneva Press Service.
— Letter to Miss I. M. Butler from Geneva Press Service, 1936. *Germ.* 51172, f. 193.

Gentleman (J. W.), *writing from Dublin on behalf of the Rev. Bolton Waller Memorial Fund.*
— Letter, etc., to Lord Cecil from J. W. Gentleman, 1936, 1937. *Signed.* 51174, ff. 99-103; 51176, ff. 54, 70.

George (David Lloyd).
— *v.* Lloyd George (David).

George (Gwilym Lloyd-).
— *v.* Lloyd-George (Gwilym).

George (Megan Lloyd).
— *v.* Lloyd George (Megan).

Gepp (*Sir* Herbert William), *Chairman of Australian Development and Migration Commission.*
— Letter to Lord Stonehaven from Sir H. W. Gepp, 1926. 51072, f. 245.

Gerard (James W.), *Chairman, The American Committee for the Independence of Armenia.*
— Correspondence between Lord Cecil and J. W. Gerard, 1921. *Signed.* 51162, ff. 127, 131, 154.

Gerlach (— von), *[head of a League of Nations Organisation in Berlin?].*
— Memorandum by Lord Cecil rel. to conversation with — von Gerlach, 1923. 51096, f. 39.

GERMANY . EMPERORS OF , *and transactions in particular reigns. THIRD REICH.*
— Memoranda rel. to refugees and political prisoners of the Third Reich, *circa* 1936. *Copies.* 51173, ff. 150-155v.

Giaever (Magnus K.), *Sec., International Nansen Monument Committee.*
— Correspondence between Lord Cecil and M. K. Giaever, 1937, 1938. *Signed.* 51177, f. 159; 51179, ff. 42, 81.

Giannini (Amadeo), *Italian politician and historian.*
— Correspondence between Lord Cecil and A. Giannini, 1936, 1937. *Signed. Fr.* 51174, f. 223; 51175, f. 3.

Giannini (Francesco), *Italian Commercial Attaché in London.*
— Correspondence between Lord Cecil and F. Giannini, 1922. *Signed.* 51095, ff. 60, 62-65.

Gibbs (Herbert Cokayne), *1st Baron Hunsdon.*
— Letters to Lord Cecil from H. C. Gibbs, 1914. 51161, ff. 146, 149.

Gibson (Harold), *Director, Finnish Aid Bureau; afterw. of the Ministry of Information.*
— Correspondence between Lord Cecil and H. Gibson, 1940. 51184, ff. 301-305v; 51185, f. 169.

Giffard (Hardinge Stanley), *1st Earl of Halsbury.*
— Correspondence between Lord Cecil and Lord Halsbury, 1909-1932. Partly *signed.* 51159, f. 187; 51160, f. 6; 51161, ff. 17, 181; 51168, ff. 4-9.

Gilchrist (E. A.), *Editor, Church Reform Chronicle.*
— Correspondence between Lord Cecil and E. A. Gilchrist, 1929. *Signed.* 51166, ff. 96, 97.

Gilchrist (Huntington), *businessman and author, of New York.*
— "The Japanese Islands: Annexation or Trusteeship", by H. Gilchrist. Reprinted from 'Foreign Affairs', 1944. *Printed,* with MS. additions. 51191, ff. 146-151v.

Gilchrist (Huntington), *businessman and author, of New York. continuation*
— Correspondence between Lord Cecil and H. Gilchrist, 1944. 51191, ff. 146-151v, 297.

Giles (Frederick C.), *of the League of Nations Union, Finchley Branch.*
— Correspondence between Lord Cecil and F. C. Giles, 1938. *Signed.* 51136, ff. 146-150; 51179, ff. 92, 96, 171, 178, 201, 249.

Gilmour (*Sir* John), *2nd Bart; P.C.; M.P.*
— Correspondence between Lord Cecil and Sir J. Gilmour, 1933. *Signed.* 51101, ff. 69-71, 101, 103-105.

Gimingham (C. A.), *of Time and Tide.*
— Letter to Lord Cecil from C. A. Gimingham, 1940. *Signed.* 51193, f. 204.

Ginsberg (*Miss* Marie), *of the International Committee for Assistance of German Refugee Professional Workers, Geneva.*
— Letters, etc., to Lord Cecil from Miss M. Ginsberg, 1933, 1936. *Signed.* 51168, ff. 48-55; 51174, ff. 191-207, 225, 227.

Gladstone (Dorothy Mary), *wife of Herbert, Viscount Gladstone.*
— Correspondence between Lord Cecil and Lady Gladstone, 1922-1941. 51163, ff. 109, 111; 51170, ff. 143-145; 51172, f. 76; 51175, f. 80; 51187, f. 78.
— Letter to Lady Gladstone from W. H. W. Roberts, 1937. *Signed.* 51175, f. 81.

Gladstone (Herbert John), *Viscount Gladstone.*
— Correspondence between Lord Cecil and Lord Gladstone, 1921-1924. 51163, ff. 43-50, 77-79, 83, 91, 104-119; 51164, ff. 18-22.

Glazebrook (*Miss* Monica), *of Limpsfield; former official of the League of Nations Union.*
— Correspondence between Lord Cecil and Miss M. Glazebrook, 1941. 51187, ff. 97, 103.

Glenconner, *1st Baron.*
— *v.* Tennant (Edward Priaulx).

Glossop (*Vice-Adm.* John Collings-Taswell).
— Correspondence between Lord Cecil and Vice-Adm. J. C.-T. Glossop, 1931. 51167, ff. 117-121, 124.

Godfrey (Helen J.), *of Ruskington.*
— Letter to Lord Cecil from H. J. Godfrey, 1940. 51185, f. 268.

Goff (Eric Noel Porter), *Vicar of Immanuel Church, Streatham.*
— Correspondence between Rev. E. N. P. Goff and Miss I. M. Butler, 1931. *Signed.* 51167, f. 58.

Goldmann (Nahum), *President of the World Jewish Congress.*
— Letter to Lord Cecil from N. Goldmann, 1937. *Signed.* 51136, f. 57; 51175, f. 155.

Gollancz (*Sir* Victor), *publisher and author.*
— Correspondence, including telegrams etc., between Lord Cecil and Sir V. Gollancz, 1933-1943. Partly *signed.* 51101, f. 80; 51168, ff. 81, 94; 51181, ff. 105-108, 114; 51182, f, 93; 51183, ff. 24-27, 167, 169; 51187, ff. 376-378, 396; 51190, ff. 33, 37, 41, 43.

Gooch (George Peabody), *historian.*
— Correspondence between Lord Cecil and G. P. Gooch, 1943, 1944. 51189, ff. 272, 273, 280; 51190, ff. 21, 297, 303, 336, 337, 393, 398; 51191, f. 5.

Goodchild (S. C.), *industrial chemist.*
— Letter to Lord Cecil from S. C. Goodchild, 1938. 51181, f. 74.

INDEX

Gordon (A.), *Sec., Anglo-Palestinian Club.*
— Letter to Lord Cecil from A. Gordon, 1943. *Signed.* 51190, f. 72.

Gordon (*Lt.-Gen. Sir* Alexander Hamilton), *K.C.B.*
— Correspondence between Lord Cecil and Lt.-Gen. Sir A. H. Gordon, 1931. *Signed.* 51167, ff. 76, 93, 110, 114.

Gordon (Thomas), *Editor of Safety News.*
— Correspondence between Lord Cecil and T. Gordon, 1939. *Signed.* 51182, ff. 137, 148.

Gore (William George Arthur Ormsby-).
— *v.* Ormsby-Gore (William George Arthur).

Gott (Florence), *of the Carnegie Endowment for International Peace.*
— Letter to Lord Cecil from F. Gott, 1941. *Signed.* 51186, f. 279.

Gottleib (Wolfram), *London correspondent of official Latvian newspaper.*
— Letter to Miss I. M. Butler from W. Gottleib, 1937. 51178, f. 104.

Goulding (Edward Alfred), *Baron Wargrave.*
— Correspondence between Lord Cecil and E. A. Goulding, 1909. 51159, ff. 23-27, 29.

Gowers (*Sir* Ernest Arthur), *G.C.B.*
— Letter to Lord Cecil from E. A. Gowers, 1912. 51160, f. 78.

Grabow (*Dr. —*), *Mayor of Memel.*
— Memorandum by Lord Parmoor rel. to conversation with Dr.—Grabow, 1924. 51097, f. 10.

Graham (F. E. A).
— Letter to Lord Cecil from F. E. A. Graham, 1909. 51159, f. 127.

Graham (James), *6th Duke of Montrose.*
— Correspondence between Lord Cecil and Duke of Montrose, 1945. *Signed.* 51192, ff. 20, 36.

Graham-Harrison (Francis), *of the Home Office.*
— Letter to Miss E. V. Lazarus from F. Graham-Harrison, 1941. *Signed.* 51187, f. 404.

Grandi (Dino), *Italian statesman and diplomatist.*
— Memorandum by Lord Cecil rel. to conversation with D. Grandi, 1931. 51100, f. 133.
— Correspondence between Lord Cecil and D. Grandi, 1931, 1935. *Signed.* 51100, f. 144; 51170, f. 111.

Grange (G.), *Sec., League of Nations Union, Upper Norwood Branch.*
— Correspondence between Lord Cecil and G. Grange, 1937. 51176, ff. 94, 100.

Grant (Neil [Forbes?]), *journalist.*
— Letter to Lord Cecil from N. [F?] Grant, 1931. *Signed.* 51167, f. 42.

Grass (B. von), *member of German minority from Poland.*
— Letter to Lord Cecil from B. von Grass, 1923. *Signed.* 51096, f. 55.

Graveson (S.), *of the Society of Friends in Hertford.*
— Correspondence between Lord Cecil and S. Graveson, 1944. *Signed.* 51191, ff. 253, 268.

Gray (*Sir* Albert), *K.C.B.*
— Letter, etc., to Lord Cecil from A. Gray, 1913. 51161, ff. 57-64.
— Legal opinions, 1913. 51161, ff. 59-64, 67-69.

Gray (*Miss* D. H. F.), *Sec. to the Council, St. Hugh's College, Oxford.*
— Correspondence between Lord Cecil and Miss D. H. F. Gray, 1940. *Signed.* 51185, ff. 276, 278.

Gray (Edmund Dwyer-).
— *v.* Dwyer-Gray (Edmund).

Gray (*Miss* F. C.), *Sec., the Commomwealth Irish Association.*
— Letter to Miss E. V. Lazarus from Miss F. C. Gray, 1943. *Signed.* 51190, f. 332.

Green (George S.), *of the League of Nations Union, Skipton Branch.*
— Letters to Lord Cecil from G. S. Green, 1941, 1944. *Signed.* 51187, f. 215; 51191, f. 224.

Green (Leonard Henry), *President, League of Nations Union, Chelsea Branch.*
— Correspondence between Lord Cecil and L. H. Green, 1938. *Signed.* 51179, ff. 39, 44.
— Letter to Lord Cecil from L. H. Green, 1943. *Signed.* 51190, f. 186.

Greenberg (Leslie Claude), *winner of the Cecil Peace Prize.*
— Correspondence between Lord Cecil and L. C. Greenberg, 1941. 51187, ff. 47, 60, 106; 51188, f. 96.

Greene (*Sir* Conyngham), *K.C.B.; Ambassador to Japan.*
— Letter to Lord Cecil from Sir C. Greene, 1918. 51093, f. 125.

Greening (Edward Owen), *Editor of The Agricultural Economist.*
— Letters to Lord Cecil from E. O. Greening, 1912. *Signed.* 51160, ff. 85, 108.

Gregory (John Duncan), *diplomatist.*
— Letter to J. D. Gregory from A. H. Bathurst, 1916. *Signed.* 51092, f. 75.

Gregory (Robert), *Dean of St. Paul's.*
— Letter to Lord Cecil from Dean of St. Paul's, 1909. 51159, f. 194.

Grenfell (*Lt.-Col.* Arthur M.).
— Correspondence between Lord Cecil and Lt.-Col. A. M. Grenfell, 1941. 51188, ff. 52, 67.

Grenfell (*Commander* Russell), *R.N.*
— Correspondence between Lord Cecil and Commander R. Grenfell, 1929. *Signed.* 51166, ff. 131-141.

Grenfell (William Henry), *Baron Desborough.*
— Letter to Lord Cecil from Lord Desborough, 1922. *Copy.* 51163, f. 57.

Grey (Charles Robert), *5th Earl Grey.*
— Letter to Lord Cecil from C. R. Grey, 1912. 51160, f. 218.

Grey (*Sir* Edward), *Viscount Grey of Falloden.*
— Letters to Sir E. Grey from A. M. Munn, 1914. *Copies.* 51073, ff. 59, 64.
— Correspondence between Lord Cecil and Lord Grey, 1914-1929. Partly *signed.* 51073, ff. 59-96.
— Letter to Lord Grey from F. Dixon, 1916. 51092, f. 115.

Grey (Mabel Laura Georgiana), *wife of Charles, 5th Earl Grey.*
— Letter to Lord Cecil, 1944. 51191, f. 275.

Grey (Roger), *10th Earl of Stamford.*
— Correspondence between Lord Cecil and Lord Stamford, 1934-1945. Partly *signed.* 51139, ff. 1-83v.

Griffin (Robert John Thurlow), *al.* (Jonathan), *author.*
— Correspondence, etc., between Lord Cecil and R. J. T. Griffin, 1935-1938. Partly *printed.* 51156, ff. 183-233.

Grimes (Francis Mortimer), *Sec., League of Nations Union, Nottingham Branch.*
— Correspondence between Lord Cecil and F. M. Grimes, 1935-1941. *Signed.* 51171, ff. 141, 148; 51182, ff. 192, 196; 51187, ff. 19, 25; 51193, ff. 107-110.

Grimes (*Dr.* Louis A.), *Sec. of State, afterw. Chief Justice, in Liberia.*
— Memoranda by Lord Cecil rel. to interviews with Dr. L. A. Grimes, 1932. 51100, ff. 159, 199.

INDEX

Grimes (*Dr.* Louis A.), *Sec. of State, afterw. Chief Justice, in Liberia. continuation*
— Correspondence between Lord Cecil and Dr. L. A. Grimes, 1932-1938. *Signed.* 51100, f. 197; 51101, f. 52; 51178, f. 154; 51179, f. 29.

Grindlinger (Pino), *Polish refugee.*
— Memorandum rel. to the case of P. Grindlinger, 1940. *Copy.* 51185, f. 284.

Grosvenor (Robert Wellesley), *2nd Baron Ebury.*
— Letter to Lord Cecil from Lord Ebury, 1909. 51159, f. 138.

Groves (*Brig.-Gen.* Percy Robert Clifford), *Sec.-General, Air League of the British Empire.*
— Correspondence between Lord Cecil and Brig.-Gen. P. R. C. Groves, 1927. *Signed.* 51165, ff. 194-196.

Grumbach (S.), *French politician.*
— Correspondence between Lord Cecil and S. Grumbach, 1940. *Signed. Fr.* 51185, ff. 2, 20.

Guani (A.), *of the Legation of Uraguay in London.*
— Letter to Lord Cecil from A. Guani, 1926. *Signed.* 51089, f. 23.

Guinness (Richard S[ydney?]), *merchant banker and company director.*
— Correspondence between Lord Cecil and R. S. Guinness, 1918. *Signed.* 51093, ff. 101-104.

Guinness (Walter Edward), *1st Baron Moyne.*
— Correspondence between Lord Cecil and Lord Moyne, 1941. *Signed.* 51187, ff. 233, 241, 338.
— Reply by Lord Moyne to Parliamentary Question of Lord Cecil rel. to speech of Mr Sumner Wells, 1941. *Signed.* 51187, f. 398.

Gullander (Åke), *of the Swedish Farmers' Union.*
— Correspondence between Lord Cecil and Å. Gullander, 1938. *Signed.* 51180, ff. 57, 86, 109, 116, 162; 51181, f. 6.

Gwyer (Barbara Elizabeth), *Principal of St Hugh's College, Oxford.*
— Letters to Lord Cecil, 1945. Partly *signed.* 51192, ff. 211-213v.

Gwynne (Howell Arthur), *journalist.*
— Letters to Lord Cecil from H. A. Gwynne, 1909, 1914. Partly *signed.* 51159, f. 92; 51160, ff. 240-242v, 265; 51161, ff. 22, 70-73v, 150, 201.

H

Hackler (Victor), *News Editor, Associated Press.*
— Correspondence between Lord Cecil and V. Hackler, 1945. *Signed.* 51192, ff. 153, 157, 181, 189, 190.

Haggard (*Sir* Henry Rider), *K.B.E.*
— Letter to Lord Cecil from H. Rider Haggard, 1911. 51160, f. 27.

Hailsham, *1st Viscount.*
— *v.* Hogg (Douglas McGarel).

Halifax, *W.R., co. York.*
— Message from Lord Cecil for Peace Week at Halifax, 1938. *Copy.* 51181, f. 121.

Halifax, *3rd Viscount and 1st Earl.*
— *v.* Wood (Edward Frederick Lindley).

Hall (*Adm. Sir* George Fowler King-).
— *v.* King-Hall (*Adm. Sir* George Fowler).

Hall (H. Duncan), *of the League of Nations Secretariate, Geneva.*
— Correspondence between Lord Cecil and H. D. Hall, 1937. 51177, ff. 161, 177.

Hall (Ida Scott Audsley), *widow of Sir A. D. Hall.*
— Correspondence, etc., between Lord Cecil and Lady Hall, 1937-1943. Partly *printed* and *signed*. 51175, ff. 15, 105; 51178, ff. 149, 167, 176; 51181, ff. 19, 20; 51187, f. 113; 51190, f. 307.

Hall (*Adm. Sir* William Reginald), *K.C.M.G.*
— Correspondence between Lord Cecil and Sir W. R. Hall, 1918. *Signed.* 51093, ff. 67-74.

Hall (William Stephen Richard King-), *Baron King-Hall.*
— *v.* King-Hall (William Stephen Richard).

Haller (Nicolas de), *pastor, of St. Livres, Switzerland.*
— Correspondence between Lord Cecil and N. de Haller, 1935. Partly *Fr.* 51170, ff. 186, 187, 192, 222, 240.
— Memorandum by Lord Cecil rel. to conversation with N. de Haller, 1935. 51170, f. 195.

Hallewell (Vernon H.), *Sec., Hitchin Division Conservative and Liberal Unionist Association.*
— Letters to Lord Cecil from V. H. Hallewell, 1918. *Signed.* 51162, ff. 60, 82.
— Letter to V. H. Hallewell from Miss M. E. Nicholson, 1918. 51162, f. 64.

Hallsworth (*Sir* Joseph), *trade unionist.*
— Letter to Lord Cecil from J. Hallsworth, 1939. *Signed.* 51184, f. 119.

Halsbury, *1st Earl of.*
— *v.* Giffard (Hardinge Stanley).

Hambleden, *2nd Viscount.*
— *v.* Smith (William Frederick Danvers).

Hambro (*Mr.* —).
— Memorandum by J. M. Keynes (?) rel. to conversation with Mr. — Hambro, 1918. *Copy.* 51093, f. 151.

Hambro (Carl Joachim), *Norwegian politician and journalist.*
— Correspondence between Lord Cecil and C. J. Hambro, 1937-1943. *Signed.* 51177, f. 181; 51182, f. 13; 51190, f. 31.

Hambro (Edvard), *son of C.J. Hambro.*
— Letter to Lord Cecil from E. Hambro, 1937. *Signed.* 51177, f. 180.

Hamilton (C. J.), *of the Labour Co-Partnership Association.*
— Letters, etc., to Lord Cecil from C. J. Hamilton, 1927. *Signed.* 51165, ff. 131-139.

Hamilton (*Lord* George Francis), *P.C.; M.P.*
— Letters to Lord Cecil from Lord G. F. Hamilton, 1904, 1909. 51158, ff. 2, 10, 13, 16; 51159, ff. 1, 181.

Hamilton (Gerald), *writing from Tangier.*
— Correspondence between Lord Cecil and G. Hamilton, 1937. *Signed.* 51175, ff. 52, 60.

Hamilton (Henry), *afterw. Professor of Political Economy, Aberdeen.*
— Correspondence between Lord Cecil and H. Hamilton, 1941-1943. *Signed.* 51187, ff. 23, 61; 51188, f. 237; 51189, ff. 257, 258; 51190, f. 6.

Hamilton (J. W.), *Founder and Sec., International Magna Carta Day Association.*
— Letter, etc., to Lord Cecil from J. W. Hamilton, 1941. *Facs. signature.* 51187, ff. 357-359.

Hamilton (Mary Agnes), *C.B.E.*
— Correspondence between Lord Cecil and M. A. Hamilton, 1941. *Signed.* 51186, f. 289; 51187, ff. 27, 39, 52.

INDEX

Hamilton (*Lt.-Col.* Roland), *afterw. M.P.*
— Correspondence between Lord Cecil and Lt.-Col. R. Hamilton, 1937. *Signed.* 51175, ff. 58-60.

Hamilton (Vereker M[onteith?]), *[artist?]*.
— Letter to Lord Cecil from V. M. Hamilton, 1915. 51161, f. 222.

Hamilton-Temple-Blackwood (Basil Sheridan), *4th Marquess of Dufferin and Ava*.
— Correspondence, partly on his behalf, with Lord Cecil, 1939. *Signed.* 51183, ff. 174, 177-181, 184.
— Reply by Lord Dufferin and Ava to Parliamentary Question of Lord Cecil rel. to Ethiopia, 1939. *Signed.* 51183, f. 179.

Hammond (John Lawrence Le Breton), *journalist*.
— Correspondence between Lord Cecil and J. L. Le B. Hammond, 1936. 51172, ff. 52, 70.

Hamrin (Agne), *Swedish journalist*.
— Letter to Miss I. M. Butler from A. Hamrin, 1936. *Signed.* 51173, f. 70.

Han Li-wu, *representative of the Chinese League of Nations Union*.
— Letter to Lord Cecil, 1944. *Copy.* 51191, f. 12.

Han Lih-wu, *of the People's Political Council, Chung King*.
— Letter, etc., to Lord Cecil from Han Lih-wu, 1940. *Signed.* 51186, ff. 107-109.

Hankey (Maurice Pascal Alers), *1st Baron Hankey*.
— Correspondence between Lord Cecil and M. P. A. Hankey, 1916-1943. Partly *signed*. 51088.
— Letter to A. J. Balfour from M. P. A. Hankey, 1918. *Signed.* 51094, f. 51.
— Telegrams between Lord Cecil and M. P. A. Hankey, 1927. 51104, ff. 87, 91-96.

Hanotaux (Gabriel), *French statesman*.
— Letter to G. Hanotaux from Lord Parmoor, 1924. *Copy.* 51097, f. 50.

Hansson (*Dr.* Michael), *of the Nansen International Office for Refugees*.
— Correspondence between Lord Cecil and Dr. M. Hansson, 1936. *Signed.* 51172, ff. 131, 140, 162, 178.

Haque (*Sir* Mohammed Aziz-ul), *High Commissioner for India in London*.
— Letter from Lord Cecil to Sir M. A. Haque, 1942. *Copy.* 51189, f. 151.

Harberton, *7th Viscount*.
— *v.* Pomeroy (Ernest Arthur George).

Harbord (Derek), *Sec., The Bentham Committee*.
— Correspondence between Lord Cecil and D. Harbord, 1938. *Signed.* 51180, ff. 52, 67-74.

Hardcastle (*Rev.* Henry Robert), *of Lyndhurst, co. Hants*.
— Correspondence between Lord Cecil and Rev. H. R. Hardcastle, 1943. *Signed.* 51190, ff. 217, 218.

Hardinge (Alexander Henry Louis), *2nd Baron Hardinge of Penshurst*.
— Correspondence between Lord Cecil and A. H. L. Hardinge, 1921, 1937. *Signed.* 51163, ff. 41, 42; 51175, ff. 203, 215; 51176, f. 2.

Hardinge (Charles), *1st Baron Hardinge of Penshurst*.
— Letters to Lord Hardinge from J. R. Rodd, 1917, 1918. 51093, ff. 56, 57 (extract), 58, 170.
— Correspondence between Lord Cecil and Lord Hardinge, 1918, 1919. 51094, ff. 4, 5, 154, 170.

Hardwicke, *6th Earl of*.
— *v.* Yorke (Albert Edward).

Hare (William Francis), *5th Earl of Listowel.*
— Correspondence, including telegram, between Lord Cecil and Lord Listowel, 1941. Partly *printed.* 51187, ff. 329, 334, 388; 51188, ff. 5-8.

Harewood, *6th Earl of.*
— *v.* Lascelles (Henry George Charles).

Harker (*Brig.* O. Allen), *of the War Office.*
— Correspondence between Lord Cecil and Brig. O. A. Harker, 1946. *Signed.* 51192, ff. 244, 245.

Harlech, *4th Baron.*
— *v.* Ormsby-Gore (William George Arthur).

Harmsworth, *1st Baron.*
— *v.* Cooper (Alfred Duff).

Harmsworth (Alfred Charles William), *Viscount Northcliffe.*
— Correspondence between Lord Cecil and Lord Northcliffe, 1909, 1914. *Signed.* Partly *extract.* 51159, ff. 136, 156, 199, 215, 220-222, 225-242, 280; 51161, ff. 195, 196.

Harmsworth (Cecil Bisshopp), *1st Baron Harmsworth.*
— Correspondence, partly on his behalf, with Lord Cecil, 1922. Partly *signed.* 51095, ff. 56, 66-67v; 51163, f. 51.

Harrington, Edwards and Cobban, *solicitors.*
— Accounts with Lord Cecil, 1925. 51164, ff. 128, 129.
— Receipt to Trustees of Cecil Peace Prize from Harrington, Edwards and Cobban (solicitors), 1944. Partly *printed.* 51191, f. 11.

Harris (Alfred W.), *J.P.; of the National Liberal Club.*
— Correspondence, including telegrams, between Lord Cecil and A. W. Harris, 1913. 51160, ff. 246-257, 261, 266.

Harris (F. W.), *of Burslem.*
— Letter to Lord Cecil from F. W. Harris, 1927. 51165, f. 149.

Harris (Henry Wilson), *journalist.*
— Correspondence between Lord Cecil and H. W. Harris, 1922-1948. Partly *signed.* 51095, ff. 73-76v; 51099, ff. 92, 94; 51164, ff. 63, 117-119; 51167, f. 25; 51188, ff. 45, 89, 91, 106, 330, 330v; 51191, ff. 109, 164, 255; 51192, ff. 52, 54, 128, 143, 295.
— Memorandum rel. to 'Headway' by H. W. Harris, 1928. *Copy.* 51166, ff. 44-48.

Harris (J. Nugent), *of Dane Hill.*
— Correspondence between Lord Cecil and J. N. Harris, 1944. 51191, ff. 198, 250.

Harris (*Sir* John Hobbis), *Sec., Anti-Slavery and Aborigines Protection Society.*
— Correspondence between Lord Cecil and Sir J. H. Harris, 1937. *Signed.* 51177, ff. 83, 103-105, 115; 51184, ff. 44, 45, 93, 104; 51185, ff. 64, 65.

Harris (Ray Baker), *U.S. author.*
— Correspondence between Lord Cecil and R. B. Harris, 1939. *Signed.* 51184, ff. 3, 69.

Harrison (Francis Graham-).
— *v.* Graham-Harrison (Francis).

Harrod (*Sir* Roy Forbes).
— Correspondence between Lord Cecil and Sir R. F. Harrod, 1940. 51185, ff. 42, 44.

Hart (*Sir* Basil Henry Liddell), *military historian and strategist.*
— Memorandum by Sir B. H. L. Hart rel. to Poland, 1939. *Copy.* 51183, ff. 216-224.
— Correspondence between Lord Cecil and Sir B. H. L. Hart, 1939. Partly *signed.* 51183, f. 229; 51184, ff. 15-18, 52, 192-201, 205, 208-212.

INDEX

Hartington, *Marquess of.*
— *v.* Cavendish (Edward William Spencer).

Harvey (Margaret), *Sec., the Women's Liberal Federation.*
— Letter to Lord Cecil from M. Harvey on behalf of G. L. Baerlein, 1937. *Signed.* 51175, f. 55.

Harvey (Oliver Charles), *1st Baron Harvey of Tasburgh.*
— Correspondence between Lord Cecil and O. C. Harvey, 1937-1941. *Signed.* 51083, ff. 140-145, 172, 174; 51175, f. 61.

Harwood (*Sir* Ralph Endersby), *K.C.B.*
— Correspondence between Lord Cecil and Sir R. E. Harwood, 1937. *Signed.* 51177, ff. 80, 110.

Haskell (Henry S.), *of the Carnegie Endowment for International Peace.*
— Letter and telegram to Lord Cecil from H. S. Haskell, 1940, 1941. *Signed.* 51186, f. 178; 51187, ff. 11, 264-272.

Haslam (George D.), *of Uckfield.*
— Correspondence between Lord Cecil and G. D. Haslam, 1939. 51183, ff. 142, 151, 155, 166, 170-173.

Havelock (Sydney), *physician.*
— Letter to Lord Cecil, 1944. *Signed.* 51191, f. 215.

Hawkes (R. S.), *President of the Union Society, University College, London.*
— Letters to Lord Cecil from R. S. Hawkes, 1936. *Signed.* 51172, ff. 11, 43, 177.

Hawkey (William John), *of Long Wittenham.*
— Correspondence between Lord Cecil and W. J. Hawkey, 1939. 51184, ff. 254, 256.

Hawkin (Robert Crawford), *barrister; Sec. of the International Arbitration League.*
— Memorandum by Lord Cecil rel. to interview with R. C. Hawkin, 1937. *Copy.* 51176, f. 131.
— Correspondence between Lord Cecil and R. C. Hawkin, 1937, 1938. *Signed.* 51176, ff. 134, 138, 150-151, 158; 51177, ff. 22, 28, 29, 120; 51178, f. 144.

Hawkins (James Harford), *of the Independent Order of Odd Fellows.*
— Letter to Lord Cecil from J. H. Hawkins, 1911. 51160, f. 36.

Haworth (*Sir* Arthur Adlington), *1st Bart.*
— Correspondence between Lord Cecil and Sir A. A. Haworth, 1938. *Signed.* 51180, ff. 133-135.

Hazlerigg (Arthur Grey), *1st Baron Hazlerigg.*
— Correspondence between Lord Cecil and A. G. Hazlerigg, 1936. *Signed.* 51173, ff. 244, 250.

Headlam-Morley (*Sir* James Wycliffe).
— Letter to W. H. M. Selby from J. W. Headlam-Morley, 1918. *Signed.* 51094, f. 31.
— Correspondence between Lord Cecil and Sir J. W. Headlam-Morley, 1923-1928. *Signed.* 51095, ff. 154, 156; 51099, ff. 105*-113, 125-130.

Heald (Stephen Alfred), *of the Royal Institute of International Affairs, London.*
— Correspondence, partly on behalf of Lord Cecil, between S. A. Heald and R. F. Wigram, 1934. 51082, ff. 215-227, 232-240, 245-260.
— Letter to S. A. Heald from C. W. Baxter, 1934. *Signed.* 51082, ff. 228-231.
— Letters to Lord Cecil from S. A. Heald, 1934. *Signed.* 51169, ff. 49, 75.

Heaton-Ellis (*Sir* Charles Henry Brabazon), *Chairman, Hitchin Division, Conservative and Unionist Association.*
— Correspondence between Lord Cecil and C. H. B. Heaton-Ellis, 1921, 1922. 51163, ff. 26-29v, 93-95.

Hemming (Arthur Francis), *of the Economic Advisory Council.*
— Letter to Rear-Adm. L. E. H. Maund from A. F. Hemming, 1932. *Signed.* 51088, f. 78.

Henderson (Arthur), *Baron Rowley; son of Arthur Henderson, P.C; M.P.*
— Correspondence between Lord Cecil and A. Henderson, 1937. *Signed.* 51081, ff. 234, 235.

Henderson (Arthur), *P.C.; M.P.*
— Correspondence between Lord Cecil and A. Henderson, 1929-1934. *Signed.* 51081, ff. 143-233.
— 'Preliminary report on the Conference for the Reduction and Limitations of Armaments at Geneva (1932-1934)' by A. Henderson, 1936. *Printed. Imperf.* 51122.

Henderson (*Sir* David), *K.C.B.; Director-General, League of Red Cross Societies.*
— Letter to Sir D. Henderson from J. S. Barnes, 1921. *Copy.* 51095, f. 22.

Henderson (J. F.), *of the Allied Maritime Transport Council.*
— Letter to A. Webber from J. F. Henderson, 1918. 51094, f. 84.

Henderson (*Sir* Nevile Meyrick), *G.C.M.G.*
— Correspondence between Lord Cecil and N. M. Henderson, 1930. *Signed.* 51100, ff. 72-76.

Henderson (Peter Bernie), *solicitor.*
— Letter to Lord Cecil, 1943, 1944. 51190, f. 80; 51191, ff. 39, 42, 82.

Henderson (William Watson), *Baron Henderson.*
— Correspondence between Lord Cecil and Lord Henderson, 1948. *Signed.* 51192, ff. 303-305.

Hendriks (*Sir* Cecil Augustus Charles John), *Private Sec. to the Leader of the House of Lords.*
— Correspondence between Miss I. M. Butler and C. A. C. J. Hendriks on behalf of Lord Halifax, 1938. *Signed.* 51084, ff. 121-123.

Henniker, *8th Baron.*
— *v.* Henniker-Major (John Patrick Edward Chandos).

Henniker-Major (John Patrick Edward Chandos), *8th Baron Henniker.*
— Correspondence between Lord Cecil and J. P. E. C. Henniker-Major on behalf of E. Bevin, 1946. *Signed.* 51192, ff. 238, 242, 246-248.

Henson (Herbert Hensley), *former Bishop of Durham.*
— Correspondence between Lord Cecil and H. H. Henson, 1943. 51190, ff. 107, 109, 119.

Henson (Isabella Caroline), *wife of H. Hensley Henson, former Bishop of Durham.*
— Correspondence between Lord Cecil and I. C. Henson, 1943. 51190, ff. 1-3, 17, 100.

Henty (E. Claude), *personal private sec. to Lord Cecil.*
— Correspondence on behalf of Lord Cecil, 1925-1927. Partly *signed.* 51097, f. 187; 51098, ff. 3-178.
— Letter to E. C. Henty from W. St. C. H. Roberts, 1926. *Signed.* 51097, f. 126.
— Correspondence between Lord Cecil and E. C. Henty, 1926-1944. Mostly *signed.* 51098, ff. 4, 32, 70; 51100, ff. 80-84, 124-127; 51191, ff. 213, 242.

INDEX

Henty (E. Claude), *personal private sec. to Lord Cecil.* continuation
— Correspondence between E. C. Henty on behalf of Lord Cecil and G. A. Innes, 1931. 51167, ff. 126-131.
— Letter to P. A. Laszlo de Lombos from E. C. Henty on behalf of Lord Cecil, 1931. 51167, f. 133.

Hepburne-Scott (Walter George), *9th Baron Polwarth.*
— Correspondence between Lord Cecil and Lord Polwarth, 1926. *Signed.* 51098, ff. 93-97.

Herbert (Aubrey Nigel Henry Molyneux), *M.P.*
— Correspondence between Lord Cecil and A. N. H. M. Herbert, 1920, 1922. *Signed.* 51141, ff. 316-319.

Herbert (*Sir* George Sidney), *Bart.*
— Letter from Lord Cecil to Sir G. S. Herbert, 1937. *Copy.* 51175, f. 26.

Herbert (H.), *Parliamentary Sec., The British Federation for the Emancipation of Sweated Women.*
— Letter to Lord Cecil from H. Herbert, 1913. *Signed.* 51161, f. 31.

Herbert (*Mrs* M.).
— Letter to Mrs M. Herbert from T. Zavalani, 1943. *Signed.* 51141, f. 331.

Herbert (Mary), *widow of A. N. H. M. Herbert.*
— Correspondence between Lord Cecil and M. Herbert, 1943-1945. 51141, ff. 320-362.

Herman-Hodge (*Rear-Adm.* Claude Preston).
— Letter to Lord Cecil from Rear-Adm. C. P. Herman-Hodge, 1928. *Signed.* 51088, f. 74.

Herriot (Edouard), *French statesman.*
— Correspondence between Lord Cecil and E. Herriot, 1945. 51192, ff. 89, 96.

Herrman (Leo), *of the Erez Israel (Palestine) Foundation Fund.*
— Letter to B. E. C. Dugdale from L. Herrman, 1945. *Signed.* 51157, f. 302.

Hertfordshire.
— Addresses, etc., by Lord Cecil to the electors of North Herts, 1918, 1923. Partly *printed.* 51162, ff. 72-76v; 51163, f. 175.

Hertz (Joseph Herman), *Chief Rabbi.*
— Letters to Lord Cecil from J. H. Hertz, 1939-1944. Mostly *signed.* 51184, ff. 81, 145; 51186, ff. 225, 282; 51188, f. 27; 51190, f. 288; 51191, f. 176.

Hervé (Gustave), *French author.*
— Statement to Press on revision of Treaty of Versailles, 1931. *Copy.* 51167, f. 89.

Herwig (Gisela), *German refugee.*
— Memorandum by Lord Cecil rel. to G. Herwig, 1940. 51184, f. 348.

Herzog (Isaac), *Chief Rabbi of Palestine.*
— Correspondence between Lord Cecil and I. Herzog, 1937. Partly *signed.* 51176, ff. 13, 51; 51177, ff. 116, 156.

Hesketh, *1st Baron.*
— *v.* Fermor-Hesketh (Thomas).

Hesketh (Thomas Fermor-).
— *v.* Fermor-Hesketh (Thomas).

Hewins (William Albert Samuel), *Sec., Tariff Commission.*
— Letter to Lord Cecil from W. A. S. Hewins, 1908. 51158, f. 283.

Hewison (R. J. P.), *of the Home Office.*
— Letter to Miss E. V. Lazarus from R. J. P. Hewison on behalf of H. S. Morrison, 1945. *Signed.* 51192, f. 68.

INDEX

Heymann (Lida Gustava), *German emigrant in Zurich.*
— Correspondence between Lord Cecil and L. G. Heymann, 1938. Partly *signed.* 51181, ff. 157, 165, 199.

Hicks (William Joynson).
— *v.* Joynson-Hicks (William).

Hicks-Beach (Michael Edward), *1st Earl St. Aldwyn.*
— Correspondence between Lord Cecil and M. E. Hicks-Beach, 1909. 51159, ff. 176, 182, 189, 193.

Hill (Andrew), *of the League of Nations Union, Oldham Branch.*
— Letter from Lord Cecil to A. Hill, 1938. *Copy.* 51178, f. 183.

Hill (Martin), *official of the League of Nations at Princeton, New Jersey.*
— Letter to Lord Cecil, 1944. *Signed.* 51191, f. 68.

Hill (*Maj.-Gen.* Walter Pitts Hendy).
— Letter to Lord Cecil from Maj.-Gen. W. P. H. Hill, 1941. *Signed.* 51187, f. 340.

Hills (John Waller), *M.P.*
— Letter to Lord Cecil from J. W. Hills, [1927?]. 51165, f. 156.

Hills (*Sir* Reginald Playfair), *barrister.*
— Memorandum and legal opinion rel. to school-building under the Appropriation Act, 1907, 1908. *Copies.* 51074, ff. 12-163, 167v-171.
— Letter to Lord Cecil from R. P. Hills, 1914. 51161, f. 102.

Hilton (John), *of the Free Trade Union.*
— Letter to Lord Cecil from J. Hilton, 1909. *Signed.* 51159, f. 197.

Hines (*Rev.* Charles Percy), *of Beaumaris, Anglesey.*
— Correspondence between Lord Cecil and Rev. C. P. Hines, 1939. 51183, ff. 185, 192.

Hinsley (Arthur), *Cardinal.*
— Correspondence, partly on his behalf, with Lord Cecil, 1935-1941. Partly *signed.* 51171, ff. 26, 27; 51179, ff. 136-139, 145-149, 153, 167, 229-231; 51182, ff. 102, 105; 51184, ff. 117, 154, 165, 168; 51187, ff. 263, 279, 328, 331.

Hirtzel (*Sir* Frederic Arthur), *K.C.B.*
— Correspondence between Lord Cecil and Sir F. A. Hirtzel, 1918. 51094, ff. 52, 57.

Hitchin, *co. Hertf.*
— Notice of public meeting to be addressed by Lord Cecil at Hitchin, 1918. *Printed.* 51162, f. 59.

Hnik (Frank M.), *of the Czechoslovak Ministry of Foreign Affairs in London.*
— Letters, etc., to Lord Cecil, 1940, 1944. Partly *signed.* 51184, ff. 319-322v; 51185, f. 69; 51191, f. 193.

Hoare (*Sir* Samuel John Gurney), *1st Viscount Templewood.*
— Correspondence between Lord Cecil and Lord Templewood, 1918-1945. Mostly *signed.* 51083, ff. 1-47.
— Memorandum by Bishop of Chichester rel. to interview with Sir S. J. G. Hoare, 1938. *Copy.* 51154 B, f. 100.

Hobhouse (Edmund Graham), *Curate, Battersea Parish Church.*
— Letter to Lord Cecil from E. G. Hobhouse, 1941. *Printed. Signed.* 51188, f. 20.

Hobhouse (Henry), *P.C.; M.P.*
— Letter to Lord Cecil from H. Hobhouse, 1909. *Signed.* 51159, f. 101.

Hodder and Stoughton Ltd., *publishers.*
— Letter from Lord Cecil to Hodder and Stoughton Ltd. (publishers), 1946. *Copy.* 51192, f. 229.

Hodge (Harold), *Editor of The Saturday Review.*
— Letter to Lord Cecil from H. Hodge, 1908. *Signed.* 51158, f. 250v.

Hodge (Rear-Adm. Claude Preston Herman-).
— *v.* Herman-Hodge (*Rear-Adm. Claude Preston*).

Hodsoll (J. Sass), *Examiner of Death Duties, Estate Duty Office.*
— Correspondence between Lord Cecil and J. S. Hodsoll, 1944. 51191, ff. 260, 274.

Hodson (H. V.), *of the Royal Institute of International Affairs.*
— Correspondence between Lord Cecil and H. V. Hodson, 1933. *Signed.* 51168, ff. 103, 127, 129-131.

Hodson (J. Wignall), *Sec., League of Nations Union, Fleetwood Branch.*
— Correspondence between Lord Cecil and J. W. Hodson, 1936. *Signed.* 51173, ff. 12, 22.

Hoegner (Wilhelm), *German lawyer and politician.*
— Correspondence between Lord Cecil and W. Hoegner, 1935, 1936. Partly *signed.* 51170, ff. 199, 211, 212; 51171, f. 237; 51172, ff. 6, 24, 29.

Hoel (Adolf), *President, International Nansen Monument Committee.*
— Letter to Lord Cecil from A. Hoel, 1937. *Signed.* 51177, f. 159.

Hoesch (Leopold Gustav Alexander von), *German diplomatist.*
— Correspondence, partly on his behalf, with Lord Cecil, 1934-1936. *Signed.* 51101, ff. 106, 197-201; 51170, ff. 171, 182, 253; 51171, f. 7; 51173, ff. 1, 9.

Hofmeyer (Jan Hendrik), *South African politician.*
— Correspondence between Lord Cecil and J. H. Hofmeyer, 1940. *Signed.* 51184, f. 339; 51185, f. 17.

Hogarth Press.
— Note to Lord Cecil rel. to royalties from the Hogarth Press, 1940. 51193, f. 183.
— *v. also* West (Margaret).

Hogg (Douglas McGarel), *1st Viscount Hailsham.*
— Correspondence, partly on his behalf, with Lord Cecil, 1936. *Signed.* 51172, ff. 83, 91, 99; 51173, ff. 218-221.

Hohler (*Sir* Thomas Beaumont), *K.C.M.G; diplomatist.*
— Correspondence between Lord Cecil and Sir T. B. Hohler, 1924. 51096, ff. 145, 152; 51167, f. 43.

Holderness (*Sir* Ernest William Elsmie), *2nd Bart.*
— Letter to Lord Cecil from Sir E. W. E. Holderness, 1938. 51182, f. 89.

Hole (Tahu), *of The Herald, Melbourne.*
— Letter to Miss I. M. Butler from T. Hole, 1941. *Signed.* 51187, f. 183.

Holke (Felix), *of the Imperial Life Assurance Company of Canada.*
— Letter to Lord Cecil from F. Holke, 1940. *Signed.* 51185, f. 217.

Holland (R.), *Sec., the National Society for Promoting Religious Education.*
— Correspondence between Lord Cecil and R. Holland, 1936. *Signed.* 51172, ff. 81, 95.

Holman (Dorothy), *wife of P. Holman, M.P.*
— Correspondence between Lord Cecil and D. Holman, 1935. 51171, ff. 183, 187.

Holmden (*Miss* Geraldine), *Sec., League of Nations Union, Hurtwood Branch.*
— Correspondence between Lord Cecil and Miss G. Holmden, 1941. 51188, ff. 113-115, 117, 121.

Holmes (V.), *engineer.*
— Letter to Lord Cecil from V. Holmes, 1938. *Signed.* 51181, f. 75.

Holsti (Rudolf), *Finnish diplomatist.*
— Correspondence between Lord Cecil and R. Holsti, 1926, 1927. *Signed. Partly Fr.* 51098, ff. 133-138; 51099, ff. 65-67.
— Memorandum by Lord Cecil rel. to conversation with R. Holsti, 1931. 51100, f. 135.

Holt (Lawrence Durning), *shipowner.*
— Correspondence between Lord Cecil and L. D. Holt, 1938. *Signed.* 51179, ff. 65, 76.

Home Office.
— *v.* Allen (Philip).
— *v.* Cooper (E. M.).
— *v.* Graham-Harrison (Francis).
— *v.* Lenfestey (*Miss* A.).
— *v.* Peterson (A. W.).
— *v.* Strutt (H. A.).

Homfray (*Miss* Ida Frances), *of Hampstead.*
— Correspondence between Lord Cecil and Miss I. F. Homfray, 1938. *Signed.* 51179, ff. 88, 102.

Hood (Alexander Fuller-Acland-).
— *v.* Fuller-Acland-Hood (Alexander).

Hooft (Willem Adolph Visser't), *General Sec., World Council of Churches.*
— Memorandum rel. to visits to Czechoslovakia and Germany, 1938. *Printed.* 51182, ff. 50-54.

Hoover (Herbert), *President of the U.S.A.*
— Correspondence between Lord Cecil and H. Hoover, 1932. *Signed.* 51100, ff. 166, 171.

Hope (*Miss* Graham), *Organising Sec., Women's Amalgamated Unionist and Tariff Reform Association.*
— Letter to Lord Cecil from Miss G. Hope, 1913. *Signed.* 51160, f. 259.

Hope (James Fitzalan), *1st Baron Rankeillour.*
— Correspondence between Lord Cecil and Lord Rankeillour, 1912-1944. Partly *signed* and *printed.* 51160, f. 77; 51161, ff. 33, 35, 61, 65, 73; 51191, ff. 270, 271.
— Memorandum rel. to Anglo-Soviet relations, 1941. *Printed.* 51186, f. 306.
— Memoranda to members of Watching Committee, 1943. *Printed.* 51189, f. 287; 51190, ff. 39, 44.

Hopkins (Harry L.), *Special Adviser to the President of the U.S.A.*
— Correspondence between Lord Cecil and H. L. Hopkins, 1941. *Signed.* 51186, f. 304; 51187, f. 4.

Horder (Thomas Jeeves), *1st Baron Horder.*
— Correspondence between Lord Cecil and Lord Horder, 1936, 1939. 51174, f. 188; 51183, f. 228; 51184, ff. 155, 157, 163.

Hore-Belisha (Leslie), *Baron Hore-Belisha.*
— Correspondence, partly on his behalf, with Lord Cecil, 1934, 1935. *Signed.* 51169, ff. 218, 242, 250; 51170, ff. 1-5, 115, 153-159, 216, 217, 232.

Hornby (*Sir* William Henry), *1st Bart.*
— Letter to Lord Cecil from Sir W. H. Hornby, 1909. *Signed.* 51159, f. 63.

Horne (Robert Stevenson), *Viscount Horne.*
— Letter to Lord Cecil from Lord Horne, 1940. *Signed.* 51186, f. 42.

Horowicz (P.), *of the Anglo-Palestinian Club.*
— Correspondence between Lord Cecil and P. Horowicz, 1942. *Signed.* 51189, ff. 136, 198.

Horsbrugh-Porter (*Sir* John Scott), *2nd Bart.*
— Letter to Lord Cecil from J. S. Horsbrugh-Porter, 1913. 51161, f. 12.

Horsman (Dorothy), *of Victor Gollancz Ltd.*
— Correspondence between Lord Cecil and D. Horsman, 1936. *Signed.* 51193, ff. 79-81.

Houghton (Alanson Bigelow), *U.S. diplomatist.*
— Memorandum by Lord Cecil rel. to conversation with A. B. Houghton, 1926. 51098, f. 15.

House (*Col.* Edward Mandell), *U.S. statesman.*
— Memoranda by Lord Cecil rel. to interviews with Col. E. M. House, 1919. 51094, ff. 168, 176.
— Correspondence, including telegrams, between Lord Cecil and Col. E. M. House, 1919-1927. *Signed.* 51094, ff. 171-175; 51095, ff. 5, 39-42, 61, 68-72v, 133, 139; 51099, ff. 86, 98, 136.

Houston (Herbert Sherman), *editor, of New York.*
— Correspondence between Lord Cecil and H. S. Houston, 1937. *Signed.* 51178, ff. 30, 31.

Howard (Esme William), *1st Baron Howard of Penrith.*
— Correspondence between Lord Cecil and Lord Howard, 1925-1936. *Signed.* 51097, ff. 101, 106; 51168, f. 44; 51173, ff. 249, 263.

Howard (George Wren), *publisher.*
— Letters to Miss I. M. Butler from G. W. Howard, 1941. *Signed.* 51187, ff. 84, 111.

Howard (Hubert John Edward Dominic), *3rd son of Esme, Baron Howard of Penrith.*
— Correspondence between Lord Cecil and H. J. E. D. Howard, 1936, 1937. *Signed.* 51172, ff. 138, 149; 51175, ff. 32, 82-84.

Howe (A. J.), *Chairman, Bromley Branch, League of Nations Union.*
— Correspondence between Lord Cecil and A. J. Howe, 1943, 1944. *Signed.* 51190, f. 65; 51191, ff. 81, 85.

Howe (P. P.), *of Hamish Hamilton Ltd.*
— Correspondence, etc., between Lord Cecil and P. P. Howe, 1941. *Signed.* 51193, ff. 209-212, 216-220, 222.
— Correspondence between P. P. Howe and Miss I. M. Butler, 1941. *Signed.* 51193, ff. 213-215, 221, 223-225.

Howick, *Viscount.*
— *v.* Grey (Charles Robert).

Hsu (Y. C.), *of the International Peace Campaign, China Branch.*
— Correspondence between Lord Cecil and Y. C. Hsu, 1938. *Signed.* 51180, ff. 120, 159.

Hubbard (John Gellibrand), *3rd Baron Addington.*
— Correspondence between Lord Cecil and Lord Addington, 1937. *Signed.* 51177, ff. 133, 140, 151.

Hudson (*Sir* Austin Uvedale Morgan), *Bart.; M.P.*
— Correspondence between Lord Cecil and Sir A. U. M. Hudson, 1936. *Signed.* 51172, ff. 58, 85.

Hudson (Manley Ottmer), *Professor of International Law, Harvard University.*
— Correspondence between Lord Cecil and M. O. Hudson, 1923, 1935. Partly *signed.* 51095, ff. 183-185; 51171, ff. 154, 180, 210.

Hughes (*Miss* Dorothea Price), *of the League of Nations Union, Holborn Branch.*
— Correspondence between Lord Cecil and Miss D. P. Hughes, 1938. *Signed.* 51182, ff. 95, 96.

Hughes (*Maj.-Gen.* Ivor Thomas Percival).
— Letters to Lord Cecil from Maj.-Gen. I. T. P. Hughes, 1907, 1908. Partly *signed.* 51158, ff. 162, 165.

Hull, *E.R., co. York.*
— Message from Lord Cecil for Peace Week at Hull, 1937. 51177, f. 40.

Hull (Cordell), *U.S. Sec. of State.*
— Memorandum by Lord Cecil rel. to conversation with C. Hull, 1937. 51178, f. 12.

Hulton (*Sir* Edward George Warris), *writer and publisher.*
— Correspondence between Lord Cecil and Sir E. G. W. Hulton, 1941. *Signed.* 51186, ff. 286, 303.

Hume (Ethel Douglas), *wife of Hedley Thomson; author.*
— Correspondence between Lord Cecil and E. D. Hume, 1940. *Signed.* 51185, ff. 92, 104.

Hume-Williams (*Sir* Ellis), *1st Bart.*
— Correspondence between Lord Cecil and Sir E. Hume-Williams, 1943, 1944. 51190, ff. 309, 322, 367-370v; 51191, f. 209.

Humphreys (John H.), *of Bromley, co. Kent.*
— Correspondence between Lord Cecil and J. H. Humphreys, 1936. *Signed.* 51174, ff. 126, 137, 171.

Humphreys (William J.), *of The New York Herald Tribune.*
— Letters, etc., to Lord Cecil from W. J. Humphreys, 1945. *Signed.* 51192, f. 93.

Hunsdon, *1st Baron.*
— *v.* Gibbs (Herbert Cokayne).

Hunt (*Mrs* J. A.), *Sec., Birmingham Council for Refugees.*
— Correspondence between Lord Cecil and Mrs J. A. Hunt, 1940. *Signed.* 51186, ff. 32-35.

Hunt (Sydney C.), *Chairman, Norwood Conservative Council.*
— Correspondence between A. J. Balfour and S. C. Hunt, 1907. Partly *draft.* 51071 A, ff. 3, 5.

Hurst (*Miss* C. C.), *writing from Bovey Tracey.*
— Correspondence between Lord Cecil and Miss C. C. Hurst, 1940. 51186, ff. 216, 226.

Hurst (*Sir* Cecil James Barrington), *G.C.M.G.*
— Correspondence between Lord Cecil and Sir C. J. B. Hurst, 1925-1944. Partly *signed.* 51090, ff. 91-138v.
— Signature, 1927. 51099, f. 24.

Huston (Howard R).
— Correspondence between E. C. Henty and H. R. Huston, 1925. 51097, f. 187.

Hutton (J. Arthur), *of James F. Hutton & Co., Manchester.*
— Letter to Lord Cecil from J. A. Hutton, 1941. *Signed.* 51187, f. 66.

Hutton (John A.), *of the Over-Seas League and Post-War Bureau.*
— Correspondence between Lord Cecil and J. A. Hutton, 1939. *Signed.* 51184, ff. 174, 214, 234, 235, 239, 242.

Huxley (*Sir* Julian Sorell), *F.R.S.*
— Letters to Lord Cecil from J. S. Huxley, 1939. Partly *signed.* 51184, ff. 100, 156.

Hyatt-Woolf (*Mrs* Elizabeth), *of the Letchworth Unionist Committee.*
— Correspondence between Lord Cecil and Mrs E. Hyatt-Woolf, 1918. *Signed.* 51162, ff. 78, 81.

INDEX

Hyde (G. Miller), *Sec., Canadian Club of Montreal.*
— Correspondence between Lord Cecil and G. M. Hyde, 1933. *Signed.* 51168, ff. 61, 69.

Hyka (—), *Czechoslovak delegate to the League of Nations.*
— Memorandum by Lord Cecil rel. to conversation with — Hyka, 1923. 51096, f. 50.

Hylton, *3rd Earl.*
— *v.* Jolliffe (Hylton George Hylton).

Hyman (Leonard), *of the Pedestrians' Association.*
— Letter to Lord Cecil, 1943. 51190, f. 375.

Hymans (Paul), *G.C.M.G; Belgian statesman.*
— Correspondence between Lord Cecil and P. Hymans, 1923. Partly *signed.* Partly *Fr.* 51095, ff. 150, 157, 164; 51097, f. 60.

I

Illingworth (Percy Holden), *M.P.*
— Letter to Lord Cecil from P. H. Illingworth, 1913. *Signed.* 51160, f. 238.

Imperial Fund.
— Papers rel. to the Imperial Fund, 1912. *Printed.* 51160, ff. 178-187.

Imperial War Relief Fund.
— Accounts, 1925. 51164, ff. 120-127v.

Imperiali (*Marchese* Guglielmo), *Italian ambassador in London.*
— Correspondence between Lord Cecil and Marchese G. Imperiali, 1918. *Signed.* 51093, ff. 83-85.
— Memorandum by Lord Cecil rel. to conversation with Marchese G. Imperiali, 1918. 51094, f. 8.

Inch (R. B.), *of the Canadian League of Nations Society.*
— Correspondence, including telegram, between Lord Cecil and R. B. Inch, 1942. 51189, ff. 101, 169, 187.

India.
— Farewell message to the people of India from Chiang Kai-shek, 1942. *Printed.* 51188, f. 216.

Industrial Co-Partnership Association.
— Bulletins nos. 2, 3, 5 published by Industrial Co-Partnership Association, 1945. *Printed.* 51192, ff. 1, 57, 106.
— *v.* also Ramsey (*Mrs* Irene S.).

Ingram (Archibald Kenneth), *Editor of The New Green Quarterly.*
— Letter to Lord Cecil from A. K. Ingram, 1936. *Signed.* 51193, f. 74.

Ingram (Arthur Foley Winnington-).
— *v.* Winnington-Ingram (Arthur Foley).

Innes (George A.), *official of the League of Nations Union.*
— Correspondence between E. C. Henty on behalf of Lord Cecil and G. A. Innes, 1931. 51167, ff. 126-131.
— Correspondence between Lord Cecil and G. A. Innes, 1931, 1935. *Signed.* 51167, ff. 126-132; 51170, f. 175.
— Memorandum rel. to Lord Cecil's Portrait Fund, 1933. *Signed.* 51167, f. 36.

Inskip (Thomas Walker Hobart), *1st Viscount Caldecote.*
— Correspondence, etc., between Lord Cecil and Lord Caldecote, 1942. Partly *printed.* 51188, ff. 349-351v, 371, 374; 51189, f. 10.

International Committee for Assistance of German Refugee Professional Workers.
— Minutes of the British Section of the International Committee for Assistance of German Refugee Professional Workers, 1933. *Copy.* 51168, ff. 141-146.
— *v. also* Ormerod (*Mrs* Mary).

International Nansen Monument Committee.
— *v.* Giaever (Magnus K.).
— *v.* Hoel (Adolf).

International Peace Campaign.
— Memoranda, etc., rel. to the International Peace Campaign, 1936-1940. Partly *printed.* Partly *Fr.* 51172, f. 211; 51173, ff. 29-36, 193-196; 51174, ff. 10, 45-48, 55-59; 51175, ff. 15, 89-97, 105, 108-111, 218, 219; 51176, ff. 93, 110, 164-175; 51177, ff. 77-79, 142; 51178, ff. 4, 105; 51179, ff. 8, 181, 184; 51181, f. 62; 51182, ff. 17-20, 186; 51183, ff. 144-150; 51184, ff. 122-130, 255; 51185, f. 250.
— Memorandum rel. to visits to Austria, etc., by E. P. Young on behalf of the International Peace Campaign, 1936. *Copy.* 51173, ff. 162-168.
— Donations to and payments by the International Peace Campaign, 1936, 1937. 51177, f. 41.
— Message from Lord Cecil to the First British Congress of the International Peace Campaign, 1937. *Copy.* 51177, f. 182.
— Resolutions of the First British Congress of the International Peace Campaign, 1937. *Printed.* 51177, ff. 190, 191.
— Telegrams between Lord Cecil and the China Branch of the International Peace Campaign, 1940. 51185, ff. 220, 221.

International Peace Campaign, *International Secretariate.*
— Letter to International Peace Campaign (International Secretariate) from Cheng Yin-fu, 1940. *Copy.* 51184, f. 345.

International Peace Campaign.
— *v. also* Allen (Elisabeth Acland).
— *v. also* Bell (Nancy E.).
— *v. also* Cohen-Stuart (A. B.).
— *v. also* Degerman (Allan).
— *v. also* Dickson (*Maj.* Dhannuil Gordon).
— *v. also* Dolivet (Louis).
— *v. also* Garnsey (*Canon* Arthur H.).
— *v. also* Hsu (Y. C.).
— *v. also* Jézéquel (Pastor J.).
— *v. also* Keeling (Guy W.).
— *v. also* Lussi (Willi).
— *v. also* Manus (*Miss* Rosa).
— *v. also* Menant (Guy).
— *v. also* Nygatan (Lilla).
— *v. also* Pouderoux (*Gen.* —).
— *v. also* Shao Li-tze.
— *v. also* Williams (F. D.).

International Student Service.
— Letter to Lord Cecil, signed by Archbishop of York and C. Weizmann on behalf of the International Student Service, 1937. *Facsimile.* 51178, f. 45.

Iran.
— Memorandum rel. to refugees and nationals of occupied countries in Iran, 1941. *Copy.* 51188, ff. 135-138.

Iremonger (Frederic Athelwold), *Dean of Lichfield.*
— Correspondence between Lord Cecil and F. A. Iremonger, 1945. *Signed.* 51192, ff. 112, 122, 124.

Irming (M. R.), *refugee from Nazi Germany.*
— Letter, etc., to Lord Cecil, 1947. *Signed.* 51192, ff. 262-267.

Irwin, *Baron.*
— *v.* Wood (Edward Frederick Lindley).

INDEX

Isaac (Walter), *J.P.*
— Correspondence between Lord Cecil and W. Isaac, 1938. *Signed.* 51181, ff. 97, 101.

Isaacs (Rufus Daniel), *1st Marquess of Reading.*
— Correspondence between Lord Cecil and Lord Reading, 1925-1931. *Signed.* 51082, ff. 1-62.

ITALY.
— Memorandum by Maj.-Gen. P. A. M. Nash rel. to coal supply for France and Italy, 1918. *Signed.* 51093, ff. 92-96.

Iwan-Müller (Ernest Bruce), *journalist.*
— Letters to Lord Cecil from E. B. Iwan-Müller, 1909. 51159, ff. 216-218.

J

Jabotinsky (Jeanne), *wife (?) of V. E. Jabotinsky, Zionist politician and author.*
— Telegram to Lord Cecil, 1940. 51185, f. 201.

Jackson (Frederick Huth), *P.C.*
— Letters to Lord Cecil from F. H. Jackson, 1909. 51159, ff. 53, 83.

Jacob (Ernest Fraser), *historian.*
— Correspondence between Lord Cecil and E. F. Jacob, 1934. *Signed.* 51169, ff. 92, 100, 104.

Jaffé (Arthur), *of the International Law Association.*
— Letter to Lord Cecil, 1944. 51191, f. 307.

Jaksch (Wenzel), *leader of German Social Democrats in Czechoslovakia.*
— Letter to Lord Cecil from W. Jaksch, 1938. *Signed.* 51154, f. 94.

James (Lionel), *of Five Ashes.*
— Correspondence between Lord Cecil and L. James, 1940. 51186, ff. 8, 31.

Jameson (Margaret Storm), *author; wife of Professor G. P. Chapman.*
— Letter to G. G. A. Murray from M. S. Jameson, 1934. *Signed.* 51132, f. 192.
— Correspondence, etc., between Lord Cecil and M. S. Jameson, 1934. Partly *printed* and *signed.* 51193, ff. 15-17, 20-32.
— Letter to Miss I. M. Butler from M. S. Jameson, 1934. *Signed.* 51193, f. 19.

Japan.
— Reply by Lord Stanhope to Parliamentary Question of Lord Cecil rel. to trade mission to Japan, 1934. 51169, f. 227.
— Memorandum rel. to the 73rd session of the Diet of Japan, 1938. *Copy.* 51179, ff. 161-166.

Jebb (*Miss* Eglantyne), *philanthropist.*
— Plan for publication of an essay by Miss E. Jebb, 1929. 51193, ff. 8-10.

Jebb (*Miss* G.), *Honorary Sec., Ray Strachey Memorial Committee.*
— Letters to Lord Cecil from Miss G. Jebb, 1941. *Signed.* 51186, ff. 247, 272; 51187, f. 69.

Jen C. Shieh, *Sec. General, The People's Foreign Relations Association of China.*
— Correspondence between Lord Cecil and Jen C. Shieh, 1940. *Signed.* 51185, f. 235; 51186, f. 81.

Jenkins (Charles Elliott Edward), *K.C.*
— Legal opinion, 1914. *Copy.* 51161, ff. 95-98v.

Jevons (Herbert Stanley), *Sec., Abyssinia Association.*
— Correspondence between Lord Cecil and H. S. Jevons, 1936-1941. *Signed.* 51173, ff. 16, 20; 51175, ff. 194, 199, 205, 217; 51176, ff. 4, 9, 45-50, 52; 51177, ff. 58, 68; 51186, ff. 276, 291.

Jeyes (Samuel Henry), *journalist.*
— Letters to Lord Cecil from S. H. Jeyes, 1908, 1909. 51158, f. 289; 51159, f. 116.

Jézéquel (*Pastor J.*), *of the International Peace Campaign, Brussels.*
— Correspondence between Lord Cecil and Pastor J. Jézéquel, 1936-1945. Partly *Fr.* 51174, f. 168; 51191, f. 305; 51192, f. 43.

Jochelman (*Dr. D.*), *Chairman, Polish Jewish Refugee Fund.*
— Correspondence, including telegrams, between Lord Cecil and Dr. D. Jochelman, 1941. *Signed.* 51187, ff. 260, 275, 280, 309, 316.

Johnson (Albin E.), *European Commissioner for the New York World's Fair.*
— Correspondence between Lord Cecil and A. E. Johnson, 1937. *Signed.* 51178, ff. 27, 32.

Johnson (Herschel Vespasian), *U.S. diplomatist.*
— Correspondence between Lord Cecil and H. V. Johnson, 1938. *Signed.* 51179, ff. 141, 144, 236, 241.

Johnson (Thomas Frank), *Assistant Commissioner for Refugees, League of Nations.*
— Letter, etc., to P. J. Noel-Baker from T. F. Johnson, 1923. *Signed.* 51095, f. 196.

Johnston (J. H. Clifford), *writer on monetary matters.*
— Correspondence between Lord Cecil and J. H. C. Johnston, 1941. *Signed.* 51187, ff. 90, 107.

Johnston (W. F.), *member of the League of Nations Union.*
— Correspondence between Lord Cecil and W. F. Johnston, 1934-1938. *Signed.* 51169, ff. 44-46; 51170, ff. 77v-80, 87v; 51181, ff. 15, 18.

Jolliffe (Hylton George Hylton), *3rd Earl Hylton.*
— Letter to Lord Cecil from Lord Hylton, 1909. 51159, f. 14.

Jones (A. Cadbury), *Sec., Societas Rosicruciana in Anglia.*
— Letter to Lord Cecil from A. C. Jones, 1908. 51158, f. 262v.

Jones (Amy Heminway), *Division Assistant, Carnegie Endowment for International Peace.*
— Letter to Lord Cecil from A. H. Jones, 1925. *Signed.* 51163, f. 115.

Jones (Arthur Stuart Duncan-).
— *v.* Duncan-Jones (Arthur Stuart).

Jones (*Sir* Clement Wakefield).
— Correspondence between Lord Cecil and C. W. Jones, 1943, 1944. *Signed.* 51190, ff. 216, 220, 222; 51191, f. 37.

Jones (*Sir* Edgar Rees), *K.B.E.; M.P.*
— Letter, etc., to I. Z. Malcolm from Sir E. R. Jones, 1918. 51094, ff. 77-83.

Jones (*Sir* Lawrence Evelyn), *5th Bart; author.*
— Correspondence between Lord Cecil and L. E. Jones, 1944. 51191, ff. 225, 238.

Jones (Rufus Matthew), *Professor of Philosophy, Haverford College, U.S.A.*
— Correspondence between Lord Cecil and R. M. Jones, 1937. Partly *signed.* 51176, f. 42; 51177, f. 64.

Jones (Vincent Duncan-).
— *v.* Duncan-Jones (Vincent).

Jones (W. Oswald), *of Willesden.*
— Correspondence between Lord Cecil and W. O. Jones, 1936. 51172, ff. 169, 172.

Jones (Walter D.), *National President, the League of Nations Society in Canada.*
— Letter to Lord Cecil, 1944. *Signed.* 51191, f. 80.

Jones (William A.), *Sec., League of Nations Union, Liverpool and Merseyside Council.*
— Letters, etc., to Lord Cecil from W. A. Jones, 1938. *Signed.* 51179, ff. 61-64, 127-131.
— Correspondence between W. A. Jones and Miss I. M. Butler, 1938. *Signed.* 51179, ff. 143, 168, 179, 202-205.

Jourdain (Francis), *Sec., Comité Mondial Contre la Guerre et le Fascisme.*
— Correspondence between Lord Cecil and F. Jourdain, 1937. Partly *signed. Fr.* 51176, ff. 111, 132; 51178, ff. 63, 99.

Jouvenel (Henri de), *French senator and diplomatist.*
— Correspondence between Lord Cecil and H. de Jouvenel, 1931. Partly *Fr.* 51100, ff. 105-107.

Jovanovic (Slobodan), *Prime Minister of Yugoslavia.*
— Letter from Lord Cecil to S. Jovanovic, 1942. *Copy.* 51188, f. 176.

Joynson-Hicks (William), *1st Viscount Brentford.*
— Correspondence, partly on his behalf, with Lord Cecil, 1908-1927. Partly *signed.* Partly *printed.* 51059, f. 259; 51096, ff. 18-19v, 23; 51097, ff. 157, 160; 51158, ff. 225, 231-234v, 240; 51165, ff. 1-9, 113, 116, 120, 122, 140, 153, 168.

Judd (Charles Wilfred), *C.B.E; of the League of Nations Union.*
— Correspondence between C. W. Judd and Miss I. M. Butler, 1934. 51169, ff. 145, 176.
— Letters to Lord Cecil, 1939-1945. *Signed.* 51184, f. 253; 51188, ff. 70-72, 105; 51189, f. 153; 51190, f. 176; 51192, ff. 125, 135; 51193, ff. 282-288.
— Letter to Dame K. D'O. Courtney from C. W. Judd, 1941. *Signed.* 51141, f. 160.
— Letter to C. W. Judd from Lord Lytton, 1944. *Copy.* 51139, f. 218.

K

Kaizer (Arnold Meer), *journalist; General Sec., Polish Jewish Refugee Fund.*
— Letter to Lord Cecil from A. M. Kaizer, 1941. *Signed.* 51187, f. 26.
— Memorandum rel. to conversation with A. M. Kaizer, 1941. 51187, f. 345.
— Letter, etc., to Miss E. V. Lazarus from A. M. Kaizer, 1941. *Signed.* 51187, ff. 346-350.

Kalina (*Dr.* Antonin S.), *Czech journalist.*
— Letters to Lord Cecil from Dr. A. S. Kalina, 1936. *Signed.* 51173, ff. 135, 142, 149.

Kano (H.), *of the Yokohama Specie Bank, London.*
— Correspondence, etc., between Lord Cecil and H. Kano, 1941. *Signed.* 51187, ff. 290-302, 307.

Keate (*Miss* Edith M.), *writing from Chelwood Gate.*
— Letters to Lord Cecil from Miss E. M. Keate, 1942. 51187, ff. 99, 131.

INDEX

Keeling (Guy W.), *of the British National Committee, International Peace Campaign.*
— Correspondence between Lord Cecil and G. W. Keeling, 1935, 1939. 51171, f. 209; 51182, ff. 166, 177, 187, 200.

Keen (Edward L.), *of the United Press Association of America.*
— Letter, etc., to Lord Cecil from E. L. Keen, 1919. *Signed.* 51162, f. 103.

Keen (Frank Noel), *barrister.*
— Correspondence, etc., between Lord Cecil and F. N. Keen, 1922-1942. 51163, ff. 122-124v; 51186, ff. 175, 184; 51189, ff. 179, 190, 203-214v, 218, 222, 231.

Keighley, W.R. co. York.
— Message from Lord Cecil for Peace Exhibition at Keighley, 1938. *Copy.* 51182, f. 7.

Keilhau (Wilhelm), *Norwegian historian and economist.*
— Correspondence, including telegrams, between Lord Cecil and W. Keilhau, 1939. *Signed.* 51184, ff. 133, 142, 159, 170, 173.

Keith (Arthur Berriedale), *Professor of Sanskrit at Edinburgh University.*
— Correspondence between Lord Cecil and A. B. Keith, 1936, 1941. *Signed.* 51173, ff. 180, 191, 200; 51188, ff. 14-16, 21.

Kellogg (Frank Billings), *U.S. statesman.*
— Correspondence between Lord Cecil and F. B. Kellogg, 1934. *Signed.* 51169, ff. 182, 191.

Kellogg (Paul), *Editor of The Survey.*
— Letter to T. W. Lamont from P. Kellogg, 1923. *Signed.* 51144, f. 15.

Kelly (*Sir* David Victor), *G.C.M.G.*
— Letter to Lord Cecil from D. V. Kelly, 1939. *Signed.* 51184, f. 151.

Kemball-Cook (*Sir* Basil Alfred), *K.C.M.G.*
— Memorandum by Lord Cecil rel. to conversation with B. A. Kemball-Cook, 1918. 51093, f. 179.

Kenderdine (*Sir* Charles Halstaff), *K.B.E.*
— Letter to Lord Cecil from C. H. Kenderdine, 1914. *Signed.* 51161, f. 107.

Kennedy (Aubrey Leo), *author and journalist.*
— Letter from Lord Cecil to A. L. Kennedy, 1948. *Draft.* 51192, f. 306.

Kennedy (Hugh Anketell Studdert), *of The International Interpreter.*
— Correspondence between Lord Cecil and H. A. S. Kennedy, 1923. *Signed.* 51163, ff. 182, 189.

Kennedy (William Paul McClure), *Professor of Law, Toronto University.*
— Correspondence between Lord Cecil and W. P. M. Kennedy, 1934. Partly *signed.* 51169, ff. 161-211 *passim.*

Kennet, *1st Baron.*
— *v.* Young (Edward Hilton).

Kentish (*Brig.-Gen.* Reginald John).
— Correspondence between Lord Cecil and Brig.-Gen. R. J. Kentish, 1943. *Mostly signed.* 51190, ff. 68-272v *passim.*

Kern (Paul), *writing from Leadenhall St., London.*
— Correspondence between Lord Cecil and P. Kern, 1941. *Signed.* 51187, ff. 412, 414.

Kerr (Philip Henry), *11th Marquess of Lothian.*
— Correspondence between Lord Cecil and Lord Lothian, 1915-1939. Partly *signed.* 51076, f. 28; 51100, f. 18; 51161, f. 203; 51168, ff. 57, 60; 51169, f. 185; 51175, f. 69; 51183, ff. 116, 117.
— Letter to P. H. Kerr from J. S. Barnes, 1921. *Copy.* 51095, f. 24.

Kerrich (G. J.), *member of the Cambridge University League of Nations Union.*
— Correspondence between Lord Cecil and G. J. Kerrich, 1936. 51174, ff. 61-63.

Keswick, *League of Nations Union Branch.*
— Correspondence with Lord Cecil, 1941. 51186, ff. 5, 22.

Keyes (*Adm. of the Fleet* Roger John Brownlow), *1st Baron Keyes.*
— Correspondence between Lord Cecil and R. J. B. Keyes, 1936. Partly *signed.* 51136, ff. 37-41; 51172, ff. 30, 33, 40, 54, 72, 73, 90, 104, 112.

Keymer (*Col.* S. L.), *of Alderley Edge.*
— Correspondence between Lord Cecil and Col. S. L. Keymer, 1938, 1939. 51180, ff. 62, 76, 85; 51183, ff. 154, 158.

Keynes (John Maynard), *Baron Keynes.*
— Memorandum by J. M. Keynes (?) rel. to conversation with Mr. — Hambro, 1918. *Copy.* 51093, f. 151.
— Correspondence between Lord Cecil and J. M. Keynes, 1938, 1939. *Signed.* 51179, ff. 93, 100; 51184, f. 162.

Keyser (John A.), *of Sevenoaks, afterw. of Shiplake; of the League of Nations Union.*
— Correspondence, etc., between Lord Cecil and J. A. Keyser, 1938, 1945. *Signed.* Partly *printed.* 51179, ff. 54, 55; 51182, ff. 64-72; 51192, ff. 105, 113.

Kilmuir, *Earl.*
— *v.* Fyfe (*Sir* David Patrick Maxwell).

Kimber (Charles Dixon), *General Sec., Federal Union.*
— Letters, partly on his behalf, to Lord Cecil, 1940, 1941. *Signed.* 51185, f. 106; 51186, ff. 183, 195, 224; 51187, ff. 51, 65, 154, 192.

Kindersley (Gladys Margaret), *wife of Robert, 1st Baron Kindersley.*
— Correspondence between Lord Cecil and Lady Kindersley, 1941. *Signed.* 51187, ff. 124, 137.

Kindersley (*Maj.* Guy Molesworth), *M.P.*
— Letter to Lord Cecil from Maj. G. M. Kindersley, 1922. *Copy.* 51163, f. 63.

King (*Sir* Henry Seymour), *Bart.*
— Letter to Lord Cecil from Sir H. S. King, 1909. 51159, f. 69.

King (William Lyon Mackenzie), *Prime Minister of Canada.*
— Correspondence between Lord Cecil and W. L. Mackenzie King, 1936-1944. *Signed.* 51172, f. 7; 51189, f. 182; 51191, ff. 95, 104, 107.

King-Hall (*Adm. Sir* George Fowler), *K.C.B.*
— Correspondence between Lord Cecil and Adm. Sir G. F. King-Hall, 1938. *Signed.* 51179, ff. 10, 26.

King-Hall (William Stephen Richard), *Baron King-Hall.*
— Correspondence between Lord Cecil and W. S. R. King-Hall, 1935. Partly *printed.* 51170, ff. 13-16.
— News-Letter Supplement No. 263 by W. S. R. King-Hall, 1941. *Printed.* 51188, f. 133.

Kirkpatrick (*Mrs* E. M.), *of Hove.*
— Letter to Lord Cecil from Mrs E. M. Kirkpatrick, 1940. 51185, f. 93.

INDEX

Kirkpatrick (*Sir* Ivone Augustine), *G.C.B.*
— Letter, etc., to Lord Cecil from I. A. Kirkpatrick, 1926. *Signed.* 51079, f. 13.

Kisch (*Sir* Cecil Hermann), *K.C.I.E.*
— Letter to W. H. M. Selby from C. H. Kisch, 1918. 51090, f. 58.
— Correspondence, etc., with Lord Cecil, partly on behalf of E. S. Montagu, 1918. Partly *signed.* 51093, ff. 196-198; 51094, f. 12.

Kiss (Helen) *née* **Hajdu**, *wife of Sigismund Kiss.*
— Correspondence between Lord Cecil and H. Kiss, 1936, 1937. Partly *signed.* 51172, ff. 57, 105, 125; 51173, ff. 67, 101, 144; 51174, ff. 144, 209; 51175, f. 54.

Kitto (John Vivian), *Librarian of the House of Commons.*
— Correspondence between Lord Cecil and J. V. Kitto, 1941. 51187, ff. 6, 53.

Kleffens ([Eelco Nicolaas?] van), *of the Dutch Foreign Office.*
— Memorandum by Lord Cecil rel. to conversation with E. N. van Kleffens, 1923. 51095, f. 162.

Knight (Hamilton Stephen Langley), *former Borough Engineer of Guildford.*
— Question by Lord Cecil rel. to case of H. S. L. Knight, 1942. *Copy.* 51189, f. 58.
— Letter to Lord Cecil from E. F. Prescott on behalf of H. S. L. Knight, 1942. *Signed.* 51189, f. 76.
— Memorandum by Lord Cecil rel. to interview with H. S. L. Knight, 1942. *Signed.* 51189, f. 143.
— Correspondence, etc., between Lord Cecil and H. S. L. Knight, 1942, 1943. 51189, ff. 68, 74, 82-95v, 105, 106, 108, 114, 119, 120, 122, 286.

Knox (Collie), *author and journalist.*
— Correspondence between Lord Cecil and C. Knox, 1942, 1943. *Signed.* 51193, ff. 277-281.

Knox (Edmund Arbuthnott), *Bishop of Manchester.*
— Telegrams to Lord Cecil from Bishop of Manchester, 1908. 51158, ff. 235-237.

Knox (*Sir* Geoffrey George), *K.C.M.G.; diplomatist.*
— Correspondence between Lord Cecil and Sir G. G. Knox, 1936. *Signed.* 51172, ff. 127, 146, 164.

Koestler (Arthur), *author.*
— Letter to Miss I. M. Butler from A. Koestler, 1938. *Signed.* 51181, f. 194.

Konitza (Mehmed), *Albanian statesman.*
— Telegram to Lord Cecil from M. Konitza, 1941. 51187, f. 389.

Koo Vi Kyuin Wellington, *Chinese diplomatist.*
— Correspondence between Lord Cecil and Dr Koo, 1942, 1945. Partly *signed.* 51188, f. 300; 51189, f. 156; 51192, f. 151.

Korean National Front.
— Letter to Lord Cecil from the General Council of the League of the Korean National Front, 1938. *Copy. Engl. transl.* 51179, f. 17.

Kruk (*Dr.* Joseph), *of Jerusalem.*
— Telegrams between Lord Cecil and Dr. J. Kruk, 1943. 51190, ff. 47, 160, 164.

Kunosi (*Dr.* Alexander), *formerly Sec., Czechoslovak Federation of League of Nations Union.*
— Correspondence between Lord Cecil and Dr. A. Kunosi, 1936, 1943. *Signed.* 51173, ff. 169, 176; 51190, f. 184; 51193, ff. 283, 287.

Künstler (*Dr.* Ernst), *of Danzig.*
— Correspondence between Lord Cecil and Dr. E. Künstler, 1934-1936. *Signed.* Partly *Fr.* 51145, ff. 78-128.

INDEX

Künstler (*Dr.* Ernst), *of Danzig.* continuation
— Correspondence between Dr. E. Künstler and Miss I. M. Butler, 1935, 1936. Mostly *signed.* 51145, ff. 81-118 *passim.*

Kurti (Lec), *Albanian diplomatist.*
— Correspondence between Lord Cecil and L. Kurti, 1937. *Signed.* 51178, ff. 5, 7.

L

La Follette (Philip F.), *Governor of Wisconsin.*
— Letter to Lord Cecil from F. D. Stuart on behalf of P. F. La Follette, 1939. *Signed.* 51182, f. 198.

Labarthe (—), *of 'Cercle des Nations', Paris.*
— Correspondence between Lord Cecil and — Labarthe, 1939. *Signed. Fr.* 51183, ff. 113, 122.

Labour Co-Partnership Association.
— Speech by Sir H. Bowden to the Labour Co-Partnership Association, 1927. *Draft.* 51165, ff. 102-112.
— *v. also* Hamilton (C. J.).
— *v. also* Mundy (Ernest W.).
— *v. also* Plaistowe (Cuthbert).

Lambart (Alfred), *of Richmond-on-Thames.*
— Letter to Lord Cecil from A. Lambart, 1941. 51187, f. 80.

Lambart (*Field-Marshal* Frederic Rudolph), *10th Earl of Cavan.*
— Correspondence between Lord Cecil and Lord Cavan, 1918-1939. 51162, ff. 85, 89; 51184, ff. 88, 109.

Lamble (Frank F. B.), *writing from Clapham.*
— Letter to Lord Cecil from F. F. B. Lamble, 1912. 51160, f. 74.

Lambton (Ann Katherine Swynford), *Professor of Persian, University of London.*
— Correspondence between Lord Cecil and his niece A. K. S. Lambton, 1936-1945. 51157, ff. 175-230.

Lambton (Claud), *son of George, 2nd Earl of Durham.*
— Letters to Lord Cecil from C. Lambton, 1909-1942. 51159, f. 67; 51187, ff. 24, 135; 51188, ff. 273, 277.

Lambton (Frederick William), *4th Earl of Durham.*
— Letter to Lord Cecil from his brother-in-law F. W. Lambton, 1907. 51158, f. 113.

Lambton (*Adm.* of the Fleet Sir Hedworth) *afterw.* **Meux**, *G.C.B.*
— Letter, etc., to Lord Cecil from Sir H. Lambton, 1909. 51159, ff. 200-210.
— Memorandum rel. to China Station by Adm. Sir H. Lambton, 1909. *Printed. Signed.* 51159, f. 208.

Lambton (John George), *3rd Earl of Durham.*
— Letter to Lord Cecil from his brother-in-law Lord Durham, 1906. 51158, f. 56.

Lamont (Florence Haskell), *wife of T. W. Lamont.*
— Correspondence between Lord Cecil and F. H. Lamont, 1923-1941. 51144, ff. 89-132v.

Lamont (Thomas William), *American banker.*
— Letter to T. W. Lamont from P. Kellogg, 1923. *Signed.* 51144, f. 15.
— Correspondence between Lord Cecil and T. W. Lamont, 1923-1944. Mostly *signed.* Partly printed. 51144, ff. 1-88v.

Lampson (Oliver Stillingfleet Locker-).
— *v.* Locker-Lampson (Oliver Stillingfleet).

Lancaster (Alan Norman), *Sec. to Lord Cecil.*
— Correspondence between Miss A. Lenfestey and A. N. Lancaster on behalf of Lord Cecil, 1940. *Signed.* 51186, ff. 155, 161, 166, 193, 220, 249.
— Letter to A. N. Lancaster from P. Allen on behalf of Miss A. Lenfestey, 1940. *Signed.* 51186, f. 220.

Lane (J. D.), *of Christchurch, co. Hants.*
— Correspondence between Lord Cecil and J. D. Lane, 1940. *Signed.* 51185, ff. 94, 102.

Lang (Cosmo Gordon), *Archbishop of York and (1928) of Canterbury; Baron Lang.*
— Correspondence, partly on his behalf, with Lord Cecil, 1909-1944. Mostly *signed.* 51154 A, ff. 1-125v.
— Memorandum rel. to his interview with the Archbishop of Canterbury and the Bishop of St. Asaph concerning the Welsh Church Act, 1915. *Copy.* 51161, ff. 237-242.

Lange (Christian Lous), *of the Nobel Committee of the Norwegian Parliament.*
— Correspondence between Lord Cecil and C. L. Lange, 1931-1938. *Signed.* 51167, ff. 103, 122, 125; 51178, ff. 139, 156; 51182, ff. 14, 25; 51193, ff. 64, 67, 69-72.
— Speech by C. L. Lange at conferment of Nobel Prize on Lord Cecil, 1937. *Printed* with MS additions. 51178, ff. 88-97.

Langley (*Sir* Walter Louis Frederick Goltz), *K.C.M.G.*
— Letter to W. H. M. Selby from Sir W. L. F. G. Langley, 1918. 51091, f. 180v.

Lansdowne, *5th Marquess of.*
— *v.* Petty-FitzMaurice (Henry Charles Keith).

Lanux (Pierre de), *author.*
— Correspondence between Lord Cecil and P. de Lanux, 1940, 1941. Partly *printed.* Partly *Fr.* 51185, ff. 11, 22, 245; 51186, f. 227; 51187, f. 287.

Lapointe (Ernest), *Canadian Minister of Justice.*
— Correspondence between Lord Cecil and E. Lapointe, 1926. *Signed.* 51098, ff. 112, 121, 123.

Lascelles (*Sir* Francis William), *K.C.B.; Clerk of the Parliaments.*
— Letter, etc., to Lord Cecil from F. W. Lascelles, 1941. 51187, f. 55.

Lascelles (Henry George Charles), *Viscount Lascelles; 6th Earl of Harewood, 1929.*
— Letter to Lord Cecil from H. G. C. Lascelles, 1913. 51161, f. 49.

Laski (Neville Jones), *judge.*
— Correspondence between Lord Cecil and A. G. Brotman, partly on behalf of N. J. Laski, 1935-1944. *Signed.* 51171, ff. 113-117, 120, 133; 51189, f. 144; 51191, f. 178.

Laszlo de Lombos (Lucy Madeleine), *wife of P. A. Laszlo de Lombos.*
— Correspondence between Lord Cecil and L. M. Laszlo de Lombos, 1931. 51167, ff. 113, 116, 123, 147.

Laszlo de Lombos (Philip Alexius), *portrait-painter.*
— Letter to P. A. Laszlo de Lombos from E. C. Henty on behalf of Lord Cecil, 1931. 51167, f. 133.
— Letter to Lord Cecil from P. A. Laszlo de Lombos, 1931. *Signed.* 51167, f. 149.

Latimer (*Maj.* W. H.), *of the War Office.*
— Correspondence between Lord Cecil and Maj. W. H. Latimer, 1939. *Signed.* 51184, ff. 78, 87.

INDEX

Lauber (*Frau* —), *of 'Frauenliga für Frieden und Freiheit' in Arbon, Switzerland.*
— Letter to Lord Cecil from Frau Lauber, 1938. *Signed.* 51182, f. 48.

Laughlin (Irwin B.), *Counsellor, U.S. Embassy in London.*
— Letter to Lord Cecil from I. B. Laughlin, 1918. *Signed.* 51094, f. 17.
— Memorandum by Lord Cecil rel. to conversation with I. B. Laughlin, 1918. 51094, f. 87.

Laurvig (*Count* Preben Ferdinand Ahlefeldt-).
— *v.* Ahlefeldt-Laurvig (*Count* Preben Ferdinand).

Laves (Walter H. C.), *Director, League of Nations Association, Chicago.*
— Letter to Lord Cecil from W. H. C. Laves, 1937. *Signed.* 51175, f. 131.

Law, *OF ENGLAND.*
— Bill to promote the adoption of Co-Partnership, 1926. *Copy.* 51164, f. 53.
— Bill to declare the independence of the judges, 1934. *Drafts.* 51169, ff. 3-6v, 22-24.
— Amendments to the Road Traffic Act (1930), 1934. *Draft.* 51169, f. 157.

Law (*Sir* Algernon), *K.C.M.G.*
— Correspondence between Lord Cecil and Sir A. Law, 1938. 51180, ff. 111, 112.

Law (Andrew Bonar), *Prime Minister.*
— Letter to Sir F. Trippel from A. Bonar Law, 1912. *Copy.* 51160, f. 182.
— Correspondence between Lord Cecil and A. Bonar Law, 1913-1918. Partly *signed.* 51093, ff. 16, 40, 133, 147, 150, 156; 51160, f. 75; 51161, ff. 21, 51, 94, 170, 194, 220, 221.
— Memorandum by Lord Cecil rel. to interview with A. Bonar Law, 1922. 51095, f. 129.

Law (Richard Kidston), *M.P.; son of A. Bonar Law.*
— Correspondence between Lord Cecil and R. K. Law, 1942-1945. *Signed.* 51188, f. 336; 51190, ff. 287, 351; 51192, ff. 46, 56.

Lawford (V. G.), *of the Foreign Office.*
— Letter to Miss E. V. Lazarus from V. G. Lawford, 1941. *Signed.* 51188, f. 25.
— Letter to Lord Cecil, 1943. *Signed.* 51190, f. 174.

Lawrence (Emmeline Pethick-).
— *v.* Pethick-Lawrence (Emmeline).

Lawrence (W. B.), *writing from Barnes.*
— Correspondence between Lord Cecil and W. B. Lawrence, 1936. Partly *signed.* 51172, ff. 77, 82, 88v, 93.

Layton (Eleanor Dorothea), *wife of Walter, 1st Baron Layton.*
— Correspondence between Lord Cecil and Lady Layton, 1939. *Signed.* 51182, ff. 141-144, 151.

Lazarus (*Miss* E. Vera), *Sec. to Lord Cecil.*
— Letter, etc., to Miss E. V. Lazarus from A. M. Kaizer, 1941. *Signed.* 51187, ff. 346-350.
— Letter to Miss E. V. Lazarus from F. Graham-Harrison, 1941. *Signed.* 51187, f. 404.
— Letter to Miss E. V. Lazarus from V. G. Lawford, 1941. *Signed.* 51188, f. 25.
— Letter to Miss E. V. Lazarus from V. D. Barker, 1941. *Signed.* 51188, f. 34.
— Correspondence, including telegram, between Lord Cecil and Miss E. V. Lazarus, 1941-1943. Partly *signed.* 51187, f. 216, 274, 281, 345, 405; 51189, f. 73; 51190, ff. 127, 149-152.

Lazarus (*Miss* E. Vera), *Sec. to Lord Cecil.* continuation
— Correspondence between P. H. Edwards and Miss E. V. Lazarus, 1943. *Signed.* 51189, f. 263; 51190, ff. 319, 320.
— Letter to Miss E. V. Lazarus from Miss F. C. Gray, 1943. *Signed.* 51190, f. 332.
— Letter to Miss E. V. Lazarus from M. R. Gale, 1944. *Signed.* 51191, f. 22.
— Letter to Miss E. V. Lazarus from S. de Madariaga, 1945. *Signed.* 51192, f. 8.
— Memorandum by Miss E. V. Lazarus rel. to conversation with Gen. M. de Baer, 1945. *Signed.* 51192, f. 18.
— Letter to Miss E. V. Lazarus from R. J. P. Hewison on behalf of H. S. Morrison, 1945. *Signed.* 51192, f. 68.
— Letter to Miss E. V. Lazarus from L. C. Prescott, 1945. *Signed.* 51192, ff. 72-74.
— Letter to C. D. W. O'Neill from Miss E. V. Lazarus, 1948. *Copy.* 51192, f. 288.

Lazarus (Hans Leo), *German lawyer, formerly of Danzig.*
— Correspondence between Lord Cecil and H. L. Lazarus, 1938. *Signed.* 51180, ff. 23-28, 31.

Le Prevost (H. W.), *Editor of Headway.*
— Letter to H. W. Le Prevost from Miss I. M. Butler, 1938. *Signed.* 51181, f. 49.
— Correspondence between Lord Cecil and H. W. Le Prevost, 1939. Partly *signed.* 51182, ff. 165, 169; 51183, ff. 132-138; 51184, ff. 185, 187.

Le Quesne (Charles Thomas), *Master of the Library, Inner Temple.*
— Letter, etc., to Lord Cecil from C. T. Le Quesne, 1942. Partly *printed.* 51188, ff. 349, 351v.

League of Nations.
— Auditors' Report on High Commission for Refugees, 1936. 51173, ff. 126-129.
— Letter to League of Nations from Chu Chia-hua, 1943. *Signed.* 51190, f. 333.
— *v. also* Abraham (*Capt.* G.).
— *v. also* Avenol (Joseph Louis Anne).
— *v. also* Buxton (*Maj.* Anthony).
— *v. also* Colban (Erik).
— *v. also* Comert (Pierre).
— *v. also* Drummond (James Eric).
— *v. also* England.
— *v. also* Felkin (Arthur Elliott).
— *v. also* Hall (H. Duncan).
— *v. also* Hill (Martin).
— *v. also* Johnson (Thomas Frank).
— *v. also* Lester (Sean).
— *v. also* Loveday (Alexander).
— *v. also* Mackenzie (Melville Douglas).
— *v. also* Palmer (John Leslie).
— *v. also* Rault (Victor).
— *v. also* Renthe-Fink (— von).
— *v. also* Smith (*Miss* Janet).
— *v. also* Sweetser (Arthur).
— *v. also* Villeri (Luigi).
— *v. also* Walters (Francis Paul).
— *v. also* Wertheimer (Egon F. Ranshofen).
— *v. also* Woods (*Col.* Arthur).

League of Nations Non-Partisan Association.
— *v.* Marburg (Theodore).

League of Nations Society.
— Publication no. 42, 'League of Nations Scheme of Organisation' by the League of Nations Society, 1918. *Printed.* 51162, ff. 38-53v.

League of Nations Union.
— Letter to Miss — Arnold on behalf of the League of Nations Union, 1942. *Copy.* 51188, f. 256.
— *v. also* names of individual members.

INDEX

Leak (J. A. Trevelyan), *Sec., League of Nations Union, Sussex Federal Council.*
— Correspondence between Lord Cecil and J. A. T. Leak, 1935, 1944. *Signed.* 51171, ff. 5, 10, 15, 18, 177, 181; 51191, ff. 181, 267.

Leay (Frederick Peter), *Consul-General in Boston, U.S.A.*
— Telegrams between F. P. Leay and G. H. Locock on behalf of F. Dixon, 1915-1917. Partly *draft.* Partly *signed.* 51092, ff. 23-288 *passim.*

Leconfield, *3rd Baron.*
— *v.* Wyndham (Charles Henry).

Lederer (Emil), *German sociologist.*
— Correspondence between Lord Cecil and E. Lederer, 1931. 51167, ff. 107, 108.

Leeds, *11th Duke of.*
— *v.* Osborne (John Francis Godolphin).

Leeds, *Duchess of.*
— *v.* Osborne (Irma).

Leeper (*Sir* Reginald Wildig Allen), *G.B.E.*
— Memorandum by J. Eppstein rel. to interview with Sir R. W. A. Leeper, 1935. *Copy.* 51171, ff. 94-98.

Lefevre (George John Shaw-).
— *v.* Shaw-Lefevre (George John).

Leftwich (Joseph), *author.*
— Letter to Miss I. M. Butler from J. Leftwich, 1936. 51174, f. 71.

Legge (William Heneage), *6th Earl of Dartmouth.*
— Letter to Lord Cecil from Lord Dartmouth, 1912. 51160, f. 167.

Leggett (Malcolm), *of Bournemouth.*
— Correspondence between Lord Cecil and M. Leggett, 1939, 1945. 51184, ff. 29, 59, 68, 70; 51192, ff. 186, 222, 226.

Legh (Thomas Wodehouse), *2nd Baron Newton.*
— Correspondence between Lord Cecil and Lord Newton, 1922-1940. Partly *signed.* 51163, f. 61; 51177, ff. 173, 183; 51185, f. 211.

Lehmann-Russbüldt (Otto), *German author.*
— Correspondence between Lord Cecil and O. Lehmann-Russbüldt, [1933?]-1939. *Signed.* Partly *Fr.* 51145, ff. 1-77.

Leigh (*Col.* J. H.), *of Chelwood Gate.*
— Letter to Lord Cecil from Col. J. H. Leigh, 1940. 51185, f. 101.

Leishman (James R.), *of the League of Nations Union, Edinburgh Branch.*
— Correspondence between Lord Cecil and J. R. Leishman, 1939, 1941. 51184, ff. 136, 139; 51187, ff. 418, 422.

Lenfestey (*Miss* A.), *of the Home Office.*
— Correspondence between Miss A. Lenfestey and A. N. Lancaster on behalf of Lord Cecil, 1940. *Signed.* 51186, ff. 155, 161, 166, 193, 220, 249.
— Letter to A. N. Lancaster from P. Allen on behalf of Miss A. Lenfestey, 1940. *Signed.* 51186, f. 220.

Leonard (Robert Maynard), *author; Sec., Secret Commissions and Bribery Prevention League.*
— Letter to Lord Cecil from R. M. Leonard, 1914. *Signed.* 51161, f. 109.

Leslie (*Sir* Norman Roderick Alexander David), *8th Bart.*
— Correspondence, partly on his behalf, with Lord Cecil, 1926, 1927. 51098, ff. 48, 177, 178.

Lester (*Miss* Muriel), *of the International Fellowship of Reconciliation.*
— Correspondence between Lord Cecil and Miss M. Lester, 1942. 51188, ff. 269, 278, 295-297.

Lester (Sean), *Sec.-General, League of Nations.*
— Correspondence, including telegram, between Lord Cecil and S. Lester, 1941, 1944. *Signed.* 51187, f. 413; 51188, ff. 23, 41; 51191, f. 217.

Letchworth Co-operative Society.
— Minutes of meeting of the Letchworth Co-operative Society, 1918. *Copy.* 51162, f. 59.

Lever (*Sir* Tresham Joseph Philip), *2nd Bart.; of Thornton Butterworth Ltd.*
— Letters from Lord Cecil to Sir T. J. P. Lever, 1929-1939. 51193, ff. 2, 114-117, 134.

Lever (*Sir* Tresham Joseph Philip).
— *v. also* Butterworth.

Lever (William Hulme), *2nd Viscount Leverhulme.*
— Correspondence between Lord Cecil and Lord Leverhulme, 1944. *Signed.* 51191, ff. 319, 321.

Leverhulme, *2nd Viscount.*
— *v.* Lever (William Hulme).

Levinson (Salmon Oliver), *U.S. lawyer.*
— Correspondence between Lord Cecil and S. O. Levinson, 1927-1939. *Signed.* 51165, ff. 189, 202; 51166, f. 163; 51167, f. 1; 51182, ff. 128, 146.

Leward (*Dr.* Theodor), *German economist and politician.*
— Correspondence between Lord Cecil (?) and Dr. T. Leward, 1924. *Signed. Partly Fr.* 51097, ff. 12-14, 20.

Lewis (Guilford Edward), *solicitor.*
— Letter to Lord Cecil from G. E. Lewis, 1912. 51160, f. 62.

Lewis (Henry Allan), *member of the Sutton Division Labour Party, Plymouth.*
— Correspondence between H. A. Lewis and Alderman W. L. Munday, 1927. 51165, ff. 124-125.

Lewis (J. B.), *of Whalley.*
— Correspondence between Lord Cecil and J. B. Lewis, 1940. 51185, ff. 100, 131, 135, 147.

Lewy (Emile), *writer on the coal industry.*
— Letter to Lord Cecil from E. Lewy, 1912. 51160, f. 113.

Leygues (Jean Claude Georges), *French politician.*
— Statement to Press rel. to Treaty of Versailles, 1931. *Copy.* 51167, f. 91.

Liberman (V.), *participant in the London International Assembly.*
— Letter to Lord Cecil, 1943. *Signed. Partly Fr.* 51190, ff. 50-56.

Liddle (Henry Weddell), *Headmaster, Bedford Modern School.*
— Letter to Lord Cecil from H. W. Liddle, 1940. *Signed.* 51185, f. 46.

Lieberman (David H.), *of Philadelphia, Pennsylvania.*
— Correspondence between Lord Cecil and D. H. Lieberman, 1945. *Signed.* 51192, ff. 152, 173.

Liem (H. D.), *of the Central News Agency of China.*
— Letters to Lord Cecil, 1942, 1943. *Signed.* 51188, f. 384; 51189, f. 23; 51190, ff. 145, 156.

Lindsay (Alexander Dunlop), *1st Baron Lindsay of Birker.*
— Correspondence between Lord Cecil and A. D. Lindsay, 1937-1944. *Signed.* 51178, f. 21; 51181, f. 151; 51187, ff. 195, 202, 206, 221; 51191, ff. 20, 25.

INDEX

Lindsay (David Alexander Edward), *27th Earl of Crawford and Balcarres.*
— Letters to Lord Cecil from D. A. E. Lindsay, 1912. *Signed.* 51160, ff. 79, 159.
— Letter to Lord Crawford from D. Cook, 1913. *Signed.* 51160, f. 267.

Lindsay (*Sir* Ronald Charles), *G.C.B.*
— Correspondence between Lord Cecil and Sir R. C. Lindsay, 1929. *Signed.* 51099, ff. 194-197.

Lister (Philip Cunliffe-), *Earl of Swinton.*
— *v.* Cunliffe-Lister (Philip).

Listowel, *5th Earl of.*
— *v.* Hare (William Francis).

Little (D'Arcy), *Chief Assistant, H.M. Land Registry.*
— Correspondence between Lord Cecil and D'A. Little, 1925. *Signed.* 51164, f. 104.

Livesey (*Sir* George Thomas), *of the South Metropolitan Gas Co.*
— Letter to Lord Cecil from Sir G. T. Livesey, 1906. 51158, f. 54.

Livingstone (*Dame* Adelaide Lord), *D.B.E.*
— Correspondence between Lord Cecil and Dame A. L. Livingstone, 1934-1944. Partly *signed.* 51142, ff. 1-59.

Livingstone (*Miss* L. M.), *Sec., Church of England Committee for 'Non-Aryan' Christians.*
— Correspondence between Miss L. M. Livingstone and Miss I. M. Butler, 1941. *Signed.* 51187, ff. 115, 116, 126, 210.

Lloyd (Edward Honoratus), *K.C.*
— Legal opinion, 1914. *Copy.* 51159, ff. 75-78v.

Lloyd (George Ambrose), *1st Baron Lloyd.*
— Memoranda by G. A. Lloyd rel. to Turkey, 1918. Partly *signed.* 51071, ff. 52-55; 51094, f. 35.

— Correspondence, partly on his behalf, with Lord Cecil, 1937-1940. Partly *signed.* 51177, ff. 102, 112, 121; 51181, ff. 79, 84; 51182, ff. 140, 154; 51185, f. 62.

Lloyd (John Henry), *Deputy Pro-Chancellor, University of Birmingham.*
— Correspondence between Lord Cecil and J. H. Lloyd, 1939. 51182, ff. 125, 126, 136.

Lloyd George (David), *1st Earl Lloyd George; Prime Minister.*
— Correspondence, partly on his behalf, with Lord Cecil, 1915-1943. *Signed.* 51076, ff. 1-77.
— Minutes of meeting between deputation of National Farmers' Union and D. Lloyd George, 1921. *Copy.* 51162, ff. 142-151.

Lloyd George (Frances Louise) *née* **Stevenson**, *2nd wife of David, 1st Earl Lloyd George.*
— Letter to Lord Cecil from F. L. Lloyd George, on behalf of her husband, 1943. *Signed.* 51076, f. 77.

Lloyd-George (Gwilym), *1st Viscount Tenby.*
— Correspondence, partly on his behalf, with Lord Cecil, 1942. Partly *signed.* 51188, ff. 354, 375; 51189, ff. 1, 22, 29, 41.

Lloyd George (Megan), *M.P.; daughter of David, 1st Earl Lloyd George.*
— Correspondence between Lord Cecil and M. Lloyd George on behalf of her father, 1936. *Signed.* 51076, ff. 66, 67.

Locker-Lampson (Oliver Stillingfleet), *M.P.*
— Letter to Lord Cecil from O. S. Locker-Lampson, 1939. *Signed.* 51183, f. 186.

Locock (*Sir* Guy Harold), *of the Foreign Office; afterw. Director, Federation of British Industries.*
— Telegrams between F. P. Leay and G. H. Locock on behalf of F. Dixon, 1915-1917. Partly *draft*. Partly *signed*. 51092, ff. 23-288 *passim*.
— Letter to G. H. Locock from R. J. Paterson, 1916. *Signed*. 51092, f. 41.
— Letter to G. H. Locock from A. H. Bathurst, 1916. *Signed*. 51092, f. 65.
— Letter to G. H. Locock from A. S. L. Farquharson, 1916. *Signed*. 51093, f. 11.
— Correspondence between Lord Cecil and Sir G. H. Locock, 1939. *Signed*. 51184, ff. 66, 71, 107, 113.

Lodge (*Sir* Oliver Joseph), *F.R.S.*
— Correspondence between Lord Cecil and Sir O. J. Lodge, 1931. 51167, ff. 162, 163.

Lodi (Ferdinand), *of the Argentine League of Nations Association.*
— Correspondence between Lord Cecil and F. Lodi, 1939. *Signed*. 51183, ff. 160-165, 175.

Loerken (*Miss* Edith), *Sec., Free German Youth in Great Britain.*
— Correspondence between Lord Cecil and Miss E. Loerken, 1943. *Signed*. 51190, ff. 42, 48.

Lombos (Lucy Madeleine Laszlo de).
— *v*. Laszlo de Lombos (Lucy Madeleine).

Lombos (Philip Alexius Laszlo de).
— *v*. Laszlo de Lombos (Philip Alexius).

London, *Bishop of.*
— *v*. Winnington-Ingram (Arthur Foley).

London Chinese Association.
— *v*. Wang Ching-ch'un.

London International Assembly.
— Minutes, agenda, reports, etc., of the London International Assembly, 1941-1943. Mainly *printed*. Partly *Fr*. 51151.

London. London Museum.
— Correspondence rel. to the London Museum, 1928. 51166, ff. 2, 31, 32.

Londonderry, *7th Marquess of.*
— *v*. Vane-Tempest-Stewart (Charles Stewart Henry).

Long (W. E.), *Chairman, League of Nations Union, Liverpool and Merseyside District Council.*
— Letter from Lord Cecil to W. E. Long, 1938. *Copy*. 51179, f. 68.

Long (Walter Hume), *1st Viscount Long.*
— Correspondence between Lord Cecil and W. H. Long, 1908-1918. Partly *signed*. 51072, ff. 50-108.

Longare (*Count* Bonin-).
— *v*. Bonin-Longare (*Count* —).

Longford, *7th Earl of.*
— *v*. Pakenham (Francis Aungier).

Longmore (*Sir* Charles Elton), *K.C.B.*
— Letter to Lord Cecil from C. E. Longmore, 1909. 51159, f. 249.

Lopes (Henry Ludlow), *2nd Baron Ludlow.*
— Correspondence between Lord Cecil and Lord Ludlow, 1905-1909. Partly *copy*. Partly *draft*. 51158, ff. 37, 173; 51159, ff. 145-154.

Lorimer (*Sir* William).
— Letter to Lord Cecil from Sir W. Lorimer, 1911. 51160, f. 41v.

Lothian, *11th Marquess of.*
— *v*. Kerr (Philip Henry).

Loucheur (Louis), *French deputy and statesman.*
— Correspondence between Lord Cecil and L. Loucheur, 1923. *Signed*. *Fr*. 51163, ff. 141, 149.

Loveday (Alexander), *League of Nations official.*
— Letter to Miss J. Smith from A. Loveday, 1943. *Copy.* 51190, f. 139.
— Letters, etc., partly on his behalf, to Lord Cecil, 1943, 1944. *Signed.* 51190, f. 380; 51191, ff. 68-79.

Lowe (*Vice-Adm.* Sidney Robert Drury-).
— *v.* Drury-Lowe (*Vice-Adm.* Sidney Robert).

Löwenstein-Wertheim-Freudenberg (*Princess* Elisabeth Zu) *afterw.* **Merton.**
— *v.* Merton (Elisabeth).

Lowther (James William), *1st Viscount Ullswater.*
— Correspondence, including telegrams, between Lord Cecil and J. W. Lowther, 1911-1914. 51160, ff. 38, 126, 162; 51161, ff. 157-163v, 174, 183-186v.

Loxley (P. N.), *of the Foreign Office.*
— Letter to Miss I. M. Butler from P. N. Loxley, 1942. *Signed.* 51189, f. 166.

Lucan, *5th Earl of.*
— *v.* Bingham (George Charles).

Lucas (Arthur B.), *chartered accountant.*
— Letter to Lord Cecil from A. B. Lucas, 1912. 51160, f. 211v.

Lucas (George William), *1st Baron Lucas of Chilworth.*
— Correspondence between Lord Cecil and Lord Lucas, 1950, 1951. 51192, ff. 335-337, 339.

Lucas (John Landfear), *of the Worshipful Company of Spectacle Makers.*
— Letter to Lord Cecil from J. L. Lucas, 1909. 51159, f. 16.

Lucas (Robert H.), *Sec., Printers' Pension, Almshouse and Orphan Asylum Corporation.*
— Correspondence between R. H. Lucas and Miss I. M. Butler, 1936. *Signed.* 51172, ff. 71, 80, 96.

Ludlow, *2nd Baron.*
— *v.* Lopes (Henry Ludlow).

Lugard (Frederick Dealtry), *Baron Lugard.*
— Correspondence, partly on his behalf, with Lord Cecil, 1925-1932. Partly *printed.* Partly *Fr.* 51097, ff. 125-215 *passim*; 51098, ff. 19, 129, 145; 51100, ff. 149-158.

Lunn (*Sir* Henry Simpson).
— Correspondence between Lord Cecil and Sir H. S. Lunn, 1937. *Signed.* 51176, f. 141; 51177, ff. 1-202 *passim.*

Lussi (Willi), *President of the Swiss Branch, International Peace Campaign.*
— Correspondence between Lord Cecil and W. Lussi, 1941. *Signed.* 51187, ff. 222, 230, 330.

Lutyens (Robert), *architect.*
— Letter to A. N. Chamberlain from R. Lutyens, 1939. *Printed.* 51182, f. 37.
— Letter, etc., to Lord Cecil from R. Lutyens, 1939. *Signed.* 51183, ff. 91-95, 102.

Lygon (William), *7th Earl Beauchamp.*
— Correspondence between Lord Cecil and Lord Beauchamp, 1928. 51166, ff. 81-84.

Lyon (Percy Hugh Beverley), *Headmaster of Rugby School.*
— Letter from Lord Cecil to P. H. B. Lyon, 1942. *Copy.* 51188, f. 244.

Lyte (*Sir* Henry Churchill Maxwell).
— *v.* Maxwell-Lyte (*Sir* Henry Churchill).

Lyte (W. Maxwell-).
— *v.* Maxwell-Lyte (W.).

Lyttelton (Alfred), *M.P.; statesman.*
— Letter to Lord Cecil from A. Lyttelton, 1912. 51160, f. 76.
Lyttelton (*Dame* Edith), *G.B.E.; widow of A. Lyttelton.*
— Correspondence between Lord Cecil and Dame E. Lyttelton, 1928. 51166, ff. 3-6.
Lyttelton (Edward), *Canon of Norwich.*
— Correspondence between Lord Cecil and E. Lyttelton, 1934-1938. 51169, ff. 115, 123; 51173, ff. 145, 146; 51174, ff. 96, 117; 51181, ff. 123, 144.
Lytton, *Countess of.*
— *v.* Bulwer-Lytton (Pamela).
Lytton (*Lady* Constance Georgina Bulwer-).
— *v.* Bulwer-Lytton (*Lady* Constance Georgina).
Lytton (Victor Alexander George Robert Bulwer-), *2nd Earl of Lytton.*
— *v.* Bulwer-Lytton (Victor Alexander George Robert).

M

Macadam (*Miss* Elizabeth), *of the League of Nations Union, Westminster Branch.*
— Correspondence between Lord Cecil and Miss E. Macadam, 1941, 1943. *Signed.* 51188, ff. 49, 51, 75; 51190, ff. 113, 122.
Macadam (*Sir* Ivison Stevenson), *K.C.V.O.*
— Correspondence between Lord Cecil and I. S. Macadam, 1933-1945. *Signed.* 51168, ff. 16, 22, 23; 51169, ff. 141, 147; 51170, ff. 135, 136, 143; 51171, ff. 175, 176, 185, 186, 192, 200; 51182, f. 46; 51191, ff. 239, 254, 257, 259; 51192, ff. 37-41, 97, 164.

MacAlister (*Sir* Ian), *Sec., Royal Institute of British Architects.*
— Letter to Lord Cecil from Sir I. MacAlister, 1937. *Signed.* 51175, f. 57.
M'Call (*Brig.-Gen.* John Buchanan Pollok).
— *v.* Pollok-M'Call (*Brig.-Gen.* John Buchanan).
McCallum (Ronald Buchanan), *historian and Master of Pembroke College, Oxford.*
— Correspondence between Lord Cecil and R. B. McCallum, 1944, 1945. 51191, f. 323; 51192, ff. 4, 71.
McCarthy (Michael John Fitzgerald), *barrister.*
— Letter to Lord Cecil from M. J. F. McCarthy, 1914. *Signed.* 51161, f. 83.
McCartny (J. F.), *of Banstead.*
— Correspondence between Lord Cecil and J. F. McCartny, 1942. *Signed.* 51189, ff. 138, 149, 159, 164.
McConnell (Francis), *Methodist bishop, New York.*
— Telegram to Lord Cecil from Bishop McConnell, 1939. 51182, f. 155.
McCordock (Robert Stanley), *of Lincoln Memorial University, Tennessee.*
— Letter to Lord Cecil from R. S. McCordock, 1936. *Signed.* 51173, f. 69.
McCoy (Frank Ross), *President, Foreign Policy Association, New York.*
— Letters and telegram to Lord Cecil, 1943. *Signed.* 51190, ff. 188, 208, 244.

INDEX

McDonald (James Grover), *High Commissioner for Refugees.*
— Correspondence, including telegram, between Lord Cecil and J. G. McDonald, 1921-1941. Partly *signed.* Partly *Fr.* 51101, f. 169; 51162, ff. 129, 158; 51164, ff. 27-30, 33-36, 136-139; 51170, ff. 7, 15; 51171, ff. 39-42, 56, 61-68, 101, 118; 51180, ff. 65, 104; 51187, f. 232.
— Letter to J. G. McDonald from O. Sargent, 1934. *Copy.* 51101, f. 169.
— Memoranda, 1934, 1935. *Copies.* 51101, ff. 189-196; 51170, ff. 10, 12.

MacDonald (James Ramsay), *Prime Minister.*
— Correspondence, partly on his behalf, with Lord Cecil, 1923-1934. Partly *signed.* 51081, ff. 1-142.
— Letter to J. Ramsay MacDonald from Lord Parmoor, 1924. *Signed.* 51081, f. 27.
— Letter to G. G. Dawson from J. Ramsay MacDonald, S. Baldwin and Lord Oxford and Asquith, 1924. *Copy.* 51097, f. 83.
— Letter to J. Ramsay MacDonald from G. G. A. Murray, 1929. *Draft. Signed.* 51081, f. 72.
— Letter to Lord Cecil from R. G. Vansittart on behalf of J. Ramsay MacDonald, 1929. *Signed.* 51081, f. 75.
— Letter to J. R. Clynes from R. G. Vansittart on behalf of J. Ramsay MacDonald, 1929. *Signed.* 51099, f. 199.
— Letter to Sir J. Stavridi from J. Ramsay MacDonald, 1932. *Signed.* 51081, f. 134.

MacDonald (Malcolm John), *P.C.; son of J. Ramsay MacDonald.*
— Correspondence between Lord Cecil and M. J. MacDonald, 1930-1940. *Signed.* 51081, ff. 90-94, 115; 51185, ff. 212, 216.

Macdonogh (*Lt.-Gen. Sir* George Mark Watson), *G.B.E.*
— Correspondence, partly on his behalf, with Lord Cecil, 1918, 1941. *Signed.* 51093, f. 201; 51094, ff. 1-3, 7, 60; 51188, ff. 77, 88.

McFadyean (*Sir* Andrew).
— Correspondence between Lord Cecil and Sir A. McFadyean, 1940. *Signed.* 51186, ff. 45, 54, 60, 67.

McFarlane (Kenneth Bruce), *historian.*
— Correspondence between Lord Cecil and K. B. McFarlane, 1940. 51184, ff. 333, 343.

Macfarlane (Peter), *of Hampstead.*
— Correspondence between Lord Cecil and P. Macfarlane, 1938. 51180, ff. 29, 39.

Macglashon (C.), *writing from Edinburgh.*
— Letter to Lord Cecil from C. Macglashon, 1914. 51161, f. 143.

MacGregor (Hugh), *Director of The Central Press Ltd.*
— Correspondence between Lord Cecil and H. MacGregor, 1938. *Signed.* 51181, ff. 35, 48, 56, 64, 80.

Macgregor (K. S.).
— Letter to Miss I. M. Butler from K. S. Macgregor, 1934. *Signed.* 51193, f. 14.

MacGregor (R.), *member of the Royal Empire Society.*
— Correspondence between Lord Cecil and R. MacGregor, 1939. 51183, ff. 96, 103, 111, 115.

Macintosh (Hugh), *Chairman, League of Nations Union, Croydon Branch.*
— Letter, etc., to Lord Cecil from H. Macintosh, 1936. *Signed.* 51173, ff. 204-207.

McIntyre (M. H.), *Sec. to President Roosevelt.*
— Letter to Lord Cecil from M. H. McIntyre, 1937. *Signed.* 51177, f. 167.

Mack (T. South), *writing from Haddiscoe Manor, Norwich.*
— Letter to Lord Cecil, 1939. *Signed.* 51184, f. 24.

Mackenzie (Dewitt), *of The Associated Press, New York.*
— Correspondence, etc., between Lord Cecil and D. Mackenzie, 1943. *Signed.* 51190, ff. 298-300.

Mackenzie (*Col.* Eric Dighton), *Comptroller to the Household of the Governor-General of Canada.*
— Letters to Lady Cecil from Col. E. D. Mackenzie, 1937. Partly *copy.* 51177, ff. 43, 118.

Mackenzie (Melville Douglas), *physician; League of Nations commissioner to Liberia.*
— Corrrespondence between Lord Cecil and M. D. Mackenzie, 1932-1943. Partly *signed.* 51100, f. 202; 51101, ff. 17-21, 29-34; 51189, ff. 44, 52, 262, 267.
— Letter, etc., to E. Barclay from M. D. Mackenzie, 1933. *Copy.* 51101, ff. 86-94.

M'Laren (Charles Benjamin Bright), *1st Baron Aberconway.*
— Letter to Sir W. Chance from Lord Aberconway, 1914. *Signed.* 51161, f. 140.

Maclay (Joseph Paton), *1st Baron Maclay.*
— Letter to Lord Cecil from J. P. Maclay, 1918. *Signed.* 51093, f. 189.

MacLeod (A. A.), *National Chairman of the Canadian League against War and Fascism.*
— Letters to Lord Cecil, 1936, 1943. *Signed.* 51173, f. 178; 51190, ff. 87, 153.

Macmillan (Hugh Pattison), *Baron Macmillan.*
— Correspondence between Lord Cecil and Lord Macmillan, 1939. *Signed.* 51184, ff. 46, 58.

Macmillan (Maurice Harold), *1st Earl of Stockton, 1984; Prime Minister.*
— Correspondence, partly on his behalf, with Lord Cecil, 1928, 1951. 51166, ff. 71-78; 51192, ff. 341, 342, 343.

Macnaghten (*Sir* Malcolm Martin), *K.B.E.; judge.*
— Correspondence between Lord Cecil and Sir M. M. Macnaghten, 1934. 51169, ff. 1-69 *passim.*

Macnair (A.), *of the Scottish Liberal Federation.*
— Letter to Miss I. M. Butler from A. Macnair, 1939. *Signed.* 51183, f. 79.

McNair (Arnold Duncan), *1st Baron McNair.*
— Correspondence between Lord Cecil and A. D. McNair, 1944. 51191, ff. 248, 264.

MacNeece (*Air Vice-Marshal* William Foster) *afterw.* **MacNeece Foster**, *British Air Representative to League of Nations Council.*
— Correspondence between Lord Cecil and Air Vice-Marshal W. F. MacNeece, 1926-1941. Mostly *signed.* 51113, ff. 158-203.
— Telegrams between Air Vice-Marshal W. F. MacNeece and the Air Ministry, 1927. 51104, ff. 78, 81, 82, 90.

MacNeill (Ronald John), *Baron Cushendun.*
— Correspondence between Lord Cecil and Lord Cushendun, 1928. *Signed.* 51166, ff. 52-54.

INDEX

Maconachie (*Sir* Richard Roy), *K.B.E.; of the B.B.C.*
— Letters to Lord Cecil, 1938-1941. *Signed.* 51193, ff. 105, 156, 160, 226.

McPhee (*Miss* —), *of the Ministry of Information.*
— Letter on behalf of Lord Cecil to Miss — McPhee, 1942. *Copy.* 51188, f. 153.

MacPhee (*Miss* Isabel), *Principal of Chelwood Gate School, Sydney.*
— Correspondence between Lord Cecil and Miss I. MacPhee, 1935. 51170, f. 251; 51171, f. 93.

Macready (*Gen. Sir* Cecil Frederick Nevil), *1st Bart.*
— Pass for Lord Cecil issued by Gen. Sir C. F. N. Macready, 1914. Partly *printed. Signed.* 51161, f. 188.

Madariaga (Salvador de), *Spanish diplomatist and author.*
— Correspondence between Lord Cecil and S. de Madariaga, 1924-1944. Partly *signed.* 51096, f. 169; 51178, ff. 106, 112; 51191, f. 64.
— Letter to Miss E. V. Lazarus from S. de Madariaga, 1945. *Signed.* 51192, f. 8.

Maddison (N. B.), *of Dane Hill.*
— Letter to Lord Cecil, 1944. 51191, f. 198.

Madol (Hans Roger), *Swedish journalist.*
— Correspondence between Lord Cecil and H. R. Madol, 1938. 51181, ff. 130-132.

Magnus (*Sir* Philip), *1st Bart.*
— Correspondence between Lord Cecil and P. Magnus, 1907. Partly *signed.* 51158, ff. 124, 138, 143-161, 164.

Mahaim (Ernest Aimé Joseph), *Belgian sociologist.*
— Letter to Lord Cecil from E. A. J. Mahaim, 1934. *Signed.* 51169, f. 78.

Maillefeu (*Vicomte de* Donville-).
— *v.* Donville-Maillefeu, *Vicomte de.*

Maisky (Ivan Mikhailovich), *Soviet diplomatist.*
— Memoranda by Lord Cecil rel. to conversation with I. M. Maisky, 1934, 1937. 51101, ff. 109, 130; 51178, f. 126.
— Correspondence, including telegrams, between Lord Cecil and I. M. Maisky, 1934-1944. *Signed.* 51101, ff. 112, 113; 51169, ff. 57, 62; 51170, ff. 19-21; 51176, ff. 130, 140; 51177, f. 69; 51178, f. 114; 51187, ff. 386, 395, 403; 51188, ff. 285, 290, 300, 376; 51189, f. 125; 51190, ff. 63, 64; 51191, f. 229.

Maitland (*Sir* Arthur Herbert Drummond Ramsay Steel-).
— *v.* Steel-Maitland (*Sir* Arthur Herbert Drummond Ramsay).

Major (John Patrick Edward Chandos Henniker-), *Baron Henniker.*
— *v.* Henniker-Major (John Patrick Edward Chandos).

Makins (Roger Mellor), *of the Foreign Office.*
— Letter, etc., to Miss I. M. Butler from R. M. Makins, 1936. 51173, ff. 77-89.

Makower (Ernest Samuel), *F.S.A.; Trustee of the London Museum.*
— Letter from Lord Cecil to E. S. Makower, 1928. *Copy.* 51166, f. 32.

Malcolm (*Sir* Ian Zachary), *K.C.M.G.; M.P.*
— Letter, etc., to I. Z. Malcolm from Sir E. R. Jones, 1918. 51094, ff. 77-83.
— Letter to I. Z. Malcolm from Sir A. H. D. R. Steel-Maitland, 1918. *Signed.* 51094, f. 86.
— Correspondence between Lord Cecil and I. Z. Malcolm, 1918, 1922. 51094, ff. 76-83; 51163, f. 60.

INDEX

Malcolm (*Maj.-Gen. Sir* Neill), *K.C.B.*
— Correspondence between Lord Cecil and Maj.-Gen. Sir N. Malcolm, 1933, 1937. *Signed.* 51168, ff. 162, 163; 51177, ff. 4, 13, 19.

Malcolmson (Vernon Austen), *writer on agriculture and imperial development.*
— Letter to Lord Cecil from V. A. Malcolmson, 1912. 51160, f. 111.

Malkin (*Sir* Herbert William), *G.C.M.G.*
— Memorandum by Lord Cecil rel. to conversation with Sir H. W. Malkin, 1940. *Copy.* 51185, f. 68.
— Correspondence between Lord Cecil and Sir H. W. Malkin, 1940-1944. *Signed.* 51184, ff. 308, 313; 51188, ff. 282, 283; 51190, f. 394; 51191, ff. 1, 7, 53, 54.

Mallery (Otto Tod), *author; of Philadelphia, Pennsylvania.*
— Letter to Lord Cecil from O. T. Mallery, 1941. *Signed.* 51181, f. 17.

Malleson (William Miles), *actor.*
— Correspondence between Lord Cecil and W. M. Malleson, 1933, 1934. *Signed.* 51168, ff. 149, 160; 51169, f. 48.

Mallet (*Sir* Charles Edward), *M.P.*
— Letters, etc., to Lord Cecil from C. E. Mallet, 1909. Partly *signed.* 51159, ff. 6, 41, 68, 81, 162-165, 247.

Mallet (William Ivo), *of the Foreign Office.*
— Letter to W. I. Mallet from Miss I. M. Butler, 1939. *Copy.* 51183, f. 99.

Malthe-Bruun (Urban), *Danish diplomatist.*
— Letters to Lord Cecil from U. Malthe-Bruun, 1925. *Signed.* 51097, ff. 165-171, 177.

Man (*Rev.* Morrice Lionel), *Rector of Chartham.*
— Correspondence between Lord Cecil and Rev. M. L. Man, 1940. *Signed.* 51185, ff. 246, 248.

Manchester, *Bishop of.*
— *v.* Knox (Edmund Arbuthnott).

Mander (*Sir* Geoffrey Le Mesurier), *M.P.*
— Correspondence between Lord Cecil and G. Le M. Mander, 1935-1940. *Signed.* 51171, ff. 53-55; 51173, ff. 105, 115, 119; 51177, f. 107; 51184, f. 19; 51185, ff. 208, 240, 244.

Mansbridge (Albert), *Chairman, Seafarers' Education Service.*
— Correspondence between Lord Cecil and A. Mansbridge, 1938. *Signed.* 51179, ff. 132, 140, 180.

Mansbridge (John), *artist.*
— Correspondence between Lord Cecil and J. Mansbridge, 1938, 1939. 51181, f. 89; 51182, ff. 135, 139.

Mansfield (Ralph Sheldon), *4th Baron Sandhurst.*
— Letter to Pedestrians' Association from Lord Sandhurst, 1938. *Signed.* 51178, f. 164.

Manus (*Miss* Rosa), *official of the International Peace Campaign.*
— Correspondence between Lord Cecil and Miss R. Manus, 1936. *Signed.* Partly *Fr.* 51143, f. 84; 51173, f. 253.

Maps and Plans.
— Map of Ethiopia, 1935. *Printed* with MS. annotations. *Fr.* and *Ital.* 51177, f. 56v.

Marburg (Theodore), *U.S. publicist; Chairman, League of Nations Non-Partisan Association.*
— Correspondence, including telegram, between Lord Cecil and T. Marburg, 1926-1945. *Signed.* 51164, ff. 157-168; 51165, f. 34; 51167, f. 18; 51192, ff. 138, 144-148.

Marchant (*Sir* James), *K.B.E.*
— Correspondence, etc., between Lord Cecil and Sir J. Marchant, 1939, 1945. 51183, ff. 202-205; 51192, ff. 64-67.

Margesson (Henry David Reginald), *1st Viscount Margesson.*
— Letter to Lord Cecil from H. D. R. Margesson, 1941. *Signed.* 51187, f. 127.

Marin (Antonio de la Cruz), *Spanish diplomatist.*
— Letter to Lord Cecil from A. de la Cruz Marin, 1937. *Signed.* 51175, f. 45.

Marinis Stendardo de Ricigliano (Alberto de), *Italian general.*
— Letter to Lord Cecil from A. de Marinis Stendardo de Ricigliano, 1927. *Fr.* 51099, f. 2.
— Memorandum by Lord Cecil rel. to conversation with A. de Marinis Stendardo de Ricigliano, 1927. 51099, f. 53.

Marinkovic (Voislav), *Yugoslav statesman.*
— Memoranda by Lord Cecil rel. to conversation with V. Marinkovic, 1930, 1931. 51100, ff. 69, 142.

Marling (*Sir* Charles Murray), *G.C.M.G.*
— Telegrams between Lord Cecil and C. M. Marling, 1918. Partly *drafts.* 51093, ff. 199, 200; 51104, ff. 11-16.

Marlow (Oliver), *writing from London, SW 13.*
— Correspondence between Lord Cecil and O. Marlow, 1940. Partly *signed.* 51185, ff. 80, 85, 108, 149.

Marriott (*Sir* John Arthur Ransome).
— Correspondence between Lord Cecil and Sir J. A. R. Marriott, 1942, 1944. 51188, ff. 263, 266; 51191, ff. 62, 66, 84.

Marsden (J. W.), *of Nottingham.*
— Correspondence between Lord Cecil and J. W. Marsden, 1935. 51170, ff. 112, 117.

Marsh (*Sir* Edward Howard), *K.C.V.O.*
— Letter to Lord Cecil from E. H. Marsh on behalf of the Duke of Devonshire, 1923. *Signed.* 51096, f. 91.

Marsh (Robert H.), *Sec., The National Association of Building Societies.*
— Correspondence between Lord Cecil and R. H. Marsh, 1936, 1937. *Signed.* 51173, ff. 95, 111, 118, 171, 173; 51177, ff. 48, 86, 91.

Marshall (Arthur Edward Willoughby), *solicitor.*
— Letter, etc., to Lord Cecil from A. E. W. Marshall, 1912. *Signed.* 51160, ff. 118-120.

Marshall (*Miss* Josephine), *of Hampstead Garden Suburb.*
— Correspondence between Lord Cecil and Miss J. Marshall, 1936. *Signed.* 51174, ff. 155, 158, 164.

Marshall (Noel Ambrose), *rector of Whippingham.*
— Correspondence between Lord Cecil and N. A. Marshall, 1945. 51192, ff. 142, 150.

Marston (*Sir* Charles), *Chairman of the Villiers Engineering Co.*
— Correspondence between Lord Cecil and Sir C. Marston, 1936. *Signed.* 51173, ff. 130, 138.

Martin (Azaj Wavqueh), *Ethiopian diplomatist.*
— Letter to Lord Cecil from A. W. Martin, 1936. *Signed.* 51174, f. 1.

Martin (Basil Kingsley), *Editor, New Statesman and Nation.*
— Correspondence between Lord Cecil and B. K. Martin, 1940. *Signed.* 51186, ff. 43, 64.

Martinez de Alva (Salvador), *Mexican diplomatist.*
— Letter to Lord Cecil from S. Martinez de Alva, 1931. 51100, f. 137.

Masaryk (Jan Garrigue), *Czech statesman.*
— Correspondence between Lord Cecil and J. G. Masaryk, 1934-1944. Partly *signed.* 51101, ff. 118, 119; 51172, ff. 56, 60, 74, 94, 100; 51173, ff. 136, 140, 143, 183; 51181, f. 102; 51182, f. 31; 51184, f. 320; 51186, f. 100; 51187, ff. 246, 351.

Masirevich (Constantin de), *Hungarian diplomatist.*
— Correspondence between Lord Cecil and C. de Masirevich, 1936, 1937. *Signed.* 51172, ff. 165, 176; 51173, f. 49; 51174, ff. 170, 173; 51175, f. 49.

Mason (D. M.), *writing from West Malvern.*
— Letters to Lord Cecil from D. M. Mason, 1940, 1941. 51186, ff. 200, 295; 51187, f. 3.

Massigli (René Lucien Daniel), *French statesman.*
— Correspondence between Lord Cecil and R. L. D. Massigli, 1930-1944. *Signed.* Partly *Fr.* 51100, ff. 46-50, 57-60v, 87; 51170, ff. 213, 219, 241; 51191, f. 315.
— Memoranda rel. to conversations with R. L. D. Massigli, 1931-1935. 51100, ff. 117-120; 51170, f. 10.

Matejka (Gerda), *wife of Dr V. Matejka.*
— Correspondence between Lord Cecil and G. Matejka, 1938, 1939. Partly *signed. Germ.* with *Engl. transl.* 51179, f. 121; 51182, ff. 74-75v, 83, 179-182.

Matejka (*Dr.* Viktor), *Austrian politician.*
— Memoranda, partly by Miss I. M. Butler, rel. to Dr. V. Matejka, 1939. 51183, ff. 17, 127.

Mathew (David), *R.C. Archbishop of Apamea.*
— Correspondence between Lord Cecil and the Archbishop of Apamea on behalf of Cardinal Hinsley, 1941. Partly *signed.* 51187, ff. 263, 279, 328, 331.

Matthews (Peter), *[writer on European affairs?].*
— Correspondence between Miss I. M. Butler and P. Matthews, 1936. 51174, ff. 5, 44.
— Letter to —, 1936. *Extract.* 51174, f. 242.

Maufe (Gareth), *of the International Student Service.*
— Letter to Lord Cecil from G. Maufe, 1936. *Signed.* 51174, f. 49.

Maugham (Frederic Herbert), *1st Viscount Maugham.*
— Memorandum to members of the Watching Committee, 1942. *Printed.* 51188, f. 208.
— Correspondence between Lord Cecil and Lord Maugham, 1942. 51188, ff. 271-272v, 298, 373, 379; 51189, ff. 5, 18-20, 40.

Maund (*Rear-Adm.* Loben Edward Harold).
— Letter to Lord Cecil from Rear-Adm. L. E. H. Maund, 1928. 51088, f. 76.
— Letter to Rear-Adm. L. E. H. Maund from A. F. Hemming, 1932. *Signed.* 51088, f. 78.

Maurice (*Maj.-Gen. Sir* Frederick Barton), *K.C.M.G.*
— Correspondence between Lord Cecil and Maj.-Gen. Sir F. B. Maurice, 1925. Partly *copy.* 51097, ff. 197, 198, 216, 217.

Max-Muller (*Sir* William Grenfell), *G.B.E.*
— Letter to Sir W. G. Max-Muller from E. Ovey on behalf of Lord Curzon, 1923. *Copy.* 51096, f. 17.

Max-Muller (*Sir* William Grenfell), *G.B.E. continuation*
— Memorandum by Lord Parmoor rel. to conversation with Sir W. G. Max-Muller, 1924. 51096, f. 144.
— Correspondence between Lord Parmoor and Sir W. G. Max-Muller, 1924. 51097, ff. 61, 65.

Maxse (*Gen. Sir* Ivor), *K.C.B.*
— Correspondence between Lord Cecil and Col. I. Maxse, 1907. 51158, ff. 133-137v.

Maxse (Leopold James), *Editor of The National Review.*
— Letters to Lord Cecil from L. J. Maxse, 1915. *Signed.* 51161, ff. 202, 206, 207.

Maxwell-Lyte (*Sir* Henry Churchill), *K.C.B.; Deputy-Keeper of the Public Records.*
— Letter to Lord Cecil from Sir H. C. Maxwell-Lyte, 1905. 51158, f. 33.

Maxwell-Lyte (W.), *of the Tariff Reform League; son of Sir H. C. Maxwell-Lyte.*
— Letter to Lord Cecil from W. Maxwell-Lyte, 1905. 51158, f. 30.

Meade (J. E.), *Sec. of Sir Arthur Salter's Election Committee, Oxford University.*
— Correspondence between Lord Cecil and J. E. Meade, 1936. Partly *printed.* 51174, ff. 38-43, 84.

Mears (Charles W.), *of Offley.*
— Correspondence between Lord Cecil and C. W. Mears, 1918. 51162, ff. 71, 80.

Mears (J. H.), *Managing Director, Joseph Mears Theatres Ltd.*
— Letter to Lord Cecil, 1943. *Signed.* 51190, f. 132.

Medland (*Miss* Elsie), *Sec., National Parliament of Youth.*
— Letter to Lord Cecil from Miss E. Medland, 1939. *Signed.* 51183, f. 20.

Medway Towns.
— Message from Lord Cecil for Peace Week in Medway Towns, [1938?]. *Copy.* 51182, f. 122.

Meiklejohn (*Miss* Rita), *Sec. to Sir D. M. Stevenson.*
— Correspondence between Lord Cecil and Miss R. Meiklejohn, 1942. *Signed.* 51188, ff. 184, 194, 199.

Melas (George V.), *C.V.O.; Greek diplomatist.*
— Letter to Lord Cecil from G. V. Melas, 1923. *Signed.* 51095, f. 131.

Melchett, *1st Baron.*
— *v.* Mond (Alfred Moritz).

Mello-Franco (Afranio de), *Brasilian diplomatist.*
— Correspondence between Lord Cecil and A. de Mello-Franco, 1923. *Signed.* Partly *Fr.* 51096, ff. 60-65.
— Memorandum by Lord Cecil rel. to conversation with A. de Mello-Franco, 1926. 51098, f. 9.

Menant (Guy), *of the International Peace Campaign, Paris.*
— Letter to G. Menant, 1937. *Copy.* 51177, f. 187.

Mendelssohn-Bartholdy (Albrecht), *German jurist.*
— Letter to H. R. H. Gascoyne-Cecil from A. Mendelssohn-Bartholdy, 1910. 51157, ff. 10-13.

Merry del Val y Zulueta (*Marques* Alfonso de), *Spanish diplomatist.*
— Memoranda by Lord Cecil rel. to conversations with Marques A. de Merry del Val y Zulueta, 1918. 51093, ff. 130, 159, 161, 173, 182, 204; 51094, ff. 117, 136, 156.

Merton (Elisabeth) *née* **Zu Löwenstein-Wertheim-Freudenberg**, *wife of R. Merton.*
— Letter from Lord Cecil to E. Merton, 1929. *Copy.* 51166, f. 130.

Merton (Richard), *German metal merchant.*
— Letter to Lord Cecil from R. Merton, 1929. *Signed.* 51166, f. 108.

Meston (James Scorgie), *1st Baron Meston.*
— Letters to Lord Cecil from Lord Meston, 1940. *Signed.* 51185, ff. 258, 272.

Meux (*Adm. of the Fleet Sir* Hedworth) *formerly* **Lambton**, *G.C.B.*
— *v.* Lambton (*Adm. of the Fleet Sir* Hedworth).

Michalakopoulos (Andrew), *Greek Foreign Minister.*
— Correspondence between Lord Cecil and A. Michalakopoulos, 1930. *Signed.* 51100, ff. 13, 26.

Michalopoulos (André), *Greek Minister of Information in London.*
— Letter to Lord Cecil, 1942. *Signed.* 51188, f. 307.

Michell (J. H.), *Sec., Junior Constitutional Club.*
— Correspondence between Lord Cecil and J. H. Michell, 1938. *Signed.* 51181, ff. 54, 68, 87, 92.

Middlemas (Robert), *cigar-importer.*
— Correspondence between Lord Cecil and R. Middlemas, 1944. *Signed.* 51191, ff. 130, 132, 134.

Midleton, *1st Earl of.*
— *v.* Brodrick (William St. John Fremantle).

Miller (David Hunter), *U.S. lawyer.*
— Correspondence between Lord Cecil and D. H. Miller, 1927, 1928. *Signed.* 51165, ff. 143, 179, 191; 51166, f. 60.

Miller (Fred), *Managing Editor, The Daily Telegraph.*
— Letter, etc., to Lord Cecil from F. Miller, 1916. *Signed.* 51093, ff. 6-8.
— Letter to F. Miller from A. Thorop, 1916. 51093, f. 7.

Millerand (Alexandre), *President of the French Republic.*
— Memorandum by Lord Cecil rel. to conversation with A. Millerand, 1923. 51095, ff. 175-177.

Millin (Sarah Gertrude), *author.*
— Correspondence between Lord Cecil and S. G. Millin, 1940. 51184, f. 330; 51185, ff. 18, 116.

Millington-Drake (*Sir* Eugen John Henry Vanderstegen), *K.C.M.G.*
— Letter to Lord Cecil from E. J. H. V. Millington-Drake, 1935. *Signed.* 51171, f. 11.

Mills (David H.), *of the League of Nations Union.*
— Letters, etc., to Lord Cecil from D. H. Mills, 1935, 1944. Partly *signed.* 51171, f. 3; 51191, f. 211.

Milne (*Sir* John Sydney Wardlaw-), *K.B.E.*
— *v.* Wardlaw-Milne (*Sir* John Sydney).

Milner (Alfred), *Viscount Milner.*
— Correspondence between Lord Cecil and Lord Milner, 1918. 51093, ff. 76, 81, 180, 181; 51094, ff. 16, 58; 51160, f. 67.

Milnes (Robert Offley Ashburton Crewe-).
— *v.* Crewe-Milnes (Robert Offley Ashburton).

Mire (*Dr.* Josef), *Jewish refugee from Austria.*
— Correspondence between Lord Cecil and Dr. J. Mire, 1938. 51180, ff. 123-125.
— Memorandum by Lord Cecil rel. to interview with Dr. J. Mire, 1938. *Signed.* 51180, f. 138.

Mitchell (*Sir* Harold Picton), *Bart.; M.P.*
— Correspondence between Lord Cecil and Col. H. P. Mitchell, 1945. *Signed.* 51192, ff. 79, 85.

INDEX

Moe (*Dr. R.*), *of the Nobel Committee of the Norwegian Parliament.*
— Correspondence between Lord Cecil and Dr. R. Moe, 1937, 1938. *Signed.* Partly *printed.* Partly *Fr.* 51178, ff. 35, 113; 51179, ff. 135, 173; 51182, f. 27.

Monbrisson (H. de), *of Neuilly St. James, France.*
— Correspondence between Lord Cecil and H. de Monbrisson, 1936, 1937. *Signed.* 51172, f. 25; 51177, ff. 178, 186.

Moncheur (*Baron* Ludovic), *Belgian diplomatist.*
— Memorandum by Lord Cecil rel. to meeting with Baron L. Moncheur, 1918. 51093, f. 156.

Mond (Alfred Moritz), *1st Baron Melchett.*
— Correspondence between Lord Cecil and Lord Melchett, 1929. *Signed.* 51166, ff. 157-162.

Money (*Sir* Leo George Chiozza).
— Letter, etc., to Lord Cecil from Sir L. G. C. Money, 1918. *Signed.* 51094, f. 53.

Monk Bretton, *2nd Baron.*
— *v.* Dodson (John William).

Monnet (Jean), *French statesman.*
— Letter to Lord Cecil from J. Monnet, 1923. 51096, f. 28.

Monod (Noel), *writing from Paris.*
— Letter to Lord Cecil, 1936. 51174, f. 79.

Montagu (Edwin Samuel), *Sec. of State for India.*
— Letter to E. Drummond from E. S. Montagu, 1916. *Signed.* 51093, f. 9.
— Correspondence, partly on his behalf, with Lord Cecil, 1918. *Signed.* 51094, ff. 59, 72-75, 111-114v, 118.
— Letter to W. H. M. Selby from J. E. Shuckburgh on behalf of E. S. Montagu, 1918. 51094, f. 114.

Montague-Barlow (*Sir* Clement Anderson), *Bart.*
— Correspondence between Lord Cecil and C. A. Montague-Barlow, 1923. *Signed.* 51095, ff. 172-174, 178.

Monteagle of Brandon, *3rd Baron.*
— *v.* Spring-Rice (Thomas Aubrey).

Montenach (Jean Daniel), *Swiss official at the League of Nations.*
— Correspondence between Lord Cecil and J. D. Montenach, 1931. *Signed.* 51100, ff. 145-148.

Montgomery (Peter), *of the B.B.C.*
— Correspondence between P. Montgomery and Miss I. M. Butler, 1942. *Signed.* 51188, ff. 166-167v, 177.

Montrose, *6th Duke of.*
— *v.* Graham (James).

Moore (Frederick E.), *former official of the University of Birmingham.*
— Letter to Lord Cecil, 1944. 51191, f. 279.

Moore (*Sir* William), *1st Bart.*
— Letter to Lord Cecil from W. Moore, [1913?]. 51161, f. 14.

Moore-Brabazon (John Theodore Cuthbert), *1st Baron Brabazon of Tara.*
— Correspondence between Lord Cecil and Lord Brabazon, 1942. 51188, ff. 341, 344, 348.

Morant (*Sir* Robert Laurie), *K.C.B.*
— Letters to Lord Cecil from Sir R. L. Morant, 1915. *Signed.* 51161, ff. 231, 234, 243, 245.

Morgenthau (Henry), *U.S. banker and diplomatist.*
— Correspondence between H. Morgenthau and M. C. Norman, 1923. *Copies.* 51096, ff. 89, 97-101.
— Correspondence between G. N. Cofinas and H. Morgenthau, 1923. *Copies.* 51096, ff. 100, 101.

Morley (*Sir* James Wycliffe Headlam-).
— *v.* Headlam-Morley (*Sir* James Wycliffe).

Morrish (Frank), *Sec., Hitchin Conservative and Liberal Unionist Association.*
— Correspondence between Lord Cecil and F. Morrish, 1924. 51164, ff. 16, 17.

Morrison (Herbert Stanley), *Baron Morrison of Lambeth.*
— Correspondence, partly on his behalf, with Lord Cecil, 1938-1945. *Signed.* 51180, ff. 36-38; 51187, ff. 320, 321, 423; 51188, f. 4; 51189, ff. 172, 174, 228, 230, 268, 274, 277-279; 51192, f. 68.
— Speech by H. S. Morrison at the Guildhall, London, 1943. *Copy.* 51189, ff. 283-284v.
— Memorandum by Lord Cecil rel. to interview with H. S. Morrison, 1943. *Copy.* 51189, f. 285.
— Letter to Miss E. V. Lazarus from R. J. P. Hewison on behalf of H. S. Morrison, 1945. *Signed.* 51192, f. 68.

Morrison (William Shepherd), *1st Viscount Dunrossil.*
— Correspondence between Lord Cecil and W. S. Morrison, 1944. *Signed.* 51191, ff. 298, 304.

Morrow (Dwight Whitney), *U.S. senator and diplomatist.*
— Memoranda by Lord Cecil rel. to conversation with D. W. Morrow, 1930, 1931. 51100, ff. 27, 113.
— Letter from Lord Cecil to D. W. Morrow, 1931. *Copy.* 51167, f. 65.

Morton (George), *Sec., League of Nations Union, Bootle, Orrell and Litherland Branch.*
— Correspondence between Lord Cecil and G. Morton, 1937. *Signed.* 51177, ff. 35, 44.

Mosley (*Lady* Cynthia Blanche), *wife of Sir O. Mosley.*
— Correspondence between Lord Cecil and Lady C. B. Mosley, 1927. *Signed.* 51165, ff. 180, 185.

Mottistone, *1st Baron.*
— *v.* Seely (John Edward Bernard).

Mount Temple, *Baron.*
— *v.* Ashley (Wilfred William).

Moyers (W. W.), *writing from Liverpool.*
— Letter to Lord Cecil from W. W. Moyers, 1912. 51160, f. 96v.

Moyne, *1st Baron.*
— *v.* Guinness (Walter Edward).

Muir (Nadejda) *née* **Stancioff**, *wife of Sir A. K. Muir.*
— Correspondence between Lord Cecil and Lady Muir, 1936. *Signed.* 51172, ff. 180, 188.

Müller (Ernest Bruce Iwan-).
— *v.* Iwan-Müller (Ernest Bruce).

Müller (Fritz), *German refugee in England.*
— Correspondence between Lord Cecil and F. Müller, 1939. 51184, ff. 120, 138.

Muller (*Sir* William Grenfell Max-).
— *v.* Max-Muller (*Sir* William Grenfell).

Müller-Sturmheim (*Dr.* Emil), *Austrian journalist.*
— Correspondence between Lord Cecil and Dr. E. Müller-Sturmheim, 1938, 1939. *Signed.* 51145, ff. 129-169.
— Correspondence between Dr. E. Müller-Sturmheim and Miss I. M. Butler, 1938, 1939. *Signed.* 51145, ff. 131-169 *passim.*

Munday (*Alderman* W. L.), *Chairman, Sutton Division Unionist Association, Plymouth.*
— Correspondence between H. A. Lewis and Alderman W. L. Munday, 1927. 51165, ff. 124-125.

INDEX

Mundy (Ernest W.), *Sec., Labour Co-Partnership Association.*
— Correspondence, etc., partly on his behalf, with Lord Cecil, 1912, 1915. *Signed.* 51160, ff. 131-133, 175, 192; 51161, ff. 2, 3.

Mundy (Lionel), *journalist.*
— Letter from Lord Cecil to L. Mundy, 1940. *Signed.* 51186, f. 141.

Munir (*Bey* Mehmed), *Turkish diplomatist.*
— Correspondence between Lord Cecil and Bey M. Munir, 1933. *Signed. Fr.* 51101, ff. 73, 74, 97.

Munn (Alfred Moore), *of the Crown and Peace Office, Londonderry.*
— Letters to Sir E. Grey from A. M. Munn, 1914. *Copies.* 51073, ff. 59, 64.

Munro-Ferguson (Ronald Crauford), *1st Viscount Novar.*
— Letter to S. Baldwin from Lord Novar, 1923. *Copy.* 51080, f. 108.

Munster, *5th Earl of.*
— *v.* FitzClarence (Geoffrey William Richard Hugh).

Murphy (*Sir* Dermod Art Pelly).
— Correspondence between Lord Cecil and D. A. P. Murphy, 1934. 51169, ff. 241-245.

Murray (Alexander William Charles Oliphant), *Master of Elibank; Baron Murray of Elibank.*
— Letter to Lord Cecil from Lord Murray, 1912. 51160, f. 157.

Murray (George Gilbert Aimé), *O.M.*
— Correspondence between Lord Cecil and G. G. A. Murray, 1922-1952. Partly *signed.* 51132-51135.
— Letter to J. Ramsay MacDonald from G. G. A. Murray, 1929. *Draft. Signed.* 51081, f. 72.
— Letter to G. G. A. Murray from M. S. Jameson, 1934. *Signed.* 51132, f. 192.
— 'A Personal Message' to members of the League of Nations Union by G. G. A. Murray, 1934. *Printed.* 51169, f. 71.
— Letter, etc., to G. G. A. Murray from W. H. Beveridge, 1939. *Signed.* 51133, ff. 122-125.
— Letter to A. G. Norris from G. G. A. Murray, 1940. *Copy.* 51186, f. 204.
— Letter to G. G. A. Murray from I. L. Evans, 1941. *Signed.* 51133, f. 223.
— Letter to G. G. A. Murray from D. M. Foot, 1941. *Signed.* 51188, f. 69.

Murray (Gideon), *2nd Viscount Elibank.*
— Correspondence between Lord Cecil and Lord Elibank, 1938. *Signed.* 51179, ff. 33-37.

Murray (*Sir* John), *K.C.V.O.*
— Letter to Lord Cecil from J. Murray, 1909. 51159, f. 186.

Murray (*Lady* Mary Henrietta), *wife of G. G. A. Murray.*
— Correspondence between Lord Cecil and Lady M. H. Murray, 1937. *Signed.* 51132, f. 246-249.

Murray (William Ewart Gladstone), *of the B.B.C.*
— Letters and telegrams to Lord Cecil, 1942, 1944. Partly *signed.* 51191, f. 183; 51193, ff. 264, 276.

N

Nabwe (Sonpon), *Sec. to the Paramount Chief of Sasstown, Liberia.*
— Correspondence, on behalf of the Paramount Chiefs, etc., of Sasstown, with Lord Cecil, 1934. 51101, ff. 114, 120, 132, 138.
— Letters and telegrams to the Sec.-General, League of Nations from S. Nabwe on behalf of Chief Nimley, 1934. *Copies.* 51101, ff. 121-129, 131, 133.

Nall (*Sir* Joseph), *1st Bart.; M.P.*
— Correspondence between Lord Cecil and Sir J. Nall, 1938. *Signed.* 51180, ff. 64, 66, 75.

Namier (*Sir* Lewis Bernstein), *historian.*
— Memorandum by Lord Cecil rel. to conversation with L. B. Namier, 1930. 51100, f. 61.
— Correspondence between Lord Cecil and L. B. Namier, 1940. *Signed.* Partly *copy.* 51157, ff. 266, 267, 268; 51186, ff. 52, 55.

Nansen (Fridtjof), *Norwegian explorer.*
— Correspondence, including telegram, between Lord Cecil and F. Nansen, 1921-1928. Partly *signed.* 51095, ff. 38, 145, 153-155; 51096, f. 2; 51097, ff. 192-196; 51099, ff. 71, 72, 77-79, 83-85, 143.
— Memorandum by Lord Cecil rel. to interview with F. Nansen, 1939. 51183, f. 55.

Napier (*Sir* Walter John), *barrister.*
— Correspondence between Lord Cecil and Sir W. J. Napier, 1934, 1935. 51169, ff. 164, 166, 167; 51170, f. 128; 51171, ff. 28-30.

Narushevich (T.), *Lithuanian diplomatist.*
— Correspondence between Lord Cecil and T. Narushevich, 1923. *Signed.* 51095, ff. 132, 135.

Nash (Bernard A.), *of The Essex County Telegraph.*
— Correspondence between Lord Cecil and B. A. Nash, 1940. 51185, ff. 98, 107, 138.

Nash (David Foot), *solicitor.*
— Correspondence between Lord Cecil and D. F. Nash, 1942. *Signed.* 51189, ff. 53, 62.

Nash (*Maj.-Gen. Sir* Philip Arthur Manley), *K.C.M.G.*
— Memorandum by Maj.-Gen. P. A. M. Nash rel. to coal supply for France and Italy, 1918. *Signed.* 51093, ff. 92-96.

Nash (Philip Curtis), *Director, League of Nations Association, New York.*
— Correspondence between Lord Cecil and P. C. Nash, 1930, 1944. *Signed.* 51167, ff. 15, 16; 51191, f. 83.

Nash (*Sir* Walter), *G.C.M.G.; afterw. Prime Minister of New Zealand.*
— Correspondence between Lord Cecil and W. Nash, 1944. *Signed.* 51191, ff. 45, 47, 51, 52.

Nathan (*Maj.* Harry Louis), *1st Baron Nathan.*
— Election address by Maj. H. L. Nathan in Cardiff, 1935. *Printed.* 51171, f. 166.
— Correspondence between Lord Cecil and Lord Nathan, 1935, 1941. *Signed.* 51171, ff. 164-167v, 170, 171, 178; 51187, ff. 82, 100.

National Broadcasting Co. of America.
— *v.* Bate (Frederick).
— *v.* Royal (John F.).

National Committee on the Cause and Cure of War.
— *v.* Catt (Carrie Chapman).
— *v.* Parsons (Alice T. L.).

National Farmers' Union.
— Minutes of meeting between deputation of National Farmers' Union and D. Lloyd George, 1921. *Copy.* 51162, ff. 142-151.

National Federation of Discharged and Demobilised Sailors and Soldiers.
— Leaflet no. 5, 'Who We Are and What We Want' by the National Federation of Discharged and Demobilised Sailors and Soldiers, 1918. *Printed.* 51162, f. 63.

National Joint Committee for Spanish Relief.
— Receipt to Lord Cecil, 1938. 51181, f. 30.
— Letters to Lord Cecil, 1942. 51179, f. 7; 51189, f. 115.
— *v. also* Garratt (Geoffrey Theodore).

National Parliament of Youth.
— v. Ward (Ronald R. S.).

National Peace Congress.
— Message from Lord Cecil to the National Peace Congress, 1938. *Copy.* 51179, f. 224.

National Peace Fund.
— Memorandum by Lord Cecil rel. to the National Peace Fund, 1939. *Copy.* 51183, f. 77.

National Society for Promoting Religious Education.
— Agenda paper of the Consultative Committee of the National Society for Promoting Religious Education, 1936. *Printed.* 51172, f. 65.

Navy, *of England.*
— Memorandum rel. to China Station by Adm. Sir H. Lambton, 1909. *Printed. Signed.* 51159, f. 208.
— Memoranda rel. to oil reserves, [1915?]. 51162, ff. 7, 8.

Naylor (Henry Darnley), *Professor of Classics at Adelaide.*
— Telegram to Lord Cecil, 1944. 51191, f. 174.

Naylor (*Miss* Margaret Darnley), *Hon. Sec., League of Nations Union, London Regional Federation.*
— Correspondence between Lord Cecil and Miss M. D. Naylor, 1939. *Signed.* 51183, ff. 182, 183, 191.

Nebuška (Otakar), *Sec., Czechoslovak Group, Union Interparlamentaire.*
— Letter to Lord Cecil from O. Nebuška, 1930. *Signed.* 51167, f. 106.

Negrin (*Dr.* Juan), *Spanish physiologist and politician.*
— Letter to Lord Cecil, 1944. 51191, f. 186.

Nelson, *co. Lancs.*
— Message from Lord Cecil for Peace Week at Nelson (?), 1937. 51177, f. 171.

Nelson (*Miss* Edith J.), *of Lingfield.*
— Correspondence with Lord Cecil, 1945. 51192, ff. 207, 209v.

Nethersole (Olga), *actress; founder of The People's League of Health.*
— Correspondence between Lord Cecil and O. Nethersole, 1935. *Signed.* 51170, ff. 54, 66.

Nevins (Allan), *U.S. author and historian.*
— Letters to A. Nevins, 1941. 51186, ff. 274, 280.

Newcombe (Bertha), *Sec., Committee of 'The Men's Declaration in support of Women's Suffrage'.*
— Letter to Lord Cecil from B. Newcombe, 1909. 51159, f. 71.

Newman (R. V.), *writing from Ightam.*
— Letter to Lord Cecil from R. V. Newman, 1911. 51160, f. 34.

Newquay, *co. Cornw.*
— Message from Lord Cecil for Peace Week at Newquay, [1938?]. *Copy.* 51182, f. 123.

Newspapers. America. *Neue Volkszeitung.*
— Correspondence between Lord Cecil and G. H. Seger, 1939. *Signed.* 51183, ff. 16, 52.

Newspapers. America. *New York Herald Tribune.*
— Letters, etc., to Lord Cecil from W. J. Humphreys, 1945. *Signed.* 51192, f. 93.

Newspapers. Canada. *The Toronto Star.*
— Correspondence between Lord Cecil and W. R. Plewman, 1943. *Partly signed.* 51189, ff. 255, 282; 51190, ff. 58-61.

Newspapers. France. *Die Zukunft.*
— Correspondence between [M. J?] Frischauer and Miss I. M. Butler, 1938. *Signed.* 51181, ff. 150, 198; 51182, f. 84.
— Letter to — from [M. J?] Frischauer, 1938. *Signed.* 51181, f. 158.

Newspapers. Germany. *Nord und Süd.*
— Correspondence between Lord Cecil and A. Vallentin, 1929. *Signed.* 51166, ff. 114, 115, 128.

Newspapers. Great Britain and Ireland.
— Correspondence between Lord Cecil and newspaper editors, 1907-1945. Partly *drafts* and *printed.* 51156, ff. 1-182; 51157, f. 113; 51177, ff. 8, 111; 51179, ff. 123, 154-159; 51181, f. 66; 51182, ff. 160, 162, 212-215; 51183, f. 195; 51186, f. 232; 51192, ff. 82-85, 195-200.
— Correspondence between Lord Cecil and Lord Northcliffe, 1909, 1914. *Signed.* Partly *extract.* 51159, ff. 136, 156, 199, 215, 220-222, 225-242, 280; 51161, ff. 195, 196.
— Letter to the Editor of 'The Daily Telegraph' from Lord Lansdowne, 1917. *Copy.* 51093, f. 46.

Newspapers. Great Britain and Ireland. *Church Reform Chronicle.*
— Correspondence between Lord Cecil and E. A. Gilchrist, 1929. *Signed.* 51166, ff. 96, 97.

Newspapers. Great Britain and Ireland. *Daily News.*
— Correspondence between Lord Cecil and L. J. Cadbury, 1928. *Signed.* 51166, ff. 49-51.

Newspapers. Great Britain and Ireland. *Federal Union News.*
— Correspondence between Lord Cecil and J. Usborne, 1940. *Signed.* 51185, ff. 133, 146, 154, 167.

Newspapers. Great Britain and Ireland. *Headway.*
— Memorandum rel. to 'Headway' by H. W. Harris, 1928. *Copy.* 51166, ff. 44-48.
— Letter to H. W. Le Prevost from Miss I. M. Butler, 1938. *Signed.* 51181, f. 49.

Newspapers. Great Britain and Ireland. *New Statesman and Nation.*
— Correspondence between Lord Cecil and B. K. Martin, 1940. *Signed.* 51186, ff. 43, 64.

Newspapers. Great Britain and Ireland. *Our Flag.*
— Letter to Lord Cecil from H. Richardson, 1914. *Signed.* 51161, f. 85.

Newspapers. Great Britain and Ireland. *Picture Post.*
— Letter to Lord Cecil from C. Fenby, 1944. *Signed.* 51191, f. 108.

Newspapers. Great Britain and Ireland. *The Countryman.*
— Correspondence between Lord Cecil and J. W. R. Scott, 1941. *Signed.* 51187, ff. 43, 49.

Newspapers. Great Britain and Ireland. *The Daily Telegraph.*
— Letter to F. Miller from A. Thorop, 1916. 51093, f. 7.
— Letter, etc., to Lord Cecil from R. Binns, 1937. *Signed.* 51177, f. 88.

Newspapers. Great Britain and Ireland. *The Essex County Telegraph.*
— Correspondence between Lord Cecil and B. A. Nash, 1940. 51185, ff. 98, 107, 138.

Newspapers. Great Britain and Ireland. *The Fortnightly.*
— Correspondence between Lord Cecil and W. H. Carter, 1938. *Signed.* 51179, ff. 113-117, 124.
— Correspondence between Lord Cecil and J. Armitage, 1941. 51193, ff. 232, 234-236, 245, 248-254.

Newspapers. Great Britain and Ireland. *The Friend.*
— Correspondence between Lord Cecil and H. W. Peet, 1935. *Signed.* 51170, ff. 91, 94.

Newspapers. Great Britain and Ireland. *The Listener.*
— Correspondence between Lord Cecil and A. E. W. Thomas, 1938, 1940. Partly *signed.* 51180, ff. 141, 145; 51186, f. 73; 51193, f. 200.

Newspapers. Great Britain and Ireland. *The Manchester Guardian.*
— Correspondence between Lord Cecil and C. P. Scott, 1921, 1922. 51162, ff. 163-166v; 51163, f. 53.
— Correspondence, including telegram, between Lord Cecil and W. P. Crozier, 1940-1943. Partly *printed. Signed.* 51185, ff. 66, 77; 51189, ff. 64, 67, 98, 100, 107, 123, 131; 51190, ff. 8, 27, 30.
— Letter to Lord Cecil from A. P. Wadsworth on behalf of W. P. Crozier, 1942. *Signed.* 51189, f. 100.

Newspapers. Great Britain and Ireland. *The New Green Quarterly.*
— Letter to Lord Cecil from A. K. Ingram, 1936. *Signed.* 51193, f. 74.

Newspapers. Great Britain and Ireland. *The Observer.*
— Correspondence between Lord Cecil and J. L. Garvin, 1929-1931. *Signed.* 51166, ff. 143-146, 151-156; 51167, ff. 7-12, 154-159.

Newspapers. Great Britain and Ireland. *The Saturday Review.*
— Letter to Lord Cecil from H. Hodge, 1908. *Signed.* 51158, f. 250v.

Newspapers. Great Britain and Ireland. *The Spectator.*
— Letters to Lord Cecil from J. St. L. Strachey, 1908-1925. Partly *signed.* 51158, ff. 184-186, 194-197, 201-203v, 206, 220; 51159, f. 47; 51162, ff. 57, 58; 51164, ff. 62, 64.

Newspapers. Great Britain and Ireland. *The Times.*
— Correspondence between Lord Cecil and G. G. Dawson, 1923-1940. *Signed.* 51156, ff. 1-38.
— Letter to G. G. Dawson from J. Ramsay MacDonald, S. Baldwin and Lord Oxford and Asquith, 1924. *Copy.* 51097, f. 83.
— Correspondence between Lord Cecil and H. W. Steed, 1932-1944. Partly *signed.* 51156, ff. 126-182.
— Correspondence between Lord Cecil and R. M'G. Barrington-Ward, 1936, 1942. *Signed.* 51156, f. 34; 51189, ff. 191, 195.

Newspapers. Great Britain and Ireland. *The Western Mail.*
— Letters, etc., to Lord Cecil from Sir W. Davies, 1908. 51074, ff. 172-179.

Newspapers. Great Britain and Ireland. *Time and Tide.*
— Letter to Lord Cecil from C. A. Gimingham, 1940. *Signed.* 51193, f. 204.

Newspapers. International. *Associated Press.*
— Correspondence between Lord Cecil and V. Hackler, 1945. *Signed.* 51192, ff. 153, 157, 181, 189, 190.

Newspapers. International. *The Christian Science Monitor.*
— Telegrams between F. P. Leay and G. H. Locock on behalf of F. Dixon, 1915-1917. Partly *draft.* Partly *signed.* 51092, ff. 23-288 *passim.*
— Correspondence, partly on his behalf, between F. Dixon and Lord Cecil, 1915-1923. Partly *signed.* 51092, ff. 1-316 *passim.*
— Letter to G. H. Locock from A. H. Bathurst, 1916. *Signed.* 51092, f. 65.

Newspapers . International . The Christian Science Monitor. continuation
— Letter to J. D. Gregory from A. H. Bathurst, 1916. *Signed.* 51092, f. 75.
— Letter to Lord Grey from F. Dixon, 1916. 51092, f. 115.

Newspapers. Norway. *Tidens Tegn.*
— Correspondence between Lord Cecil and R. Thommessen, 1921. *Signed.* 51163, ff. 19, 20.

Newspapers . Sweden . *Stockholms Tidningen.*
— Correspondence between Lord Cecil and E. Swenne, 1937. *Signed.* 51178, ff. 42, 56, 98.

Newspapers. Sweden. *Svenska Morgonbladet.*
— Telegram to Lord Cecil from Svenska Morgonbladet, 1935. 51170, f. 6.

Newton, 2nd Baron.
— *v.* Legh (Thomas Wodehouse).

Newton (George Douglas Cochrane), Baron Eltisley.
— Correspondence between Lord Cecil and Lord Eltisley, 1937. Partly *signed.* 51176, ff. 97, 108.

Ney (*Maj.* Fred J.), *M.C.; Sec., National Council of Education, Canada.*
— Correspondence between Lord Cecil and Maj. F. J. Ney, 1933. 51168, ff. 43, 65, 67, 72, 86, 91.

Nias (F. H.), *Chairman, Uckfield Rural District Council.*
— Correspondence between Lord Cecil and F. H. Nias, 1941. Partly *printed* and *signed.* 51187, ff. 96, 105, 147.

Nicholson (*Miss* M. E.), *of Letchworth.*
— Letter to A. Wright from Miss M. E. Nicholson, 1918. 51162, f. 63.
— Letter to V. H. Hallewell from Miss M. E. Nicholson, 1918. 51162, f. 64.

Nicolson (*Sir* Harold George), *K.C.V.O.*
— Memorandum by H. G. Nicolson rel. to prospects of peace with Turkey, 1918. *Copy.* 51094, f. 37.
— Correspondence between Lord Cecil and H. G. Nicolson, 1925-1942. Partly *signed.* 51097, ff. 109, 110, 118; 51171, ff. 162, 172; 51186, ff. 65, 72, 82, 87, 91; 51189, ff. 147, 152.
— Memorandum by Lord Cecil rel. to interview with H. G. Nicolson, 1940. *Copy.* 51186, f. 83.

Nield (*Sir* Herbert), *M.P.*
— Letter to Lord Cecil from Sir H. Nield, 1925. *Signed.* 51163, f. 76.

Niemeyer (*Sir* Otto Ernst), *G.B.E.*
— Memorandum by Lord Cecil rel. to conversation with Sir O. E. Niemeyer, 1924. 51097, ff. 71-73.
— Correspondence between Lord Cecil and Sir O. E. Niemeyer, 1943. *Signed.* 51190, ff. 78, 99.

Nimley (Juah), *Paramount Chief of Sasstown, Liberia.*
— Correspondence on his behalf with Lord Cecil, 1934. 51101, ff. 114, 120, 132, 138.
— Letters and telegrams to the Sec.-General, League of Nations from S. Nabwe on behalf of Chief Nimley, 1934. *Copies.* 51101, ff. 121-129, 131, 133.

Ninčić (Momcilo), *Yugoslav statesman.*
— Record by Lord Cecil of conversation with M. Ninčić, 1923. 51096, f. 43.

Nitti (*Dr.* Giuseppe), *organiser of Conference Internationale des 11 et 12 Decembre 1937, Paris.*
— Letter, etc., to Lord Cecil from Dr. G. Nitti, 1937. *Fr.* 51178, ff. 61-67.

Nobel Committee.
— *v.* Moe (*Dr.* R.).

Nobel Foundation, Stockholm.
— *v.* Sohlman (Ragnar).

Nobel Foundation, Stockholm.
continuation
— *v.* Tiselius (D.).

Noel-Baker (Francis Edward), *son of Philip, Baron Noel-Baker.*
— Correspondence between Lord Cecil and F. E. Noel-Baker, 1941, 1945. Partly *signed.* 51186, ff. 265, 270, 290; 51192, ff. 100-101v, 103.

Noel-Baker (Philip John) *formerly* **Baker,** *P.C.; M.P.; Baron Noel-Baker.*
— Correspondence between Lord Cecil and P. J. Noel-Baker, 1921-1948. Partly *signed.* 51100, f. 108; 51106-51109.
— Correspondence, mostly on behalf of Lord Cecil, between P. J. Noel-Baker and E. Colban, 1922-1924. 51115, ff. 3-189 *passim.*
— Correspondence between F. P. Walters and P. J. Noel-Baker, partly on behalf of Lord Cecil, 1922-1937. Mostly *signed.* 51106, f. 130; 51114, ff. 4-30v, 103.
— Letter, etc., to P. J. Noel-Baker from T. F. Johnson, 1923. *Signed.* 51095, f. 196.
— Correspondence between P. J. Noel-Baker and A. E. Zimmern, 1923. 51106, ff. 74-76.
— Letter to P. J. Noel-Baker from J. R. Rodd, 1923. 51106, f. 78.
— Correspondence between P. J. Noel-Baker and Dame R. E. Crowdy, 1923. *Signed.* 51106, ff. 120-122.
— Correspondence between J. A. Salter and P. J. Noel-Baker on behalf of Lord Cecil, 1923, 1924. *Signed.* 51106, ff. 162-167; 51113, ff. 15-24.
— Correspondence between P. J. Noel-Baker and H. A. Rolin, 1924. *Signed.* Partly *Fr.* 51106, ff. 169-171, 205.

— Letter to P. J. Noel-Baker from J. E. Drummond, 1924. *Signed.* 51106, f. 206.
— Letters to P. J. Noel-Baker from L. Dolivet, 1936-1941. *Signed.* Partly *copy.* Mostly *Fr.* 51143, ff. 93, 175, 180.

Noel-Buxton (Noel Edmund) *formerly* **Buxton,** *1st Baron Noel-Buxton.*
— Correspondence between Lord Cecil and Lord Noel-Buxton, 1928-1944. Partly *signed.* 51140, ff. 209-247.

Norman (C. H.), *of Highgate Hill, London, N 6.*
— Correspondence between Lord Cecil and C. H. Norman, 1943. 51190, ff. 158, 165, 170.

Norman (Montagu Collet), *Baron Norman of St. Clere; Governor of the Bank of England.*
— Correspondence between H. Morgenthau and M. C. Norman, 1923. *Copies.* 51096, ff. 89, 97-101.
— Letter to M. C. Norman from G. N. Cofinas, 1923. *Copy.* 51096, f. 97.
— Memorandum by Lord Cecil rel. to conversation with M. C. Norman, 1931. 51100, f. 97.

Norris (Albert G).
— Letter to A. G. Norris from G. G. A. Murray, 1940. *Copy.* 51186, f. 204.

Norsk Forening For Nordisk Samarbeide.
— *v.* Oslo, Norden Association.

Northcliffe, *Viscount.*
— *v.* Harmsworth (Alfred Charles William).

Northcote (Henry Stafford), *Baron Northcote.*
— Letter to Lord Cecil from Lord Northcote, 1906. 51158, f. 58.

NORWAY. SOVEREIGNS OF, *and transactions in particular reigns*. *HAAKON VII.*
— Correspondence, including telegrams, of the Nobel Committee of the Norwegian Parliament with Lord Cecil, 1934-1940. 51169, f. 7; 51175, ff. 18, 28; 51178, ff. 25, 29, 35, 54, 113, 125, 136, 175; 51179, ff. 54, 58; 51184, f. 115; 51185, f. 16.

Norwich, *1st Viscount.*
— *v.* Cooper (Alfred Duff).

Nosworthy (*Sir* Richard Lysle), *K.C.M.G.*
— Correspondence between R. L. Nosworthy and W. H. M. Selby, 1918. *Signed.* 51093, ff. 165-168v.

Novar, *Viscount.*
— *v.* Munro-Ferguson (Ronald Crauford).

Nygatan (Lilla), *of the International Peace Campaign, Swedish Committee.*
— Telegram to Lord Cecil from L. Nygatan, 1942. 51188, f. 140.

O

O'Doneven, *The.*
— *v.* O'Doneven (Ernest Anthony Verlyn Hart).

O'Doneven (Ernest Anthony Verlyn Hart), *The O'Doneven.*
— Correspondence between Lord Cecil and The O'Doneven, 1936. 51172, f. 210; 51173, f. 8.

Ogden (*Mrs* Margery), *writing from Liverpool.*
— Letter to Lord Cecil from Mrs M. Ogden, 1939. 51184, f. 178.

Ogilvie (*Sir* Frederick Wolff), *Director-General of the B.B.C.*
— Letter to Lord Cecil, 1941. *Signed.* 51193, f. 247.

Ogilvy (Christine), *of the International Student Service.*
— Letter to Miss I. M. Butler from C. Ogilvy, 1936. *Signed.* 51174, f. 163.

O'Gorman (Mervyn Joseph Pius), *writer on aeronautics and traffic problems.*
— Correspondence between Lord Cecil and M. J. P. O'Gorman, 1936, 1937. Partly *signed.* 51174, ff. 167, 172; 51178, ff. 101, 129.

O'Grady (*Sir* James), *K.C.M.G.*
— Letter to J. O'Grady, 1913. *Draft.* 51160, f. 230.

Olden (Rudolf), *German lawyer and writer.*
— Correspondence between Lord Cecil and R. Olden, 1935. *Signed.* 51170, ff. 181, 185.

Oldham, *co. Lanc.*
— Message from Lord Cecil for Peace Week at Oldham, 1938. *Copy.* 51178, f. 183.

Oldham (Joseph Houldsworth), *Editor, The Christian News-Letter.*
— Correspondence between Lord Cecil and J. H. Oldham, 1942. *Signed.* 51188, ff. 152, 163.

Oliphant (*Sir* Lancelot), *K.C.M.G.*
— Correspondence between L. Oliphant and W. H. M. Selby, 1918. 51091, ff. 180, 180v; 51094, ff. 6, 6v, 58.
— Correspondence between Lord Cecil and Sir L. Oliphant, 1918, 1938. Partly *signed.* 51089, ff. 115-120; 51094, f. 58.

Oliver (Frederick Scott), *of Messrs. Debenham and Freebody; barrister and author.*
— Correspondence, partly on his behalf, with Lord Cecil, 1912-1918. Mostly *signed.* 51090, ff. 1-42v.

Oliver (George Harold), *M.P.*
— Letter to Lord Cecil, 1946. *Signed.* 51192, f. 257.

INDEX

Oliver (J. W.), *chaplain, Canadian Army.*
— Letter to Lord Cecil, 1943. 51190, f. 120.

Olivier (Sydney), *Baron Olivier.*
— Correspondence between Lord Cecil and Lord Olivier, 1935. 51171, ff. 12, 24.

Olson (Margaret), *Sec., Commission to Study the Organisation of Peace, New York.*
— Letters, etc., to Lord Cecil from M. Olson, 1941. *Signed.* 51187, ff. 212, 247.

Olsson (H. William), *of the B.B.C.*
— Correspondence between Lord Cecil and H. W. Olsson, 1941. *Signed.* 51193, ff. 256, 257.

O'Malley (*Sir* Owen St. Clair), *K.C.M.G.; diplomatist.*
— Letter to Lord Cecil from O. St. C. O'Malley, 1936. *Signed.* 51173, f. 45.

O'Moloney (William), *of the Union Internationale des Associations pour la Société des Nations.*
— Correspondence between Lord Cecil and W. O'Moloney, 1923. *Signed.* 51096, f. 102; 51163, f. 183.

O'Neill (*Sir* Con Douglas Walker), *G.C.M.G.*
— Letter to C. D. W. O'Neill from Miss E. V. Lazarus, 1948. *Copy.* 51192, f. 288.

O'Neill (Denis), *of the Ministry of Transport.*
— Correspondence between Lord Cecil and D. O'Neill, 1941. *Signed.* 51187, ff. 194, 197.

Onslow (Richard William Alan), *5th Earl of Onslow.*
— Correspondence between Lord Cecil and Lord Onslow, 1926, 1927. Partly *signed.* 51099, ff. 15, 35; 51164, f. 150.

Opočensky (Jan), *of the Czech Ministry of Foreign Affairs in London.*
— Letters to Lord Cecil, 1944. *Signed.* 51193, ff. 291, 292.

Ormerod (*Mrs* Mary), *of the International Committee for Assistance of German Refugee Professional Workers.*
— Letters to Miss I. M. Butler from Mrs M. Ormerod, 1933, 1938. Partly *signed.* 51168, f. 97; 51180, f. 44.
— Correspondence between Lord Cecil and Mrs M. Ormerod, 1938, 1939. 51180, ff. 63, 84, 140; 51184, ff. 5-8.

Ormsby-Gore (William George Arthur), *4th Baron Harlech.*
— Correspondence between Lord Cecil and W. G. A. Ormsby-Gore, 1921-[1926?]. *Signed.* 51095, f. 30; 51097, ff. 17, 161, 172; 51098, f. 151; 51163, f. 21.

Osborne (Irma), *wife of John, 11th Duke of Leeds.*
— Telegram to Lord Cecil from Duchess of Leeds, 1941. 51188, f. 19.

Osborne (John Francis Godolphin), *11th Duke of Leeds.*
— Letter from Lord Cecil to Duke of Leeds, 1941. *Copy.* 51188, f. 93.

Osborne (W[alter?] V.), *Assistant Sec., The British Constitution Association.*
— Letter to Lord Wolmer from W. V. Osborne, 1913. *Signed.* 51161, f. 20.

Oslo, *in Norway.*
— Menu for dinner in honour of Lord Cecil at Oslo, 1938. *Printed.* 51180, f. 14.

Oslo, *Norden Association.*
— Correspondence with Lord Cecil, 1936-1938. 51179, f. 57; 51193, ff. 73, 111, 112.

Osuský (*Dr.* Štéfán), *Czech diplomatist.*
— Correspondence between Lord Cecil and Dr. S. Osuský, 1935, 1944. Partly *signed.* 51171, ff. 205, 206, 228; 51191, f. 191.

Oswestry, *co. Salop.*
— Message from Lord Cecil for Peace Week at Oswestry, [1938?]. *Copy.* 51182, f. 124.

Ovey (*Sir* Esmond), *G.C.M.G.*
— Letter to Sir W. G. Max-Muller from E. Ovey on behalf of Lord Curzon, 1923. *Copy.* 51096, f. 17.

Owen (John), *Bishop of St. Davids.*
— Letter to Lord Cecil from the Bishop of St. Davids, 1911. 51160, f. 37.

Oxford, *University of.*
— Papers rel. to proposed nomination of J. A. Salter as Representative of Oxford University, 1936. *Printed.* 51174, ff. 38-43.

Oxford and Asquith, *1st Earl of.*
— *v.* Asquith (Herbert Henry).

Oxford and Asquith, *Countess of.*
— *v.* Asquith (Emma Alice Margaret).

P

Page (Ernest), *K.C.*
— Letter to Lord Cecil from E. Page, 1912. 51160, f. 82.

Page (Walter Hines), *U.S. diplomatist.*
— Correspondence between Lord Cecil and W. H. Page, 1917, 1918. 51093, f. 83; 51162, ff. 9, 11.

Paget (Almeric Hugh), *Baron Queenborough.*
— Correspondence between Lord Cecil and Lord Queenborough, 1928, n.d. Mostly *signed.* 51166, ff. 38-48; 51192, f. 321.

Paish (*Sir* George).
— Correspondence with Lord Cecil, 1937, 1944. 51177, f. 193; 51191, ff. 55-57v, 208.

Pakenham (Francis Aungier), *7th Earl of Longford.*
— Correspondence between Lord Cecil and F. A. Pakenham, 1947. 51192, ff. 278, 279.

Palmer (Beatrix Maud), *wife of William, 2nd Earl of Selborne.*
— Correspondence between Lord Cecil and his sister Lady Selborne, 1909-1945. 51157, f. 124-174.

Palmer (Francis Beaufort-).
— *v.* Beaufort-Palmer (Francis).

Palmer (Gerald E. H.), *of the Royal Institute of International Affairs.*
— Correspondence between Lord Cecil and G. E. H. Palmer, 1933. Mostly *signed.* 51168, ff. 17-85 *passim.*

Palmer (John Leslie), *writer; League of Nations official.*
— Letter to J. L. Palmer from F. P. Walters, 1919. *Copy.* 51114, f. 1.
— Correspondence between Lord Cecil and J. L. Palmer, 1922-1934. *Signed.* 51095, ff. 104-108; 51096, ff. 20, 75, 81; 51101, ff. 134, 135.

Palmer (Roundell Cecil), *Viscount Wolmer; 3rd Earl of Selborne, 1942.*
— Letter to Lord Wolmer from W. V. Osborne, 1913. *Signed.* 51161, f. 20.
— Correspondence, including telegram, between Lord Cecil and Lord Wolmer, 1913-1942. *Signed.* 51161, ff. 1-11; 51166, f. 90; 51177, ff. 131, 138, 143; 51188, ff. 206, 212, 246, 310, 377; 51189, ff. 7, 24-27v, 30, 51.

INDEX

Palmer (William Jocelyn), *son of William, 2nd Earl of Selborne.*
— Correspondence between Lord Cecil and his nephew, W. J. Palmer, 1941. 51187, ff. 229, 242.

Palmer (William Waldegrave), *2nd Earl of Selborne.*
— Correspondence between Lord Cecil and his brother-in-law, Lord Selborne, 1909-1937. Partly *signed.* 51157, ff. 66-123.

Palmstierna (*Baron* Erik Kule), *Swedish diplomatist.*
— Correspondence between Lord Cecil and Baron E. K. Palmstierna, 1933-1936. *Signed.* Partly *Fr.* 51101, ff. 98, 99, 107, 108; 51173, f. 72.

Pange (*Comtesse* Pauline Laure Marie de), *author.*
— Correspondence between Lord Cecil and Comtesse P. L. M. de Pange, 1936. *Fr.* 51172, ff. 12, 32.

Pankhurst (Christabel Harriette), *suffragette.*
— Letters to Lord Cecil from C. H. Pankhurst, 1907. 51158, ff. 93, 109.

Pankhurst (Estelle Sylvia), *suffragette and author.*
— Correspondence between Lord Cecil and E. S. Pankhurst, 1936-1943. *Signed.* 51174, ff. 52, 60; 51185, ff. 7, 13, 48-50; 51188, ff. 97-100, 144, 156; 51189, ff. 265-266v.

Paravicini (Charles Rodolphe), *Swiss diplomatist.*
— Letter to Lord Cecil from C. R. Paravicini, 1935. *Signed.* 51170, f. 188.

Paris.
— Memoranda rel. to visits by Lord Davies to Paris and Switzerland, 1939. *Copies.* 51184, ff. 217-228, 229-233.

Parkes (Charles W.), *of Bristol.*
— Correspondence between Lord Cecil and C. W. Parkes, 1935. 51170, ff. 145, 149.

Parliament, *of England.*
— Memorandum, legal opinions, etc., rel. to the Appropriation Act, 1907. *Copies.* 51074, ff. 1-171v.
— Reply by Lord Lucan to Parliamentary Question of Lord Cecil rel. to German refugees, 1933. *Signed.* 51168, f. 87.
— Reply by Lord Stanhope to Parliamentary Question of Lord Cecil rel. to trade mission to Japan, 1934. 51169, f. 227.
— Reply by Lord Stanhope to Parliamentary Question of Lord Cecil rel. to trade in arms, 1935. Partly *printed. Signed.* 51170, ff. 82-84.
— Question by Lord Cecil rel. to trade in arms, 1935. *Copy.* 51170, f. 109.
— Questions by Lord Cecil rel. to motoring offences, 1936. *Copies.* 51173, ff. 179, 220.
— Reply by Lord Swinton to Parliamentary Question of Lord Cecil rel. to Royal Commission under presidency of Sir J. E. Banks, 1936. *Signed.* 51174, f. 231.
— Amendments by Lord Cecil to Marriage Bill, 1937. *Copies.* 51176, ff. 68, 163.
— Question by Lord Cecil rel. to possible Government action concerning refugees at the League of Nations Assembly, 1937. *Copy.* 51176, f. 156.
— Reply by Lord Erne to Parliamentary Question of Lord Cecil rel. to Western Avenue at Acton, 1938. *Signed.* 51180, f. 166.
— Reply by Lord Munster to Parliamentary Question of Lord Cecil rel. to refugees, 1938. *Signed.* 51182, f. 117.
— Question by Lord Cecil rel. to Ethiopia, 1939. *Copy.* 51183, f. 159.

Parliament, *of England.*
continuation
— Reply by Lord Dufferin and Ava to Parliamentary Question of Lord Cecil rel. to Ethiopia, 1939. *Signed.* 51183, f. 179.
— Question by Lord Cecil rel. to telephone service, 1941. *Copy.* 51187, f. 374.
— Question by Lord Cecil rel. to speech of Mr Sumner Wells, 1941. *Copy.* 51187, f. 375.
— Declaration rel. to Christian Education by members of both Houses of Parliament, 1941. *Printed.* 51187, ff. 383-385.
— Reply by Lord Snell to Parliamentary Question of Lord Cecil rel. to telephone service, 1941. *Signed.* 51187, ff. 392, 393.
— Reply by Lord Moyne to Parliamentary Question of Lord Cecil rel. to speech of Mr Sumner Wells, 1941. *Signed.* 51187, f. 398.
— Letter to Lord Beaverbrook from the Watching Committee of Parliament, 1941-1942. *Draft. Printed.* 51188, f. 241*.
— Question by Lord Cecil rel. to case at Liverpool Assizes, 1942. 51188, ff. 242, 243.
— Motion on the liability of the Crown in torts by Lord Cecil, 1942. *Draft.* 51188, f. 248.
— Reply by Lord Sherwood to Parliamentary Question of Lord Cecil rel. to case of Aircraftsman Swanson, 1942. *Signed.* 51188, f. 275.
— Question by Lord Cecil rel. to case of H. S. L. Knight, 1942. *Copy.* 51189, f. 58.
— Question by Lord Cecil rel. to Draft Agreement on Post-War Rehabilitation, 1943. *Copy.* 51190, f. 161.
— Amendments by Lord Cecil to Education and Rural Water Supplies and Sewerage Bills, 1944. *Copy.* 51191, f. 118.
— Question by Lord Cecil rel. to commercial buildings close to Durham Cathedral, 1944. *Copy.* 51191, f. 141.
— Question by Lord Cecil rel. to plans for new international organisation, 1945. *Copy.* 51192, f. 102.

Parmoor, *1st Baron.*
— *v.* Cripps (Charles Alfred).

Parnell (*Miss* Nancy Stewart), *of the League of Nations Union.*
— Letter to Miss I. M. Butler from Miss N. S. Parnell, 1940. *Signed.* 51184, f. 314.
— Correspondence between Lord Cecil and Miss N. S. Parnell, 1940. Partly *printed.* 51185, ff. 145, 165.

Parry (L. A.), *physician, of Hove.*
— Letters from Lord Cecil to L. A. Parry, 1937. *Copies.* 51177, ff. 157, 170.

Parsons (Alice T. L.), *wife of Edgerton Parsons; of the National Committee on the Cause and Cure of War, New York.*
— Letter to Lord Cecil from A. T. L. Parsons, 1937. *Signed.* 51178, f. 34.

Partington (C. F.), *produce broker.*
— Letters, etc., to Lord Cecil from C. F. Partington, 1909, 1914. 51159, f. 255; 51161, ff. 117-122.

Pascall (Sydney W.), *Chairman, Convention Committee, Rotary International.*
— Letters to Lord Cecil from S. W. Pascall, 1931. *Signed.* 51167, ff. 45-47.

Paskin (*Sir* Jesse John), *K.C.M.G.*
— Letter, etc., to E. C. Henty, 1926. *Signed.* 51098, ff. 70-71v.

Passfield, *Baron.*
— *v.* Webb (Sidney James).

Paterson (Graeme M.).
— Letter to Lord Cecil, 1912. *Signed.* 51193, f. 1.

INDEX

Paterson (Robert J.), *of The Christian Science Monitor, London.*
— Letter to G. H. Locock from R. J. Paterson, 1916. *Signed.* 51092, f. 41.

Paton (Herbert James), *Professor of Moral Philosophy at Oxford.*
— Correspondence between Lord Cecil and H. J. Paton, 1939, 1940. 51184, ff. 65, 72; 51186, f. 66.

Paton (*Rev.* William), *D.D.; of the World Council of Churches.*
— Letter, etc., to Lord Cecil from Rev. W. Paton, 1940. *Signed.* 51186, ff. 94-96.

Patterson (Ernest Minor), *President of the American Academy of Political and Social Science.*
— Correspondence between Lord Cecil and E. M. Patterson, 1940. *Signed.* 51193, ff. 155, 161, 162, 164, 168-182.

Patterson (J. H.), *of the Cavalry Club.*
— Correspondence between Lord Cecil and J. H. Patterson, 1937. *Signed.* 51175, ff. 6, 11.

Paul-Boncour (Joseph), *French statesman.*
— Correspondence between Lord Cecil and J. Paul-Boncour, 1925-1940. *Signed.* Partly *Fr.* 51097, f. 210; 51099, ff. 3-5, 45, 47, 93, 97; 51174, ff. 208, 215; 51179, f. 79; 51180, ff. 95, 99; 51184, ff. 226, 299, 323.

Peace Pledge Union.
— *v.* Browne (Nancy).
— *v.* Walker (Roy).

Peake (Osbert), *M.P.*
— Correspondence, partly on his behalf, with Lord Cecil, 1940, 1941. *Signed.* 51185, ff. 283, 288; 51186, ff. 194, 221, 268, 285.

Pearson (R. Meynell), *dentist and author.*
— Correspondence between Lord Cecil and R. M. Pearson, 1935. 51170, ff. 162, 178.

Pearson (Weetman Dickinson), *1st Viscount Cowdray.*
— Letter from Lord Cecil to Lord Cowdray, 1921. *Copy.* 51163, f. 6.

Peart (George), *retired stonemason, of Wakefield.*
— Letter to Lord Cecil from G. Peart, 1912, 1913. 51160, ff. 195, 204, 268.

Peat (David A.), *of Ditchling.*
— Correspondence between Lord Cecil and D. A. Peat, 1937. Partly *signed.* 51175, ff. 72, 78, 79.

Pedestrians' Association.
— Memoranda and other papers rel. to the Pedestrians' Association, 1929-1943. *Copies.* Partly *printed.* 51153.
— Letter to Pedestrians' Association from Lord Sandhurst, 1938. *Signed.* 51178, f. 164.
— *v. also* Dean (J. S.).
— *v. also* Foley (Thomas C.).
— *v. also* Hyman (Leonard).
— *v. also* Thomas (H. Wynne).

Pedestrians' League.
— *v.* Turle (Aubrey).

Peel (Arthur George Villiers), *2nd son of Arthur, 1st Viscount Peel.*
— Letters to Lord Cecil from A. G. V. Peel, 1941, 1947. *Signed.* 51187, f. 46; 51192, f. 258.

Peel (*Sir* Sidney Cornwallis), *Bart.*
— Letter to Lord Cecil from S. C. Peel, 1913. 51160, f. 263.
— Correspondence between S. C. Peel and W. H. M. Selby, 1918. 51091, f. 200.

Peet (Hubert William), *Editor of The Friend.*
— Correspondence between Lord Cecil and H. W. Peet, 1935. *Signed.* 51170, ff. 91, 94.

Pelletier (Hector Rooney), *of the Canadian Broadcasting Corporation.*
— Letter to Lord Cecil, 1942. *Signed.* 51193, f. 263.

Pelletier (Hector Rooney), *of the Canadian Broadcasting Corporation. continuation*
— Correspondence between H. R. Pelletier and Miss I. M. Butler, 1942. *Signed.* 51193, ff. 267-270.

Percy (Eustace), *Baron Percy of Newcastle.*
— Letters to Lord Cecil from E. Percy, [1918?], 1922. Partly *copy.* 51093, f. 174; 51163, f. 59.

Percy (*Lord* Henry Algernon George), *M.P.*
— Letter to Lord Cecil from Lord H. A. G. Percy, 1905. 51158, f. 28.

Perry (Ellen C.), *Sec., Conservative and Unionist Women's Franchise Association, Irish Branch.*
— Letter to Lord Cecil from E. C. Perry, 1912. 51160, f. 121.

Perth, *16th Earl of.*
— *v.* Drummond (James Eric).

Perth, *Countess of.*
— *v.* Drummond (Angela).

Peterson (A. W.), *of the Home Office.*
— Letter to Lord Cecil from A. W. Peterson, 1942. *Signed.* 51189, f. 174.
— Letter to A. W. Peterson from Miss I. M. Butler, 1942. *Copy.* 51189, f. 228.

Peterson (Edward Whittred Iltyd), *solicitor.*
— Letters to Lord Cecil from E. W. I. Peterson, 1906. *Signed.* 51158, ff. 86-90.

Peterson (*Sir* Maurice Drummond), *G.C.M.G.*
— Correspondence, etc., between Lord Cecil and Sir M. D. Peterson, 1932-1943. *Signed.* Partly *printed.* 51091, ff. 1-144v.

Pethick-Lawrence (Emmeline), *wife of F. W. Pethick-Lawrence, Baron Pethick-Lawrence.*
— Correspondence between Lord Cecil and E. Pethick-Lawrence, 1943. *Signed.* 51190, ff. 173, 178.

Peto (*Sir* Basil Edward), *1st Bart.*
— Letter to Lord Cecil from B. E. Peto, 1915. *Signed.* 51161, f. 210.

Petty-FitzMaurice (Henry Charles Keith), *5th Marquess of Lansdowne.*
— Letters to Lord Cecil from Lord Lansdowne, 1907-1922. Partly *signed.* Partly *copy.* 51158, f. 114; 51159, f. 219; 51161, ff. 18, 88, 112, 172; 51163, f. 62.
— Letter to the Editor of 'The Daily Telegraph' from Lord Lansdowne, 1917. *Copy.* 51093, f. 46.

Phelan (Edward Joseph), *of the International Labour Office.*
— Correspondence, partly on his behalf, with Lord Cecil, 1936-1942. Partly *signed.* 51173, ff. 75, 90, 91, 96, 97; 51188, f. 90; 51189, f. 184.

Philip, *Prince; Duke of Edinburgh.*
— *v.* England.

Phillimore (Walter George Frank), *1st Baron Phillimore.*
— Correspondence between Lord Cecil and Lord Phillimore, 1920-1922. *Signed.* 51095, ff. 1, 11, 122, 125.
— Letter to Lord Phillimore from Sir A. G. M. Cadogan, 1924. *Copy.* 51096, f. 155.
— Letter to Lord Phillimore from Lord Parmoor, 1924. *Copy.* 51097, f. 16.
— Memorandum by Lord Cecil rel. to conversation with Lord Phillimore, 1924. 51097, ff. 55-58.

Phillips (A. Gwyn), *organiser of relief in Spain.*
— Correspondence between Lord Cecil and A. G. Phillips, 1936-1939. 51174, f. 145; 51179, ff. 12, 27, 41; 51182, ff. 176, 184.

INDEX

Phillips (*Mrs* Dorothy Una McGrigor), *of Temple Sowerby Manor.*
— Correspondence between Lord Cecil and Mrs D. U. McG. Phillips, 1937. 51175, ff. 146, 172.

Phillips (John Searles Ragland), *journalist.*
— Letters to Lord Cecil from J. S. R. Phillips, 1908, 1913. Partly *signed.* 51158, f. 187; 51160, f. 237.

Phillips (*Mrs* Mary F.), *of Middleton, co. Lancs.*
— Correspondence between Lord Cecil and Mrs M. F. Phillips, 1938. 51181, ff. 110-113.

Phipps (*Sir* Eric Clare Edmund), *P.C.; G.C.B.*
— Correspondence between Lord Cecil and Sir E. C. E. Phipps, 1931. *Signed.* 51100, ff. 128, 128*.

Pichon (Stephen Jean Marie), *French diplomatist.*
— Memoranda by Lord Cecil rel. to conversation with S. J. M. Pichon, 1918. 51094, ff. 92, 97-99, 101, 104, 135.
— Letter from Lord Cecil to S. J. M. Pichon, 1918. *Draft.* 51094, f. 93.

Pickard (*Lt.-Col.* Jocelyn Arthur Adair), *General Sec., The Royal Society for the Prevention of Accidents.*
— Correspondence between Lord Cecil and Lt.-Col. J. A. A. Pickard, 1941. *Signed.* 51188, ff. 50-54, 64.

Picton-Turbervill (Edith), *O.B.E.; author; former M.P.*
— Correspondence between Lord Cecil and E. Picton-Turbervill, 1944. 51191, ff. 128, 133.

Picture Post.
— Note rel. to fee paid to Lord Cecil for published contribution to 'Picture Post', 1940. Partly *printed.* 51193, f. 201.

Pierlot (Hubert), *Belgian politician.*
— Correspondence between Lord Cecil and H. Pierlot, 1942. *Signed.* 51188, ff. 190, 198.

Pierrefeu (*Countess* Alain Dedons de).
— Correspondence between Lord Cecil and Countess A. D. de Pierrefeu, 1937. 51175, ff. 19-24, 34.

Pinsent ([Gerald Hume Saverie]), *[C.B.; of the Treasury?].*
— Letters to Lord Cecil from [G. H. S.?] Pinsent, 1931. *Signed.* 51100, ff. 93-96.
— Memorandum by Lord Cecil rel. to interview with [G. H. S.?] Pinsent, 1931. 51100, f. 99.

Plaistowe (Cuthbert), *Sec., Labour Co-Partnership Association.*
— Correspondence between Lord Cecil and C. Plaistowe, 1925-1927. *Signed.* 51164, ff. 74, 75, 148; 51165, ff. 101-112.

Platt (*Sir* Thomas) afterw. **Comyn-Platt.**
— Letter to Lord Cecil from T. Platt, 1911. *Signed.* 51160, f. 44.

Platt (Wilfrid), *writing from London, SE 27.*
— Correspondence between Lord Cecil and W. Platt, 1935. 51170, ff. 92, 98; 51171, ff. 214, 215.

Plaud (René), *President, Communauté Universelle de la Jeunesse pour la Paix, Paris.*
— Correspondence between Lord Cecil and R. Plaud, 1936. *Signed. Fr.* 51173, ff. 23, 39.

Plewman (W. R.), *of The Toronto Star.*
— Correspondence between Lord Cecil and W. R. Plewman, 1943. Partly *signed.* 51189, ff. 255, 282; 51190, ff. 58-61.

Plunkett (*Sir* Horace Curzon), *K.C.V.O.*
— Letter to Lord Cecil from Sir H. C. Plunkett, 1914. 51161, f. 93.

Plymouth, *2nd Earl of.*
— *v.* Windsor-Clive (Ivor Miles).
Poetry. *ENGLISH.*
— 'Ulster's Defence' by J. T., 1892. *Printed.* 51161, f. 200.
Poincaré (Raymond), *French statesman.*
— Memorandum by Lord Cecil rel. to interview with R. Poincaré, 1922. *Draft.* 51095, ff. 94-96.
Polak (Alfred Laurence), *solicitor.*
— Correspondence, etc., with Lord Cecil, 1944, 1945. *Signed.* 51191, ff. 261-263v, 290; 51192, ff. 44, 55, 59.
Poland.
— Memorandum by Sir B. H. L. Hart rel. to Poland, 1939. *Copy.* 51183, ff. 216-224.
Poland (—), *of the Belgian Relief Committee.*
— Memoranda rel. to conversations with — Poland, 1918. *Copies.* 51093, ff. 193-194.
Politis (Nicolas Socrate), *Greek statesman.*
— Letter to Sir J. Stavridi from N. S. Politis, 1932. *Signed.* 51101, f. 35.
Polk (Frank L.), *Under-Sec. of State in U.S.A.*
— Telegram to Lord Cecil from F. L. Polk, 1923. 51095, f. 133.
Pollard (C. A.), *of Doubleday, Doran & Co., New York.*
— Letter to Lord Cecil, 1943. *Signed.* 51190, f. 304.
Pollock (*Sir* Frederick), *1st Bart.; K.C.*
— Correspondence between Lord Cecil and Sir F. Pollock, 1935. 51170, ff. 148, 150.
Pollok-M'Call (*Brig.-Gen.* John Buchanan).
— Letter to Lord Cecil from Brig.-Gen. J. B. Pollok-M'Call, 1941. 51186, f. 281; 51187, f. 63.

Polwarth, *9th Baron.*
— *v.* Hepburne-Scott (Walter George).
Pomeroy (Ernest Arthur George), *7th Viscount Harberton.*
— Letter to Lord Cecil from Lord Harberton, 1912. 51160, f. 149.
Ponsonby (Arthur Augustus Harry), *1st Baron Ponsonby.*
— Correspondence between Lord Cecil and Lord Ponsonby, 1930, 1934. *Signed.* 51167, ff. 23, 24; 51169, ff. 74, 76, 79-83, 122, 126.
Ponsonby (*Sir* Charles Edward), *1st Bart.; M.P.*
— Letters to Lord Cecil from C. E. Ponsonby, 1942, 1945. *Partly printed.* 51188, f. 287; 51192, ff. 191, 203, 205, 206.
Ponsonby (*Maj.-Gen. Sir* John), *K.C.B.*
— Letter to Lord Cecil, 1944. 51191, f. 207.
Ponsonby (Vere Brabazon), *9th Earl of Bessborough.*
— Correspondence, including telegrams, between Lord Cecil and Lord Bessborough, 1933. 51168, ff. 63, 64, 68, 71.
Poole (Norman H.), *Sec., British Universities League of Nations Society.*
— Letter from Lord Cecil to N. H. Poole, 1934. *Copy.* 51169, f. 178.
Porter (*Sir* John Scott Horsbrugh-).
— *v.* Horsbrugh-Porter (*Sir* John Scott).
Portland, *9th Duke of.*
— *v.* Cavendish-Bentinck (Victor Frederick William).
Pouderoux (*Gen.* —), *Treasurer of the International Peace Campaign, Paris.*
— Letter to Lord Cecil from Gen. — Pouderoux, 1936. *Signed. Fr.* 51172, f. 113.
Powell (Robert Stephenson Baden-).
— *v.* Baden-Powell (Robert Stephenson).

Power (*Sir* Ivan McLannahan Cecil), *2nd Bart.*
— Letter to Lord Cecil, 1945. 51192, f. 121.

Power (*Sir* John Cecil), *1st Bart.*
— Correspondence between Lord Cecil and Sir J. C. Power, 1935, 1938. *Signed.* 51171, ff. 157, 159-161; 51182, f. 34.

Poynton (Arthur Blackburne), *Senior Fellow of University College, Oxford.*
— Correspondence between Lord Cecil and A. B. Poynton, 1923. 51163, ff. 121, 125, 126.

Pratt (*Sir* John William).
— Correspondence between Lord Cecil and Sir J. W. Pratt, 1936. 51174, ff. 83, 90.

Prescott (Ernest Fare), *of Wimbledon.*
— Letter to Lord Cecil from E. F. Prescott on behalf of H. S. L. Knight, 1942. *Signed.* 51189, f. 76.
— Memorandum by Lord Cecil rel. to interview with E. F. Prescott, 1942. *Signed.* 51189, f. 143.

Prescott (L. C.), *of the Ministry of Health.*
— Letter to Miss E. V. Lazarus from L. C. Prescott, 1945. *Signed.* 51192, ff. 72-74.

Prevost (H. W. Le).
— *v.* Le Prevost (H. W.).

Priestley (*Sir* Raymond Edward), *Vice-Chancellor, Birmingham University.*
— Correspondence between Lord Cecil and R. E. Priestly, 1940, 1942. *Signed.* 51185, ff. 222, 225, 226; 51188, ff. 289, 299, 329.

Primrose League.
— *v.* Bennett (*Sir* Reginald).

Pringle (A. S.), *of the National Unionist Association.*
— Correspondence between Lord Cecil and A. S. Pringle, 1914. *Signed.* 51161, ff. 108, 116.

Pringsheim (Louise), *refugee(?); writing from Brentford.*
— Letter to Lord Cecil, 1940. 51185, f. 84.

Printed Matter.
— 'Ulster's Defence' by J. T., 1892. *Printed.* 51161, f. 200.
— Leaflet, 'Votes for Women' by the Women's Social and Political Union, 1907. *Printed.* 51158, f. 95.
— Publication no. 42, 'League of Nations Scheme of Organisation' by the League of Nations Society, 1918. *Printed.* 51162, ff. 38-53v.
— Notice of public meeting to be addressed by Lord Cecil at Hitchin, 1918. *Printed.* 51162, f. 59.
— Leaflet no. 5, 'Who We Are and What We Want' by the National Federation of Discharged and Demobilised Sailors and Soldiers, 1918. *Printed.* 51162, f. 63.
— Address by Lord Cecil, 'To the Electors of North Herts', 1918. *Printed.* 51162, f. 73.
— Memorandum, 'The Foreign Policy of His Majesty's Government in the United Kingdom' by the Foreign Office, 1931. *Printed.* 51089, ff. 58-82.
— Ballot form "Peace or War" issued by 'The Ilford Recorder', 1934. *Printed.* 51169, f. 39.
— 'A Personal Message' to members of the League of Nations Union by G. G. A. Murray, 1934. *Printed.* 51169, f. 71.
— 'Liberty and Democratic Leadership' by A. Barratt Brown, etc., 1934. *Printed.* 51169, ff. 117-120v.
— 'Preliminary report on the Conference for the Reduction and Limitations of Armaments at Geneva (1932-1934)' by A. Henderson, 1936. *Printed. Imperf.* 51122.

Printed Matter. *continuation*
— Notice of demonstration, 'Act for Spain' by the Left Wing Book Club, etc., 1937. *Printed.* 51178, f. 165.
— Notice of protest meeting rel. to Abyssinia, 1938. *Printed.* 51179, f. 199.
— Menu for dinner in honour of Lord Cecil at Oslo, 1938. *Printed.* 51180, f. 14.
— 'The Spirit of Czechoslovakia', no. 1, 1939. *Printed.* 51184, ff. 321-322v.
— News-Letter Supplement No. 263 by W. S. R. King-Hall, 1941. *Printed.* 51188, f. 133.
— 'Federal Union News', no. 88, 1942. *Printed.* 51188, ff. 361-370v.
— Article, "The Children of Germany and Permanent Peace", by F. S. Churchill, reprinted from 'Cape Cod Standard-Times', 1943. *Printed.* 51190, ff. 195-199v.
— The British Way and Purpose booklet 18, 'Today and Tomorrow. Britain and the Peace' by W. Arnold-Forster, 1944. *Printed.* 51140, ff. 144-163v.
— "The Japanese Islands: Annexation or Trusteeship", by H. Gilchrist. Reprinted from 'Foreign Affairs', 1944. *Printed,* with MS. additions. 51191, ff. 146-151v.
— Labour Party booklet, 'The United Nations Charter Examined' by W. Arnold-Forster, 1946. *Printed.* 51140, ff. 177-202v.

Pritchard (*Sir* Harry Goring), *solicitor.*
— Correspondence between Lord Cecil and Sir H. G. Pritchard, 1937. *Signed.* 51175, ff. 87, 99, 101.

Pritchard (W. T.), *Treasurer, League of Nations Union, London Regional Federation.*
— Letter, etc., to Lord Cecil from W. T. Pritchard, 1934. *Signed.* 51169, f. 70.

Privat (Edmond), *Esperantist; afterw. Professor at Neuchatel.*
— Correspondence between Lord Cecil and E. Privat, 1922, 1937. 51095, ff. 109, 120; 51178, ff. 115, 130.

Privy Council.
— Documents rel. to Lord Cecil's appointment as Privy Councillor, 1915. *Printed,* with MS. additions. 51161, ff. 250, 251.
— Summons to the Privy Council, 1936. Partly *printed.* 51172, f. 15.
— *v. also* Fitzroy (*Sir* Almeric William).

Prochazka (Adolf), *Czech lawyer and politician.*
— Letters to Lord Cecil, 1943, 1944. *Signed.* 51190, f. 183; 51191, f. 214.

Proctor (*Col.* James), *C.B.E.*
— Letter from Lord Cecil to Col. J. Proctor, 1923. 51096, f. 67.

Prothero (*Sir* George Walter), *K.B.E.*
— Correspondence between Lord Cecil and G. W. Prothero, 1918. *Signed.* 51094, ff. 69, 128-134.

Prothero (Rowland Edmund), *Baron Ernle.*
— Correspondence between Lord Cecil and R. E. Prothero, 1918. 51094, ff. 67-69, 71.

Pryse (*Capt.* Gerald Spencer-).
— *v.* Spencer-Pryse (*Capt.* Gerald).

Pye (*Miss* E. M.).
— Memorandum by Lord Cecil rel. to conversation with Miss E. M. Pye, 1942. *Copy.* 51188, f. 245.

Pye (Edith Mary), *writer.*
— Correspondence between Lord Cecil and E. M. Pye, 1931. *Signed.* 51167, ff. 160, 164.

Q

Queenborough, *Baron.*
— *v.* Paget (Almeric Hugh).
Quesne (Charles Thomas Le).
— *v.* Le Quesne (Charles Thomas).
Quickswood, *Baron.*
— *v.* Gascoyne-Cecil (Hugh Richard Heathcote).
Quinones de León (José Maria), *Spanish diplomatist.*
— Letter from Lord Cecil to J. M. Quinones de León, 1925. *Copy.* 51097, f. 188.
— Memoranda by Lord Cecil rel. to conversation with J. M. Quinones de León, 1926. 51098, f. 9.
Quo Tai-chi, *Chinese diplomatist.*
— Letter to President Beneš from Quo Tai-chi, 1934. *Copy.* 51101, f. 153.
— Correspondence between Lord Cecil and Quo Tai-chi, 1934-1943. Partly *signed.* 51101, ff. 173-188; 51169, ff. 41, 42; 51172, ff. 27, 31; 51173, ff. 103, 117; 51178, f. 134; 51179, ff. 161-166, 176, 190; 51180, f. 136; 51182, ff. 26, 43; 51183, ff. 118, 121, 123, 126, 206-208; 51189, f. 243; 51190, f. 90.

R

Radev (Simeon), *Bulgarian diplomatist.*
— Correspondence between Lord Cecil and S. Radev, 1936. *Signed.* 51172, ff. 158, 175.
Raemaekers (Louis), *Dutch cartoonist and artist.*
— Correspondence between Lord Cecil and L. Raemaekers, 1927-1931. Partly *signed.* 51165, ff. 173, 174; 51166, ff. 7-12; 51167, ff. 54-57.
Rafferty (Frank Walter), *Recorder of High Wycombe.*
— Correspondence between Lord Cecil and F. W. Rafferty, 1943-1945. *Signed.* 51190, ff. 313, 317, 321; 51191, f. 110; 51192, ff. 126, 137.
Railing (*Mrs* Clare), *of the Women's Voluntary Service for Civil Defence.*
— Correspondence between Lord Cecil and Mrs C. Railing, 1940. 51185, ff. 260, 261.
'Raimond, C. E.', *pseudonym.*
— *v.* Robins (Elizabeth).
Raine ([G?] E.), *of Constitutional Press Services.*
— Letters to Lord Cecil, 1912. *Signed.* 51160, ff. 91, 100, 107.
Rajchman (Ludwik), *Polish physician.*
— Memorandum by Lord Cecil rel. to conversation with L. Rajchman, 1930. 51100, f. 15.
Ramsey (*Mrs* Irene S.), *Sec., Industrial Co-Partnership Association.*
— Correspondence between Lord Cecil and Mrs I. S. Ramsey, 1943-1945. *Signed.* 51190, f. 349; 51191, ff. 169, 256; 51192, ff. 21, 42, 87, 90.

Randle (*Miss* Maud), *pianist.*
— Correspondence between Lord Cecil and Miss M. Randle, 1938. 51179, ff. 20, 25.

Ranger (Pierre), *official of the Wartime Information Board, Ottawa.*
— Correspondence, etc., between Lord Cecil and P. Ranger, 1945. *Signed.* Partly *Fr.* 51192, ff. 23-34, 49, 60-63.

Rankeillour, *1st Baron.*
— *v.* Hope (James Fitzalan).

Rankin (Andrew), *Q.C.*
— Correspondence between Lord Cecil and A. Rankin, 1945, 1946. Partly *signed.* 51192, ff. 225, 228, 230.

Ransome (Patrick), *of Federal Union.*
— Correspondence between Lord Cecil and P. Ransome, 1939, 1940. *Signed.* 51184, ff. 250, 341; 51185, ff. 1, 19, 23.

Rappard (William Emmanuel), *Swiss historian and economist.*
— Correspondence between Lord Cecil and W. E. Rappard, 1924-1945. *Signed.* 51097, ff. 93, 99; 51099, f. 96; 51186, f. 253; 51187, f. 416; 51188, ff. 40, 55; 51192, f. 161.

Rassemblement Universal pour la Paix.
— *v.* International Peace Campaign.

Rasta Fari *al.* **Haile Selassie.**
— *v.* Ethiopia.

Rathbone (Eleanor), *M.P.*
— Correspondence, including telegram, between Lord Cecil and E. Rathbone, 1913-1944. *Signed.* 51141, ff. 262-315.

Rault (Victor), *French representative at the League of Nations.*
— Letter from Lord Cecil to V. Rault, 1923. *Copy.* 51096, f. 127.

Reading, *1st Marquess of.*
— *v.* Isaacs (Rufus Daniel).

Reber (Samuel), *U.S. delegate to the League of Nations.*
— Telegram to S. Reber, 1932. *Copy.* 51101, f. 39.
— Correspondence between Lord Cecil and S. Reber, 1933, 1937. 51101, f. 42; 51176, f. 143.

Redding (H. R.), *General Sec., Australian Natives Association.*
— Letter, etc., to Lord Cecil, 1944. *Signed.* 51191, ff. 152-155, 276.

Reeve (Alan), *artist.*
— Correspondence between A. Reeve and Miss I. M. Butler, 1939. 51182, ff. 178, 183.

Reeves (F. G.), *of Ludlow.*
— Letter to Lord Cecil, 1938. 51181, f. 136.

Reeves (Myra), *wife of F. G. Reeves.*
— Correspondence between Lord Cecil and M. Reeves, 1938. 51181, ff. 118, 127.

Reid (Escott), *Sec., Canadian Institute for International Affairs.*
— Letter to Lord Cecil on behalf of E. Reid, 1933. 51168, f. 102.

Reith (Charles), *writing from London W 11.*
— Letter to Lord Cecil, 1942. 51189, f. 14.

Reith (John Charles Walsham), *1st Baron Reith.*
— Correspondence between Lord Cecil and J. C. W. Reith, 1933-1936. *Signed.* 51168, ff. 25-28; 51170, ff. 38, 51, 56-65, 68, 234, 239; 51174, ff. 214, 219.

Remnant (James Farquharson), *1st Baron Remnant.*
— Letter to Lord Cecil, 1908. 51158, f. 245.

Rendel (*Sir* George William), *K.C.M.G.*
— Memorandum by Lord Cecil rel. to conversation with G. W. Rendel, 1931. 51100, f. 88.

Rennell, *Baron.*
— *v.* Rodd (James Rennell).

INDEX

Renthe-Fink (— von), *League of Nations official.*
— Letter, etc., to Lord Cecil, 1932. *Signed.* 51100, ff. 203-215; 51101, f. 6.

Réquin (Edouard), *French general.*
— Correspondence between Lord Cecil and E. Réquin, 1924-1929. Partly *Fr.* 51097, f. 84; 51098, f. 118; 51099, ff. 148-166, 171.
— Memorandum by Lord Cecil rel. to conversation with E. Réquin, 1926. 51098, f. 17.

Ressel (Léon), *Sec., The American Club of Paris.*
— Letter to Lord Cecil, 1936. *Signed.* 51173, f. 132.

Revesz (*Dr.* I.), *of the Co-operation Press Service, Geneva.*
— Correspondence between Lord Cecil and Dr. I. Revesz, 1936, 1937. *Signed.* 51172, f. 111; 51175, f. 47.

Reynolds (*Sir* Alfred), *of Welwyn.*
— Letter to Lord Cecil, 1918. *Signed.* 51162, f. 79.

Rhodes (Thomas), *writing from London SW 8.*
— Correspondence between Lord Cecil and T. Rhodes, 1937. *Signed.* 51176, ff. 53, 64.

Rice (Thomas Aubrey Spring-).
— *v.* Spring-Rice (Thomas Aubrey).

Richards (A. H.), *of Defence of Freedom and Peace, London.*
— Correspondence between Lord Cecil and A. H. Richards, 1937. Partly *signed.* 51175, ff. 136, 142, 145; 51176, ff. 57-61, 118-124.

Richardson (Herbert), *Editor of Our Flag.*
— Letter to Lord Cecil from H. Richardson, 1914. *Signed.* 51161, f. 85.

Richardson (W. L.), *of Sidmouth.*
— Correspondence between Lord Cecil and W. L. Richardson, 1940, 1941. *Signed.* 51186, ff. 206-214v, 251, 257, 267, 269, 294.

Richmond (*Adm. Sir* Herbert William), *K.C.B.*
— Correspondence between Lord Cecil and Rear-Adm. Sir H. W. Richmond, 1927. 51165, ff. 181, 187.

Riddell (George Allardice), *Baron Riddell.*
— Correspondence between Lord Cecil and Lord Riddell, 1929. *Signed.* 51166, ff. 116-122, 124-127, 129.

Rideal (*Sir* Eric Keightley), *Professor of Colloid Science, Cambridge.*
— Correspondence between Lord Cecil and E. K. Rideal, 1936. *Signed.* 51172, ff. 61, 79.

Ridley (Matthew White), *1st Viscount Ridley.*
— Letters to Lord Cecil, 1909. Partly *signed.* 51159, ff. 94, 142.

Ripka (*Dr.* Robert), *Czech journalist.*
— Correspondence, including telegram, between Lord Cecil and Dr. R. Ripka, 1937. 51193, ff. 92-94.

Ritchie (David F.), *formerly of the League of Nations Union staff.*
— Letter to Lord Cecil, 1939. *Signed.* 51183, f. 84.

Rivett-Carnac (Wilfrid Theodore), *writing from Kew.*
— Letter, etc., to Lord Cecil from W. T. Rivett-Carnac, 1923. 51163, ff. 153-163.

Rivis (*Maj.* R. G. L.), *R.A.S.C.*
— Correspondence between Lord Cecil and Maj. R. G. L. Rivis, 1945. 51192, ff. 75, 76, 81.

Roberts (Cecil Edric Mornington), *author.*
— Correspondence between Lord Cecil and C. E. M. Roberts, 1937. *Signed.* 51178, ff. 108, 111.

Roberts (Isaac), *writing from Brooklyn, New York.*
— Correspondence between Lord Cecil and I. Roberts, 1938. 51181, ff. 59, 93.

Roberts (*Sir* Walter St. Clair Howland), *K.C.M.G.*
— Correspondence, partly on his behalf, with Lord Cecil, 1925-1927. *Signed.* 51097, ff. 199-203; 51098, ff. 1, 32-38; 51099, ff. 16-24.
— Letter to E. C. Henty from W. St. C. H. Roberts, 1926. *Signed.* 51097, f. 126.
— Memorandum to Sir A. G. M. Cadogan (?) from W. St. C. H. Roberts, 1926. *Copy.* 51098, f. 42.

Roberts (Weldon), *of the Weldon Roberts Rubber Company, Newark, New Jersey.*
— Correspondence between Lord Cecil and W. Roberts, 1943. *Signed.* 51190, ff. 96, 200.

Roberts (Wilfrid Hubert Wace), *M.P.*
— Letter to Lady Gladstone from W. H. W. Roberts, 1937. *Signed.* 51175, f. 81.
— Correspondence between Lord Cecil and W. H. W. Roberts, 1937, 1939. *Signed.* 51176, ff. 66, 69, 72, 76; 51183, ff. 5, 15.

Robertson (*Sir* Benjamin), *K.C.M.G.*
— Letter to Sir B. Robertson from Maj. H. Barnes, 1922. *Copy.* 51163, f. 80.
— Letter from Lord Cecil to Sir B. Robertson, 1922. *Copy.* 51163, f. 82.

Robertson (*Sir* Charles Grant), *Vice Chancellor, Birmingham University.*
— Correspondence between Lord Cecil and Sir C. G. Robertson, 1933-1944. Partly *signed.* 51168, ff. 95, 96, 117; 51170, ff. 17, 74-76, 81; 51191, f. 181.

Robertson (L. Ker), *of the Glasgow Peace Week Committee.*
— Correspondence between Lord Cecil and L. K. Robertson, 1937. *Signed.* 51176, f. 115; 51177, ff. 6-12.

Robertson (*Sir* Malcolm Arnold), *G.C.M.G.*
— Correspondence between Lord Cecil and Sir M. A. Robertson, 1938, 1942. *Signed.* 51181, ff. 72, 77; 51189, f. 96.

Robertson (*Field-Marshal Sir* William Robert), *1st Bart.*
— Letter, etc., to Lord Cecil, 1917. Partly *printed.* 51093, ff. 21-39.

Robertson-Scott (John William).
— *v.* Scott (John William Robertson).

Robiette (N.), *retired Belgian professor.*
— Corrrespondence between Lord Cecil and N. Robiette, 1938. *Signed.* 51180, ff. 126, 130, 151, 158; 51181, f. 14.
— Memorandum by Lord Cecil rel. to conversation with N. Robiette, 1938. *Copy.* 51180, f. 129.

Robins (Elizabeth) *al.* 'C. E. Raimond'.
— Correspondence between Lord Cecil and C. E. Raimond, 1935-1940. Partly *signed.* 51171, f. 46; 51173, ff. 65, 76; 51175, ff. 88, 98, 112, 126; 51185, f. 273.

Robinson (Anne E.), *wife of N. L. Robinson; Sec., League of Nations Union, Darlington Branch.*
— Correspondence between Lord Cecil and A. E. Robinson, 1941. 51188, ff. 1-3, 35, 39.

Robinson (Geoffrey George) *afterw.* **Dawson.**
— *v.* Dawson (Geoffrey George).

Robinson (Roy), *Sub-Treasurer of the Inner Temple.*
— Correspondence between Lord Cecil and R. Robinson, 1945. Partly *printed.* Partly *signed.* 51192, ff. 104, 119, 120.

Robinson (Vandeleur), *author.*
— Letter to Lord Cecil, 1941. *Signed.* 51187, f. 143.

INDEX

Robson (A. O.), *Chairman, Christian Youth Committee for Peace, Sydney.*
— Correspondence between Lord Cecil and A. O. Robson, 1935. *Signed.* 51170, f. 151; 51171, f. 158; 51193, ff. 58-62.

Röchling (Hermann), *commercial counsellor.*
— Correspondence between Lord Cecil and H. Röchling, 1924. *Signed.* 51096, ff. 159, 170; 51097, ff. 88-92.

Rockefeller (John Davison), *philanthropist.*
— Letter to Lady Cecil from J. D. Rockefeller, 1925. 51164, f. 65.
— Correspondence between Lord Cecil and R. B. Fosdick, partly on behalf of J. D. Rockefeller, 1936-1938. *Signed.* 51173, f. 21; 51174, ff. 113, 166; 51175, f. 35; 51178, ff. 184-203.

Rockley, *1st Baron.*
— *v.* Cecil (Evelyn).

Rodd (James Rennell), *1st Baron Rennell.*
— Letters to Lord Hardinge from J. R. Rodd, 1917, 1918. 51093, ff. 56, 57 (extract), 58, 170.
— Correspondence between Lord Cecil and J. R. Rodd, 1917-1923. 51093, ff. 58, 89, 105, 122, 131, 134-146, 162; 51094, ff. 115, 119; 51096, ff. 76, 82; 51163, ff. 139, 144.
— Letter to P. J. Noel-Baker from J. R. Rodd, 1923. 51106, f. 78.
— Statement to Press on revision of Treaty of Versailles, 1931. *Copy.* 51167, f. 80.

Roey (*Card.* Joseph Ernest van), *Archbishop of Malines.*
— Correspondence between Lord Cecil and Card. J. E. van Roey, 1936. *Signed.* 51173, ff. 247, 261.

Rolin (Henri A.), *of L'Union Belge pour La Société des Nations.*
— Correspondence between P. J. Noel-Baker and H. A. Rolin, 1924. *Signed.* Partly *Fr.* 51106, ff. 169-171, 205.
— Correspondence between Lord Cecil and H. A. Rolin, 1942, 1943. Partly *Fr.* 51189, f. 157; 51190, ff. 73-75, 180-182v, 191.

Rolleston (Eliza), *widow of Sir J. F. L. Rolleston.*
— Correspondence between Lord Cecil and Lady Rolleston, 1938. 51179, ff. 83, 87.

Rolleston (*Sir* John Fowke Launcelot), *M.P.*
— Letter to Lord Cecil, 1912. 51160, f. 190.

Ronaldshay, *Earl of.*
— *v.* Dundas (Lawrence John Lumley).

Ronan (*Miss* K.), *housekeeper.*
— Letter to Lord Cecil, 1938. 51179, f. 160.

Roosevelt (Anna Eleanor), *wife of President F. D. Roosevelt.*
— Letter from Lord Cecil to A. E. Roosevelt, 1942. *Copy.* 51189, f. 150.

Roosevelt (Franklin Delano), *President of the U.S.A.*
— Correspondence, partly on his behalf and including telegrams, with Lord Cecil, 1923-1941. *Signed.* 51095, f. 133; 51167, ff. 19, 20, 22; 51175, ff. 100, 197; 51176, ff. 71-125, 145; 51177, f. 167; 51178, f. 152; 51179, f. 226; 51182, f. 127; 51183, f. 107; 51186, f. 128; 51187, ff. 134, 258; 51188, f. 132.
— Memoranda by Lord Cecil rel. to conversation with F. D. Roosevelt, 1937. 51178, ff. 12-20.

Root (Elihu), *U.S. senator.*
— Telegram to Lord Cecil, 1930. 51167, f. 17.

142 INDEX

Rose (Charles Archibald Walker), *diplomatist and traveller.*
— Letter to Lord Cecil, 1930. *Signed.* 51100, f. 64.

Rose (F. de), *French diplomatist.*
— Letter to Miss I. M. Butler from F. de Rose, 1939. *Signed.* 51183, f. 119.

Rosenstein (Paul), *physician; formerly of Berlin.*
— Correspondence, partly on his behalf, with Lord Cecil, 1938, 1939. Partly *signed.* 51182, f. 87; 51183, ff. 109, 110; 51184, ff. 31-40, 77, 121.

Rosenthal (A.), *member of the Tariff Reform League.*
— Letter to Lord Cecil, 1908. 51158, f. 180.

Rosselli (Marion) *née* **Cave**, *widow of Carlo Rosselli.*
— Letter to Lord Cecil, 1937. *Signed.* 51178, ff. 64-67.

Rostron (Laurence William Simpson), *barrister.*
— Letters to Lord Cecil, 1912. 51160, ff. 87, 92, 105, 114, 123.

Roth (Cecil), *Reader in Jewish Studies at Oxford.*
— Correspondence between Lord Cecil and C. Roth, 1943. *Signed.* 51190, ff. 77, 95, 108, 118.

Rothenberg (Morris), *President, Zionist Organisation of America.*
— Correspondence between Lord Cecil and M. Rothenberg, 1934. 51169, ff. 221, 262.

Rothschild (Anthony Gustav de).
— Correspondence between Lord Cecil and A. G. de Rothschild, 1943, 1944. *Signed.* 51190, f. 385; 51191, ff. 21, 24.

Rothschild (James Armand de), *of Waddesdon Manor.*
— Letter to Lord Cecil, 1942. 51189, f. 194.

Rothschild (Nathaniel Mayer Victor), *3rd Baron Rothschild.*
— Letter from Lord Cecil to Lord Rothschild, 1942. *Copy.* 51188, f. 303.

Rousseau (Theodore), *President of the American Club in Paris.*
— Letter to Lord Cecil, 1936. *Signed.* 51172, f. 109; 51173, ff. 99, 115.

Rowe-Dutton (*Sir* Ernest), *K.C.M.G.*
— Letter to Lord Cecil from E. Rowe-Dutton, 1926. *Signed.* 51098, f. 100.

Rowell (Newton Wesley), *K.C.; Canadian statesman.*
— Memorandum by Lord Cecil rel. to conversation with N. W. Rowell, 1925. 51097, f. 111.
— Correspondence, including telegram, between Lord Cecil and N. W. Rowell, 1926-1941. *Signed.* 51164, ff. 144, 147; 51167, ff. 167, 186-190; 51168, ff. 70, 133, 144, 148; 51173, ff. 237, 243; 51174, f. 212; 51175, f. 5; 51188, f. 92.

Rowley, *Baron.*
— *v.* Henderson (Arthur).

Rowntree (Arnold Stephenson), *director, Westminster Press.*
— Correspondence between Lord Cecil and A. S. Rowntree, 1935. *Signed.* 51171, ff. 193, 195.

Roxburgh (John Fergusson), *Headmaster of Stowe School.*
— Letter to Lord Cecil, 1935. 51170, f. 152.

Royal (John F.), *Vice-President of the National Broadcasting Co. of America.*
— Telegram to Lord Cecil, 1936. 51172, f. 151.

Royden (Agnes Maude), *D.D.; wife of G. W. H. Shaw.*
— Correspondence between Lord Cecil and A. M. Royden, 1935, 1938. *Signed.* 51170, ff. 183, 194; 51180, f. 132; 51181, ff. 11, 16, 21, 25, 71, 81.

INDEX

Royston (Henry), *of the League of Nations Union, Rowlands Castle branch.*
— Correspondence between Lord Cecil and H. Royston, 1937. 51175, ff. 180, 189, 192.

Ruegger (Paul), *Swiss diplomatist.*
— Telegram to Lord Cecil, 1944. 51191, f. 219.

Rumbold (*Sir* Horace George Montagu), *9th Bart.*
— Correspondence, including telegram, between Lord Cecil and Sir H. G. M. Rumbold, 1918-1939. Partly *signed.* 51093, f. 119; 51099, f. 144; 51081, ff. 69, 76, 149; 51082, ff. 1, 30; 51184, ff. 95, 111, 131, 141, 153.

Runciman (Walter), *1st Viscount Runciman.*
— Correspondence between Lord Cecil and W. Runciman, 1921. 51095, ff. 8, 13; 51163, ff. 10, 15.

Rushton (Gerald Wynne), *author and playwright.*
— Correspondence between Lord Cecil and G. W. Rushton, 1939. 51184, ff. 22-28, 48.
— Letter to A. N. Chamberlain from G. W. Rushton, 1939. *Draft.* 51184, f. 24.

Russbüldt (Otto Lehmann-).
— *v.* Lehmann-Russbüldt (Otto).

Russel (*Mrs* Colin), *of the Women's Canadian Club of Montreal.*
— Telegrams between Lord Cecil and Mrs C. Russel, 1933. 51168, ff. 82, 84.

Russell (*Sir* Claud Frederick William), *K.C.M.G.*
— Correspondence between Haile Selassie as heir to the throne of Ethiopia and C. F. W. Russell, 1923. *Copies.* 51096, ff. 78, 79.

Russell (*Miss* Flora), *writing from Oxford Sq., London W 2.*
— Correspondence between Lord Cecil and Miss F. Russell, 1938. 51180, ff. 97, 98.

Russell (Hastings William Sackville), *12th Duke of Bedford.*
— Correspondence, etc., between Lord Cecil and the Duke of Bedford, 1942, 1943. *Signed.* 51189, ff. 42, 50, 225, 234, 237-241, 250.

Rutherford (*Sir* John), *Bart.*
— Letter to Lord Cecil, 1909. 51159, f. 257.

'Rutherford, Mark', *pseudonym.*
— *v.* White (William Hale).

Ruyssen (Théodore), *French sociologist.*
— Letter, etc., to T. Ruyssen, 1935. 51171, ff. 79-83.

S

Sadd (*Sir* Clarence Thomas Albert), *of the Midland Bank.*
— Correspondence between Lord Cecil and C. T. A. Sadd, 1944. *Signed.* 51191, ff. 131, 136.

Sadd (Renée Georgette Elizabeth), *wife of Sir C. T. A. Sadd.*
— Letter to Lord Cecil, 1944. 51191, f. 137.

Sadleir (Michael), *author and publisher.*
— Correspondence between Lord Cecil and M. Sadleir, 1942. *Signed.* 51193, ff. 274, 275.

Saerchinger (César), *of the Columbia Broadcasting System.*
— Letters to Lord Cecil, 1935, 1937. *Signed.* 51171, ff. 87, 122; 51193, ff. 82-84.

Saint.
— For titles beginning thus, *v.* St.

144 INDEX

Sale (George Samuel), *Professor of Classics, Otago.*
— Letter to Lord Cecil, 1912. 51160, f. 80.

Salisbury, *4th Marquess of.*
— *v.* Gascoyne-Cecil (James Edward Hubert).

Salisbury, *5th Marquess of.*
— *v.* Gascoyne-Cecil (Robert Arthur James).

Salter (James Arthur), *Baron Salter.*
— Correspondence between Lord Cecil and J. A. Salter, 1918-1945. Partly *signed*. 51113, ff. 1-114v.
— Correspondence between J. A. Salter and P. J. Noel-Baker on behalf of Lord Cecil, 1923, 1924. *Signed*. 51106, ff. 162-167; 51113, ff. 15-24.
— Papers rel. to proposed nomination of J. A. Salter as Representative of Oxford University, 1936. *Printed*. 51174, ff. 38-43.

Samson (*Mrs* Millecent), *of Kew.*
— Correspondence between Lord Cecil and Mrs M. Samson, 1941. 51187, ff. 177, 205.

Samuel (Herbert Louis), *1st Viscount Samuel.*
— Correspondence between Lord Cecil and Lord Samuel, 1923-1944. Partly *signed*. 51095, ff. 170, 179; 51101, f. 26; 51168, f. 40; 51175, f. 193; 51180, f. 174; 51191, ff. 194, 233.

Sandars (John Satterfield), *Sec. to A. J. Balfour.*
— Letter to Lord Cecil, 1909. 51071, ff. 13, 14.

Sandford (*Brig.* Daniel Arthur), *adviser to the Emperor of Ethiopia.*
— Correspondence between Lord Cecil and Brig. D. A. Sandford, 1936. *Signed*. 51173, f. 254; 51174, ff. 7, 9, 12, 15, 18.
— Memorandum by Lord Cecil rel. to Brig. D. A. Sandford, 1936. 51174, f. 13.

Sandhurst, *4th Baron.*
— *v.* Mansfield (Ralph Sheldon).

Sankey (John), *Viscount Sankey.*
— Correspondence between Lord Cecil and Lord Sankey, 1936-1944. 51172, ff. 42, 44; 51188, f. 385; 51190, f. 35; 51191, f. 16.

Sargent (*Sir* Orme), *G.C.M.G.*
— Letter to J. G. McDonald from O. Sargent, 1934. *Copy*. 51101, f. 169.
— Correspondence between Lord Cecil and Sir O. Sargent, 1948. *Signed*. 51192, ff. 309-311.

Sato (Naotake), *Japanese diplomatist.*
— Correspondence between Lord Cecil and N. Sato, 1927. *Copies*. Partly *Fr*. 51099, ff. 58-61.

Saunders (*Sir* Alexander Morris Carr-).
— *v.* Carr-Saunders (*Sir* Alexander Morris).

Saunders (Hilary Aidan St. George), *writer; Librarian of the House of Commons.*
— Correspondence between Lord Cecil and H. A. St. G. Saunders, 1922-1932. *Signed*. 51095, ff. 51, 77, 83, 147, 149, 166; 51098, ff. 167, 176; 51099, ff. 131, 132; 51100, ff. 161-164, 168, 173-176, 216; 51101, ff. 2-5.

Saunders (*Capt.* W. Eric P.), *writing from Tramore in Waterford.*
— Correspondence between Lord Cecil and Capt. W. E. P. Saunders, 1936. *Signed*. 51172, ff. 45, 86, 87.

Saussure (Jean de), *pastor, of Geneva.*
— Letter, etc., to Lord Cecil, 1935. *Fr*. 51170, ff. 190-191v.
— Memorandum by Lord Cecil rel. to conversation with J. de Saussure, 1935. 51170, f. 195.

INDEX

Savage (Michael Joseph), *Prime Minister of New Zealand.*
— Letter to Lord Cecil, 1938. *Signed.* 51182, f. 61.

Scammell (J. B.), *merchant.*
— Letter to Lord Cecil, 1909. 51159, f. 98.

Schenk (Vilem), *Czech refugee in England.*
— Correspondence between Lord Cecil and V. Schenk, 1940. 51185, ff. 10, 29.

Scherpenberg (Albert Hilger von), *German diplomatist.*
— Memoranda by Lord Cecil rel. to interviews with A. H. von Scherpenberg, 1935. 51170, ff. 71, 198.
— Letter to Lord Cecil, 1935. *Signed.* 51170, f. 182.

Schnee (*Dr.* [Albert Heinrich?]), *President, Deutsche Gesellschaft für Völkerbundfragen.*
— Correspondence between Lord Cecil and Dr. [A. H?] Schnee, 1935-1937. *Signed.* Partly *Germ.* 51170, ff. 52, 53, 67; 51174, f. 222; 51175, ff. 9, 10.

Schnepp (*Fräulein* Marta), *writing from Frauenfeld, in Switzerland.*
— Correspondence between Lord Cecil and Fräulein M. Schnepp, 1938. *Signed.* 51182, ff. 24, 29.

Schofield (Frank W.), *of Guelph, Ontario.*
— Correspondence between Lord Cecil and F. W. Schofield, 1943. 51190, ff. 278-279v, 311.

Scholz (*Dr.* —), *representative of German minorities in Poland.*
— Memorandum by Lord Cecil rel. to conversation with Dr. — Scholz, 1924. 51097, f. 8.

Schutz (*Dr.* Rolf), *journalist.*
— Letter, etc., to Lord Cecil, 1944. *Signed.* 51191, ff. 301-303.

Scott (Charles Prestwich), *Editor of The Manchester Guardian.*
— Correspondence between Lord Cecil and C. P. Scott, 1921, 1922. 51162, ff. 163-166v; 51163, f. 53.

Scott (John William Robertson), *Editor of The Countryman.*
— Correspondence between Lord Cecil and J. W. R. Scott, 1941. *Signed.* 51187, ff. 43, 49.

Scott (*Sir* Samuel Edward), *6th Bart.*
— Correspondence between Lord Cecil and Sir S. E. Scott, *circa* 1906-1909. 51158, f. 210; 51159, ff. 104, 140, 279.

Scott (Walter George Hepburne-).
— *v.* Hepburne-Scott (Walter George Hepburne-).

Scutari, *City of.*
— Correspondence of the President of the Municipal Council with Lord Cecil, 1921, 1922. *Signed. Fr.* 51162, ff. 128, 157; 51163, ff. 64, 92.

Secretan (Hubert Arthur), *C.B.E.; of the Ministry of Shipping.*
— Memorandum by Lord Cecil rel. to conversation with H. A. Secretan, 1918. 51093, f. 179.

Sedgwick (Gertrude G. Scott), *of Oxford.*
— Letter, etc., to Lord Cecil, 1946. 51192, ff. 259.

Seebohm (Hugh Exton), *banker.*
— Correspondence between Lord Cecil and H. E. Seebohm, 1912, 1938. Partly *signed.* 51160, f. 128; 51178, ff. 169-174; 51179, ff. 1, 14, 32.

Seeckt (Hans von), *German general.*
— Paper on modern armies, 1929. *Copy. Fr.* 51099, ff. 151-163.

Seely (Hugh Michael), *Baron Sherwood.*
— Reply by Lord Sherwood to Parliamentary Question of Lord Cecil rel. to case of Aircraftsman Swanson, 1942. *Signed.* 51188, f. 275.

Seely (John Edward Bernard), *1st Baron Mottistone.*
— Correspondence between Lord Cecil and Lord Mottistone, 1909, 1938. *Signed.* 51159, f. 125; 51179, ff. 38, 251.

Seger (Gerhart H.), *Editor of Neue Volkszeitung, New York.*
— Correspondence between Lord Cecil and G. H. Seger, 1939. *Signed.* 51183, ff. 16, 52.

Selassie (Haile), *Emperor of Ethiopia.*
— *v.* Ethiopia.

Selborne, *2nd Earl of.*
— *v.* Palmer (William Waldegrave).

Selborne, *3rd Earl of.*
— *v.* Palmer (Roundell Cecil).

Selborne, *Countess of.*
— *v.* Palmer (Beatrix Maud).

Selby (W. A.), *Assistant Sec., British Group of the Inter-Parliamentary Union.*
— Letter to Miss I. M. Butler from W. A. Selby, 1936. *Signed.* 51173, f. 124.

Selby (*Sir* Walford Harmood Montague), *K.C.M.G.*
— Correspondence between Sir H. J. Creedy and W. H. M. Selby, 1918. 51090, ff. 53-54v.
— Letter to W. H. M. Selby from C. H. Kisch, 1918. 51090, f. 58.
— Letter to W. H. M. Selby from Sir W. L. F. G. Langley, 1918. 51091, f. 180v.
— Correspondence between L. Oliphant and W. H. M. Selby, 1918. 51091, ff. 180, 180v; 51094, ff. 6, 6v, 58.
— Correspondence between S. C. Peel and W. H. M. Selby, 1918. 51091, f. 200.
— Correspondence between R. L. Nosworthy and W. H. M. Selby, 1918. *Signed.* 51093, ff. 165-168v.
— Letter, etc., to W. H. M. Selby from Sir W. Spens, 1918. *Signed.* 51093, ff. 175-178.
— Letter to W. H. M. Selby from J. W. Headlam-Morley, 1918. *Signed.* 51094, f. 31.
— Letter to W. H. M. Selby from J. E. Shuckburgh on behalf of E. S. Montagu, 1918. 51094, f. 114.
— Correspondence, partly on his behalf, with Lord Cecil, 1918-1944. Partly *signed.* 51081, f. 42; 51082, f. 61; 51090, ff. 43-90; 51091, f. 173.

Sempill (William Francis Forbes-).
— *v.* Forbes-Sempill (William Francis).

Sergeant (John Middlemore), *curate, St. Peter's, Battersea.*
— Letter to Lord Cecil, 1941. Printed. Signed. 51188, f. 20.

Seton-Watson (Robert William), *Masaryk Professor of Central European History, London.*
— Letter to Lord Cecil, 1938. *Printed,* with MS. additions. 51181, f. 99.

Seymour (*Sir* Horace James), *G.C.M.G.*
— Letter to Lord Cecil from H. J. Seymour on behalf of E. D. Simon, 1934. *Signed.* 51082, f. 266.

Sforza (*Count* Carlo), *Italian statesman.*
— Correspondence between Lord Cecil and Count C. Sforza, 1935, 1936. *Signed.* 51171, f. 236; 51172, f. 2.

Shaftesbury, *9th Earl of.*
— *v.* Ashley-Cooper (Anthony).

Shann (E. A.), *of Barnet.*
— Letter to Lord Cecil, 1940. 51185, f. 269.

Shao Li-tze, *of the China Branch, International Peace Campaign.*
— Correspondence between Lord Cecil and Shao Li-tze, 1943, 1944. *Signed.* 51190, f. 340; 51191, f. 19.

INDEX

Sharpe (Cecil P.), *Chairman, League of Nations Union, Ilford Branch.*
— Letters to Lord Cecil, 1934-1937. *Signed.* 51169, f. 25; 51172, f. 48; 51173, f. 110; 51175, ff. 46, 50.

Shaw (Agnes Maude) *formerly* **Royden.**
— *v.* Royden (Agnes Maude).

Shaw (Edward Domett), *Assistant Bishop and Archdeacon of Oxford.*
— Correspondence between Lord Cecil and E. D. Shaw, 1926. 51165, ff. 19-21.

Shaw-Lefevre (George John), *Baron Eversley.*
— Correspondence between Lord Cecil and Lord Eversley, 1928. *Signed.* 51166, ff. 19-23.

Shawcross (Hartley William), *Baron Shawcross 1959.*
— Correspondence between Lord Cecil and H. W. Shawcross, 1947. 51192, ff. 276, 280, 282.

Sheppard (Hugh Richard Lawrie), *Canon of St. Paul's.*
— Letter to Lord Cecil, 1936. *Signed.* 51172, f. 128.

Sherwood, *Baron.*
— *v.* Seely (Hugh Michael).

Short (Wilfred Maurice), *Sec. to A. J. Balfour.*
— Letters to Lord Cecil, 1908, 1913. *Signed.* 51071, ff. 7, 24.

Shotwell (James Thomson), *Professor of History, Columbia University; President, Carnegie Endowment for International Peace.*
— Correspondence between Lord Cecil and J. T. Shotwell, 1928-1944. *Signed.* 51165, ff. 93-95; 51169, ff. 151-154, 170; 51189, f. 180; 51191, f. 86.

Shuckburgh (*Sir* John Evelyn), *K.C.M.G.*
— Letter to W. H. M. Selby from J. E. Shuckburgh on behalf of E. S. Montagu, 1918. 51094, f. 114.

Sibthorpe (Mary), *of the National Committee for Rescue from Nazi Tyranny.*
— Letters, etc., to Lord Cecil, 1943. *Signed.* 51190, ff. 24-26.

Sieff (Rebecca), *wife of I. M. Sieff, Baron Sieff.*
— Letter from Lord Cecil to Lady Sieff, 1937. *Copy.* 51178, f. 135.

Sifton (Clifford), *of the Canadian League of Nations Society.*
— Correspondence between Lord Cecil and C. Sifton, 1937. *Partly printed.* 51178, ff. 69-87.

Silberstein (*Dr.* —), *[refugee physician?].*
— Letter to Lord Cecil, 1936. *Signed.* 51172, f. 166.

Silverman (Leo), *writing from London NW 3.*
— Correspondence between Lord Cecil and L. Silverman, 1936, [1937?]. *Partly signed.* 51172, f. 1; 51174, ff. 224, 228.

Simmons (E. B.), *of the Ministry of Supply.*
— Correspondence between Lord Cecil and E. B. Simmons, 1942. *Signed.* 51188, ff. 259, 262.

Simon (Ernest Darwin), *1st Baron Simon.*
— Letter to Lord Cecil from H. J. Seymour on behalf of E. D. Simon, 1934. *Signed.* 51082, f. 266.
— Letter, etc., to Lord Cecil, 1940. *Signed.* 51185, ff. 3-6.

Simon (John Allsebrook), *1st Viscount Simon.*
— Correspondence, partly on his behalf, with Lord Cecil, 1931-1945. *Mostly signed. Partly printed.* 51082, ff. 63-295; 51188, f. 279.

Simopoulos (Charalambos John), *Greek diplomatist.*
— Correspondence between Lord Cecil and C. J. Simopoulos, 1941. *Signed.* 51187, ff. 313, 317.

INDEX

Simpson (*Mrs* E. W.), *of Blackpool.*
— Correspondence between Lord Cecil and Mrs E. W. Simpson, 1941. 51187, ff. 149, 164, 209.

Sinclair (Archibald Henry Macdonald), *1st Viscount Thurso.*
— Correspondence between Lord Cecil and A. H. M. Sinclair, 1936-1940. *Signed.* 51174, ff. 77, 82, 89, 131, 138, 140; 51175, ff. 127, 129, 135, 140; 51181, ff. 152, 179, 188, 197; 51182, f. 21; 51184, f. 161; 51185, f. 214.
— Memoranda by Lord Cecil rel. to interviews with A. H. M. Sinclair, 1938. *Copies.* 51180, f. 167; 51181, f. 51.

Sinclair (Marigold), *wife of Archibald, 1st Viscount Thurso.*
— Telegram to Lord Cecil, 1939. 51184, f. 103.

Skinner (Roy A.), *of Dallas, Texas.*
— Correspondence between Lord Cecil and R. A. Skinner, 1942. *Signed.* 51189, ff. 168, 224.

Skirmunt (Constantine), *Polish diplomatist.*
— Correspondence between Lord Cecil and C. Skirmunt, 1923. *Signed.* 51096, ff. 59, 66.
— Memorandum by Lord Parmoor rel. to conversation with C. Skirmunt, 1924. 51096, ff. 167, 168.

Skrbenski (Rudolf von), *member of German minority from Poland.*
— Letter to Lord Cecil, 1923. *Signed.* 51096, f. 55.

Slade (*Lady* Janet), *widow of Sir J. R. Slade.*
— Correspondence between Lord Cecil and Lady J. Slade, 1918. 51162, ff. 27-29.

Smeed (Vernon), *of Petersfield.*
— Correspondence between Lord Cecil and V. Smeed, 1942. *Signed.* 51189, ff. 196, 201.

Smit (Jacobus Stephanus), *South African statesman.*
— Correspondence between Lord Cecil and J. S. Smit, 1926. *Signed.* 51098, ff. 89, 92, 104.

Smith (Abel Henry), *M.P.*
— Letters to Lord Cecil from and on behalf of A. H. Smith, 1909. 51159, ff. 19, 43v-46, 90, 102, 122, 129, 160.
— Telegram to Lord Cecil, 1909. 51159, f. 107.

Smith (Alexander Nicoll), *of Springfield, Massachusetts.*
— Letters to Lord Cecil, 1943, 1944. 51189, f. 248; 51190, ff. 232, 292, 330; 51191, ff. 43, 91.

Smith (*Adm. Sir* Aubrey Clare Hugh), *K.C.V.O.*
— Correspondence between Lord Cecil and Vice-Adm. A. C. H. Smith, 1925, 1927. 51097, f. 208; 51099, ff. 46, 49-52.
— Signature, 1927. 51099, f. 24.
— Correspondence with Lord Cecil, on behalf of King George's Fund for Sailors, 1935. *Signed.* 51171, ff. 220, 233.

Smith (Charles Howard), *C.M.G.; of the Foreign Office.*
— Correspondence between Lord Cecil and C. H. Smith, 1925, 1932. Partly *signed.* 51082, ff. 171-173; 51097, f. 122; 51100, ff. 19-24.

Smith (*Lt.-Col.* E. Clementi), *of Furners Green.*
— Letter to Lord Cecil, 1940. 51186, f. 156.

Smith (*Sir* Edmund Wyldbore-).
— *v.* Wyldbore-Smith (*Sir* Edmund).

Smith (Frederick Edwin), *1st Earl of Birkenhead.*
— Correspondence between Lord Cecil and Lord Birkenhead, 1925, 1926. *Signed.* 51097, f. 148; 51098, ff. 72-83.

INDEX

Smith (*Sir* George Adam), *Chaplain to the King in Scotland; Vice Chancellor of Aberdeen University.*
— Letter to Lord Cecil, 1928. 51166, f. 28.

Smith (*Sir* Hubert Llewellyn), *G.C.B.*
— Letters to Lord Cecil, 1918. 51093, f. 205 (copy); 51094, f. 88 (signed).

Smith (Isabella Anna), *wife of A. H. Smith.*
— Letter to Lord Cecil, 1909. 51159, f. 90.

Smith (*Miss* Janet), *League of Nations official.*
— Letter to Miss J. Smith from A. Loveday, 1943. *Copy.* 51190, f. 139.
— Correspondence between Lord Cecil and Miss J. Smith, 1944. 51191, ff. 187, 240.

Smith (L. Eaton), *Sec., Archbishops' Commission on relations between Church and State.*
— Letter to Lord Cecil, 1934. *Signed.* 51169, f. 94.

Smith (Lilian), *wife of Sir G. A. Smith.*
— Letter to Lord Cecil, 1926. 51164, f. 132.

Smith (Nowell Charles), *former Headmaster of Sherborne School; author.*
— Correspondence, partly on his behalf, with Lord Cecil, 1938-1943. 51180, ff. 149, 152, 169; 51181, f. 1; 51186, f. 254; 51187, ff. 235-240, 255, 273, 281, 308, 315; 51188, ff. 276, 280, 284; 51190, ff. 116, 124, 237, 241, 246.

Smith (Philip), *Sec., International Student Service, London.*
— Letters, etc., to Lord Cecil, 1936, 1937. Partly *printed.* Partly *signed.* 51174, ff. 174-181; 51177, f. 135; 51178, f. 109.

Smith (Rennie), *Sec., 'Friends of Europe'.*
— Correspondence between Lord Cecil and R. Smith, 1940, 1941. Partly *signed.* 51185, ff. 168, 181; 51187, ff. 62, 325-327v, 336.

Smith (Stanley), *of The Globe.*
— Letter to Lord Cecil, 1912. *Signed.* 51160, f. 188.

Smith (William Frederick Danvers), *2nd Viscount Hambleden.*
— Correspondence between Lord Cecil and Lord Hambleden, 1908-1927. Partly *signed.* 51158, f. 174; 51159, ff. 10, 65; 51165, ff. 170, 171, 175.

Smolka (Harry Peter) *afterw.* **Smollett**, *journalist.*
— Letter to Lord Cecil, 1935. *Signed.* 51170, f. 116.

Smollett (Harry Peter).
— *v.* Smolka (Harry Peter).

Smuts (*Field-Marshal* Jan Christiaan), *S. African Prime Minister.*
— Correspondence, partly on his behalf, with Lord Cecil, 1918-1948. Partly *signed.* 51076, ff. 78-153.

Snell (Henry), *Baron Snell.*
— Correspondence between Lord Cecil and Lord Snell, 1938, 1939. 51180, ff. 143, 156; 51181, f. 96; 51184, f. 86.
— Reply by Lord Snell to Parliamentary Question of Lord Cecil rel. to telephone service, 1941. *Signed.* 51187, ff. 392, 393.

Snowden (Ethel), *widow of Philip, Viscount Snowden.*
— Letter to Lord Cecil, 1937. 51175, f. 216.

Snowden (Percival Lovell), *curate at Kirkheaton, co. Yorks.*
— Letter to Lord Cecil, 1912. 51160, f. 169.

Sobanski (*Count* —), *of the Polish National Committee.*
— Memorandum by Lord Cecil rel. to conversation with Count — Sobanski, 1918. 51094, f. 108.

Sohlman (Ragnar), *of the Nobel Foundation, Stockholm.*
— Correspondence between Lord Cecil and R. Sohlman, 1937. *Signed.* 51178, ff. 43, 53.

Sommerfelt (*Dr.* Alf), *Norwegian philologist; of the Norwegian Ministry of Education in London.*
— Letter to Lord Cecil, 1944. *Signed.* 51191, f. 205.

Sousa Dantas (L. M. de), *Brazilian diplomatist.*
— Letter to Lord Parmoor from L. M. de Sousa Dantas, 1924. *Signed. Fr.* 51097, f. 4.

SPAIN.
— Lord Cecil's proposals, through the League of Nations, for a settlement of the Civil War in Spain, 1938. *Copy.* 51178, f. 204.

Speaight (Richard Langford), *of the Foreign Office.*
— Letter from Lord Cecil to R. L. Speaight, 1939. *Copy.* 51183, f. 129.

Spears (*Maj.-Gen. Sir* Edward Louis), *Bart.*
— Correspondence between Lord Cecil and E. L. Spears, 1918, 1935. *Signed.* 51093, f. 148; 51171, ff. 163, 173, 174, 182.

Speeches.
— Speech by B. Disraeli on installation as Lord Rector of Glasgow University, 1873. *Copy, 20th cent.* 51174, ff. 25-37.
— Addresses, speeches and broadcast talks by Lord Cecil, with related correspondence, *circa* 1897-1949, n.d. *Copies, drafts,* etc. 51162, ff. 108-116; 51180, ff. 1-13; 51193-51204 *passim.*
— Addresses by Woodrow Wilson to Congress at Mount Vernon, 1918. *Printed.* Partly *extracts.* 51093, ff. 60, 79, 80, 188.
— Speech by Sir H. Bowden to the Labour Co-Partnership Association, 1927. *Draft.* 51165, ff. 102-112.
— Speech by L. G. Curtis to the Conference of the Institute of Pacific Relations, Shanghai, 1931. *Printed.* 51167, ff. 170-184.
— Speech by C. L. Lange at conferment of Nobel Prize on Lord Cecil, 1937. *Printed* with MS additions. 51178, ff. 88-97.
— Notes by V. O. Bartlett for speech at Peace Campaign meeting in Leeds, 1938. *Copy.* 51179, f. 109.
— Speech by F. Stang at the presentation of the Nobel Peace Prize to Lord Cecil, 1938. *Printed.* 51180, ff. 16-19.
— Speech by Sir L. F. Behrens to the National League of Young Liberals at Bradford, 1941. *Printed.* 51187, f. 284.
— Memorial Address by Lord Lytton for Maj. A. J. C. Freshwater, 1943. *Copy.* 51139, f. 186.
— Speech by H. S. Morrison at the Guildhall, London, 1943. *Copy.* 51189, ff. 283-284v.

Spencer (*Rev.* Malcolm), *Sec., The Christian Social Council.*
— Correspondence between Lord Cecil and Rev. M. Spencer, 1938. *Signed.* 51179, ff. 151, 169, 209, 218, 220, 228.

Spencer-Churchill, *Baroness.*
— *v.* Churchill (Clementine Ogilvy).

Spencer-Churchill (*Lord* Ivor Charles).
— *v.* Churchill (*Lord* Ivor Charles Spencer).

Spencer-Churchill (*Sir* Winston Leonard).
— *v.* Churchill (*Sir* Winston Leonard Spencer).

Spencer-Pryse (*Capt.* Gerald), *of the Savile Club.*
— Correspondence, etc., between Lord Cecil and Capt. G. Spencer-Pryse, 1940. *Signed.* 51185, ff. 117-129, 157.

INDEX

Spender (Hugh Frederick), *journalist*.
— Letter to Lord Cecil, [1924?]. 51164, f. 56.

Spender (John Alfred), *journalist*.
— Correspondence between Lord Cecil and J. A. Spender, 1921. 51163, ff. 12, 17.

Spens (*Sir* Will), *Sec., Foreign Trade Department, Foreign Office*.
— Correspondence between Sir A. S. J. Block and W. Spens, 1918. 51093, ff. 174-176.
— Letter, etc., to W. H. M. Selby from Sir W. Spens, 1918. *Signed*. 51093, ff. 175-178.

Spens (William Patrick), *1st Baron Spens*.
— Memorandum to members of the Watching Committee, 1941. *Printed*. 51187, ff. 371-373.

Speyer (*Mme* —), *wife of Professor H. L. J. Speyer*.
— Letter from Lord Cecil to Mme — Speyer, 1934. *Copy*. 51169, f. 51.

Speyer (*Sir* Edgar), *Bart*.
— Letter to Lord Cecil, 1909. *Signed*. 51159, f. 80.

Speyer (*Professor* Herbert Louis Jean), *of the University of Brussels*.
— Correspondence between Lord Cecil and Professor H. L. J. Speyer, 1934, 1935. Partly *signed*. 51169, ff. 34, 37, 127, 138, 140, 150; 51171, ff. 190, 196, 198, 208, 212; 51172, ff. 9, 14, 192.

Spooner (*Commander* Ernest John), *R.N.*
— Correspondence between Lord Cecil and Commander E. J. Spooner, 1929. *Signed*. 51166, ff. 131-141.

Spring-Rice (Thomas Aubrey), *3rd Baron Monteagle of Brandon*.
— Minute, 1927. *Copy*. 51099, f. 75.

St. Aldwyn, *1st Earl*.
— *v.* Hicks-Beach (Michael Edward).

St. Asaph, *Bishop of*.
— *v.* Edwards (Alfred George).

St. Audries, *1st Baron*.
— *v.* Fuller-Acland-Hood (Alexander).

St. Davids, *Bishop of*.
— *v.* Owen (John).

St. Edmundsbury and Ipswich, *Bishop of*.
— *v.* Whittingham (Walter Godfrey).

Stainton (H. H.), *Representative, League of Nations Union, Midland Region*.
— Letter to H. H. Stainton from Capt. E. G. W. Vaughan, 1935. *Signed*. 51171, f. 86.
— Correspondence between Lord Cecil and H. H. Stainton, 1935, 1939. *Signed*. 51171, ff. 85, 91, 132, 134, 147; 51184, ff. 50, 171, 172.

Stamford, *10th Earl of*.
— *v.* Grey (Roger).

Stammfest (*Dr.*— Braun-).
— *v.* Braun-Stammfest (*Dr.* —).

Stamp (Josiah Charles), *1st Baron Stamp*.
— Correspondence between Lord Cecil and Lord Stamp, 1939. *Signed*. 51154, ff. 105, 140.

Stancioff (Nadejda) *afterw.* **Muir**.
— *v.* Muir (Nadejda).

Stancomb (Ernest Henry Murly), *physician; of the League of Nations Union, Southampton Branch*.
— Correspondence between Lord Cecil and E. H. M. Stancomb, 1938. 51181, ff. 26v, 31.

Stang (Frederik), *Norwegian jurist; President of the Nobel Committee of the Norwegian Parliament*.
— Correspondence, including telegrams, between Lord Cecil and F. Stang, 1937, 1938. *Signed*. 51175, ff. 18, 28; 51178, ff. 25, 29, 35, 54, 113, 125, 136; 51179, ff. 53, 56.

INDEX

Stang (Frederik), *Norwegian jurist; President of the Nobel Committee of the Norwegian Parliament. continuation*
— Speech by F. Stang at the presentation of the Nobel Peace Prize to Lord Cecil, 1938. *Printed.* 51180, ff. 16-19.

Stanhope (James Richard), *7th Earl Stanhope.*
— Reply by Lord Stanhope to Parliamentary Question of Lord Cecil rel. to trade mission to Japan, 1934. 51169, f. 227.
— Reply by Lord Stanhope to Parliamentary Question of Lord Cecil rel. to trade in arms, 1935. *Partly printed. Signed.* 51170, ff. 82-84.

Stanley (Albert Henry), *Baron Ashfield.*
— Correspondence, etc., partly on his behalf, with Lord Cecil, 1918. Mostly *signed*. 51093, ff. 75, 195; 51094, ff. 139, 140-153; 51162, ff. 37-39v.

Stanley *(Sir* Arthur), *G.C.V.O.*
— Letter from Lord Cecil to A. Stanley, 1914. 51161, f. 189.

Stanley (Edward George Villiers), *17th Earl of Derby.*
— Correspondence between Lord Cecil and Lord Derby, 1918-1926. *Signed.* 51093, ff. 91-96; 51094, ff. 11, 15; 51163, f. 174; 51164, f. 169.

Stanley (Oliver Frederick George), *P.C.; M.P.*
— Letters from Lord Cecil to O. F. G. Stanley, 1937. *Copies.* 51175, ff. 177, 186.

Stansfield (J.), *former Sec., League of Nations Union, Enfield; of Ladybrand, Orange Free State.*
— Correspondence between Lord Cecil and J. Stansfield, 1944, 1945. 51191, f. 310; 51192, f. 6.

Stansgate, *1st Viscount.*
— *v*. Benn (William Wedgwood).

Starkey (H. Walton), *organiser of the Penny-a-Week Fund, Lytham.*
— Letter to Lord Cecil, 1944. *Signed.* 51191, f. 190.

Starky (Geraldine Haynton), *of Torrington.*
— Correspondence between Lord Cecil and G. H. Starky, 1940. 51185, ff. 114, 147.

Stavridi (Annina Olga), *wife of Sir J. Stavridi.*
— Letter, etc., to Lord Cecil, 1942. 51188, ff. 227-229.

Stavridi *(Sir* John), *solicitor.*
— Letter to Sir J. Stavridi from J. Ramsay MacDonald, 1932. *Signed.* 51081, f. 134.
— Letter to Sir J. Stavridi from N. S. Politis, 1932. *Signed.* 51101, f. 35.
— Letter to Sir J. Stavridi from E. Beneš, 1932. *Signed.* 51101, f. 37.
— Correspondence between Lord Cecil and Sir J. Stavridi, 1933, 1942. *Signed. Partly extract.* 51168, f. 108; 51188, ff. 207, 215, 234.

Steed (Henry Wickham), *Editor of The Times.*
— Correspondence between Lord Cecil and H. W. Steed, 1932-1944. Partly *signed.* 51156, ff. 126-182.

Steel-Maitland *(Sir* Arthur Herbert Drummond Ramsay), *1st Bart.*
— Correspondence between Lord Cecil and Sir A. H. D. R. Steel-Maitland, 1911-1927. Partly *signed.* 51071 B; 51094, f. 154.
— Letter to I. Z. Malcolm from Sir A. H. D. R. Steel-Maitland, 1918. *Signed.* 51094, f. 86.
— Letter to H. H. Asquith from Sir A. H. D. R. Steel-Maitland, 1921. *Copy.* 51071, f. 74.
— Letter to Lord Salisbury on behalf of Sir A. H. D. R. Steel-Maitland, 1926. *Copy.* 51085, f. 180.

INDEX

Stenger (*Dr.* J.), *of Groningen.*
— Correspondence between Lord Cecil and Dr. J. Stenger, 1936. 51172, f. 208; 51173, ff. 6, 27.

Stephen (*Dr.* Adrian).
— Letter from Lord Cecil to Dr. A. Stephen, 1936. 51174, f. 213.

Stephen (*Sir* Harry Lushington), *3rd Bart.*
— Letter to Lord Cecil, 1944. 51191, f. 210.

Stephens (*Maj.* —), *of the Governing Commission of the Saar.*
— Memorandum by Lord Cecil rel. to conversation with Maj. — Stephens, 1924. 51097, f. 51.

Stephens (John Sturge), *of the University of Birmingham.*
— Correspondence between Lord Cecil and J. S. Stephens, 1940. 51184, ff. 332, 337.

Stern (Gustave), *of London NW 8.*
— Correspondence between Lord Cecil and G. Stern, 1940. *Signed.* 51186, ff. 186, 197.

Sternbach (*Baron* Paul von).
— Memoranda rel. to arrest, etc., of Baron P. von Sternbach, 1935. Partly *printed. Germ.* and *Engl. transl.* 51170, ff. 108, 129, 144.

Sternberger (Estelle M.), *Executive Director, World Peaceways, New York.*
— Letter to Lord Cecil, 1935. *Signed.* 51171, f. 138.

Stevens (E.), *florist, of Westminster.*
— Letter to Lord Cecil, 1908. 51158, f. 281.

Stevens (*Mrs* M. Gladys), *of the League of Nations Union, London Regional Federation.*
— Correspondence between Lord Cecil and Mrs M. G. Stevens, 1944. *Signed.* 51191, ff. 114-117.

Stevenson (*Sir* Daniel Macaulay), *Bart.*
— Correspondence, partly on his behalf, with Lord Cecil, 1927-1942. *Signed.* 51165, ff. 148v, 158; 51175, ff. 85, 86; 51188, ff. 169, 184, 194, 199.

Stevenson (Frances Louise) *afterw.* **Lloyd George.**
— *v.* Lloyd George (Frances Louise).

Stewart (Charles Stewart Henry Vane-Tempest-).
— *v.* Vane-Tempest-Stewart (Charles Stewart Henry).

Stewart (*Sir* Gershom), *K.B.E.*
— Letters to Lord Cecil, 1908. 51158, ff. 255-261.

Stewart (*Miss* Helen G.), *Sec., League of Nations Union, Dunoon and District.*
— Correspondence between Lord Cecil and Miss H. G. Stewart, 1940. 51185, ff. 230-232, 234.

Stewart (*Lady* Philippa), *wife of Sir E. Stewart.*
— Letter to her brother Lord Fitzalan from Lady P. Stewart, 1919. 51162, f. 97.

Stewart-Murray (Katherine Marjorie), *wife of John, 8th Duke of Atholl.*
— Correspondence, including telegrams, between Lord Cecil and the Duchess of Atholl, 1936-1944. Partly *signed.* 51142, ff. 220-271.

Sthamer (Friedrich), *German diplomatist.*
— Letter to F. Sthamer from Lord Parmoor, 1924. *Copy.* 51097, f. 59.

Stimson (Henry Lewis), *U.S. Sec. of State.*
— Correspondence, including telegrams, between Lord Cecil and H. L. Stimson, 1929-1940. *Signed.* 51099, f. 201; 51101, ff. 43, 62; 51170, f. 218; 51171, ff. 135-137, 152; 51179, f. 58; 51184, ff. 325, 329.

Stimson (Henry Lewis), *U.S. Sec. of State. continuation*
— Memorandum by Lord Cecil rel. to conversation with H. L. Stimson, 1930. 51100, f. 27.

Stockton, *1st Earl of.*
— *v.* Macmillan (Maurice Harold).

Stockton and Thornaby, *N.R., co. York.*
— Message from Lord Cecil for Peace Week at Stockton and Thornaby, 1938. *Copy.* 51181, f. 98.

Stone (Alfred T.), *Sec., Sale Peace Week.*
— Correspondence between Lord Cecil and A. T. Stone, 1937. *Signed.* 51177, ff. 113, 126.

Stoneham (Herbert S.), *stockbroker.*
— Letter to Lord Cecil, 1913. *Signed.* 51160, f. 278.

Stonehaven, *1st Viscount.*
— *v.* Baird (John Lawrence).

Stoney (*Miss* P. F.), *Sec., League of Nations Union, Paddington Branch.*
— Letter to Lord Cecil, 1940. *Signed.* 51185, f. 191.

Storr (*Lt.-Col.* Lancelot), *C.B.; Assistant Sec., Imperial War Cabinet.*
— Letters to Lord Cecil, 1918, 1924. *Signed.* 51077, f. 32; 51085, f. 124.

Storr (M.), *of London, WC 1.*
— Letter to Lord Cecil, 1940. 51185, f. 274.

Storr (T.), *of London WC 1.*
— Letter to Lord Cecil, 1940. *Signed.* 51185, f. 270.

Storrs (*Sir* Ronald), *K.C.M.G.*
— Correspondence between Lord Cecil and Sir R. Storrs, 1925, 1926. *Signed.* 51097, f. 218; 51098, f. 2.

Strachan (Lionel Richard Mortimer), *lecturer in German, Birmingham University.*
— Correspondence between Lord Cecil and L. R. M. Strachan, 1940. 51185, ff. 180, 182, 215, 218, 249, 251, 252.

Strachey (John St. Loe), *Editor of The Spectator.*
— Memorandum rel. to Lord Cromer and the Unionist Free Trade Party, 1908. *Draft.* 51158, ff. 284-288.
— Letters to Lord Cecil from J. St. L. Strachey, 1908-1925. *Partly signed.* 51158, ff. 184-186, 194-197, 201-203v, 206, 220; 51159, f. 47; 51162, ff. 57, 58; 51164, ff. 62, 64.

Strachey (*Miss* Philippa), *Sec., the London and National Society for Women's Service.*
— Letter to Lord Cecil, 1937, 1944. *Partly signed.* 51175, f. 187; 51176, f. 92; 51191, ff. 142, 144, 159, 222.

Strakosch (*Sir* Henry), *G.B.E.*
— Memorandum by Lord Cecil rel. to conversation with Sir H. Strakosch, 1924. 51097, ff. 71-73.

Strang (J. Logan), *of Edinburgh.*
— Correspondence between Lord Cecil and J. L. Strang, 1942. *Signed.* 51189, ff. 134, 146.

Streatham, *co. Surr.*
— Message from Lord Cecil for Peace Week at Streatham, 1937. *Copy.* 51178, f. 6.

Street (Jessie Mary Grey), *wife of Sir K. W. Street.*
— Correspondence between Lord Cecil and J. M. G. Street, 1938. *Partly signed.* 51179, ff. 206, 242.

Stresemann (Gustav), *German statesman.*
— Letter to Lord Cecil, 1929. *Signed. Germ.* 51099, ff. 167-169.

Strick (F. Boyle), *writing from Blackheath.*
— Letter to Lord Cecil, 1912. 51160, f. 103.

Stronski (Stanislaw), *Polish writer and politician.*
— Letter to Lord Cecil, 1944. 51191, f. 197.

INDEX

Strother (Walter J.), *writing from Blackburn.*
— Letter to Lord Cecil, 1912. 51160, f. 81.

Strutt (H. A.), *of the Home Office.*
— Letter to Miss I. M. Butler from H. A. Strutt, 1942. *Signed.* 51189, f. 230.

Stuart (A. B. Cohen-).
— *v.* Cohen-Stuart (A. B.).

Stuart (*Sir* Campbell), *G.C.M.G.*
— Correspondence between Lord Cecil and Sir C. Stuart, 1933. 51168, ff. 20, 21.

Stuart (F. D.).
— Letter to Lord Cecil from F. D. Stuart on behalf of P. F. La Follette, 1939. *Signed.* 51182, f. 198.

Stuart (Horatius Bonar), *of the Manor of Sutton by Guildford.*
— Correspondence between Lord Cecil and H. B. Stuart, 1940, 1943. 51185, ff. 86, 99; 51190, ff. 211-214.

Stumer (A. M.), *of Copenhagen.*
— Letter, etc., to Lord Cecil, 1938. *Signed.* 51181, ff. 206-209.

Sturmheim (*Dr.* Emil Müller-).
— *v.* Müller-Sturmheim (*Dr.* Emil).

Sturt (E. N. L.), *of the British Council.*
— Letters to Lord Curzon from E. N. L. Sturt, 1942. *Signed.* 51189, ff. 128, 230.

Styles (Philip), *historian; of the University of Birmingham.*
— Correspondence between Lord Cecil and P. Styles, 1941-1943. 51187, ff. 21, 59; 51189, ff. 215, 258; 51190, f. 4.

Summerhill (*Rev.* A. J.), *of Petersfield.*
— Letter from Lord Cecil to Rev. A. J. Summerhill, 1939. *Copy.* 51182, f. 168.

Sun Ching-ling, *widow of Dr. Sun Yat-sen.*
— Correspondence between Lord Cecil and Sun Ching-ling, 1939. *Signed.* 51184, ff. 176, 237, 238.

Surguy (W.), *of Dagenham.*
— Letter to Lord Cecil, 1938. 51180, f. 93.

Svenska Morgonbladet.
— Telegram to Lord Cecil from Svenska Morgonbladet, 1935. 51170, f. 6.

Swan (Thomas F.), *former detainee under Regulation 18B.*
— Correspondence between Lord Cecil and T. F. Swan, 1942. *Signed.* 51189, ff. 110-113, 118.

Swanson (—), *aircraftsman.*
— Question by Lord Cecil rel. to case of Aircraftsman Swanson, 1942. 51188, f. 275.

Sweetser (Arthur), *of the League of Nations Secretariate; afterw. President of the Woodrow Wilson Foundation.*
— Correspondence between Lord Cecil and A. Sweetser, 1923-1945. Mostly *signed.* 51113, ff. 204-251.

Swenne (Eric), *London Editor of Stockholms Tidningen.*
— Correspondence between Lord Cecil and E. Swenne, 1937. *Signed.* 51178, ff. 42, 56, 98.

Swing (Raymond Gram), *U.S. journalist.*
— Letter to Lord Cecil, 1938. *Signed.* 51181, f. 53.

Swinton, *Earl of.*
— *v.* Cunliffe-Lister (Philip).

Swire (Joseph), *author.*
— Correspondence, including telegram, between Lord Cecil and J. Swire, 1936. *Signed.* 51172, ff. 101, 143, 148, 152-157, 173, 198, 209; 51173, f. 4.

INDEX

Switzerland.
— Memoranda rel. to visits by Lord Davies to Paris and Switzerland, 1939. *Copies.* 51184, ff. 217-228, 229-233.

Sykes (*Lt.-Col. Sir* Mark), *6th Bart.*
— Correspondence between Lord Cecil and Lt.-Col. Sir M. Sykes, 1918. *Signed.* 51094, ff. 66, 70.

Symons (H.), *of the Corporation of the Church House, Westminster.*
— Letter to Lord Cecil, 1941. *Signed.* 51188, f. 76.

Syrett (Herbert Sutton), *solicitor; Chairman, League of Nations Union, City of London branch.*
— Correspondence between Lord Cecil and H. S. Syrett, 1935-1945. Mostly *signed.* 51137, ff. 1-175.

Sze Sao-ke Alfred, *Chinese diplomatist.*
— Memorandum by Lord Cecil rel. to conversation with Mr Sze, 1931. 51100, f. 136.

Szechenyi (*Count* Lazlo), *Hungarian diplomatist.*
— Letter from Lord Cecil to Count L. Szechenyi, 1936. *Copy.* 51172, f. 126.

T

Talbot (Edmund Bernard) *afterw.* **Fitzalan-Howard**, *1st Viscount Fitzalan-Howard.*
— *v.* Fitzalan-Howard (Edmund Bernard).

Talbot (*Sir* George John), *P.C.*
— Letters to Lord Cecil, [1906?]. 51158, ff. 80-82.

Talbot (*Mrs* Jane), *of Brentwood.*
— Correspondence between Lord Cecil and Mrs J. Talbot, 1936. 51172, ff. 167, 187.

Talbot (John Gilbert), *M.P.; P.C.*
— Correspondence between Lord Cecil and J. G. Talbot, 1906, 1909. 51158, f. 60; 51159, ff. 170, 188, 191, 243.

Talbot (*Mrs* Josephine), *of Chester Terrace, Eaton Square, London, SW 1.*
— Correspondence between Lord Cecil and Mrs J. Talbot, 1938. 51180, ff. 87, 88.

Talbot (*Dame* Meriel), *D.B.E.*
— Correspondence between Lord Cecil and Dame M. Talbot, 1941, 1943. 51187, ff. 57, 64; 51190, ff. 138, 155.

Tallents (*Sir* Stephen), *K.C.M.G.; of the B.B.C.*
— Letter to Lord Cecil, 1940. *Signed.* 51193, f. 202.

Tauchert (H. E.), *engineer.*
— Letters, etc., to Lord Cecil, 1942. *Signed.* 51189, f. 154.

Taunton, *co. Som.*
— Message from Lord Cecil for Peace Week at Taunton, 1937. 51177, f. 141.

Taylor (Edward H.), *manufacturer of bee hives.*
— Letter to Lord Cecil, 1918. *Signed.* 51162, f. 77.

Taylor (J. E.), *writing from Stamford Hill.*
— Letter to Lord Cecil, 1913. *Signed.* 51160, f. 280.

Taylor (Theodore Cooke), *J.P.; woollen manufacturer.*
— Correspondence between Lord Cecil and T. C. Taylor, 1944. 51191, ff. 156, 157.

te Water (Charles Theodore).
— *v.* Water (Charles Theodore te).

INDEX

Temperley (*Maj.-Gen.* Arthur Cecil), *C.B.*
— Correspondence between Lord Cecil and Maj.-Gen. A. C. Temperley, 1926-1937. *Signed.* 51079, ff. 184, 188; 51098, f. 147; 51099, ff. 6-14, 25-34, 55, 90; 51177, ff. 195, 201.
— Signature, 1927. 51099, f. 24.

Temple (William), *Archbishop of York and (1942) Canterbury.*
— Correspondence between Lord Cecil and Archbishop Temple, 1931-1943. Partly *signed.* 51154 A, ff. 126-172; 51154 B, ff. 1-81v.
— Letter to Lord Cecil, signed by Archbishop of York and C. Weizmann on behalf of the International Student Service, 1937. *Facsimile.* 51178, f. 45.

Templemore, *4th Baron.*
— *v.* Chichester (Arthur Claud Spencer).

Templewood, *1st Viscount.*
— *v.* Hoare (Samuel John Gurney).

Tenby, *1st Viscount.*
— *v.* Lloyd-George (Gwilym).

Tennant (Edward Priaulx), *1st Baron Glenconner.*
— Correspondence between Lord Cecil and Lord Glenconner, 1918. 51093, ff. 164, 171.

Terrell (Thomas), *K.C.*
— Correspondence between Lord Cecil and T. Terrell, 1909. 51159, ff. 7, 12.

Thomas (Alan Ernest Wentworth), *Editor of The Listener.*
— Correspondence between Lord Cecil and A. E. W. Thomas, 1938, 1940. Partly *signed.* 51180, ff. 141, 145; 51186, f. 73; 51193, f. 200.

Thomas (Cecil), *sculptor.*
— Letter to Lord Cecil, [1922-1923?]. 51163, f. 131.

Thomas (Cyril Leonard Ross), *former teacher of history.*
— Correspondence between Lord Cecil and C. L. R. Thomas, 1940. 51185, ff. 183, 188.

Thomas (*Sir* Godfrey John Vignoles), *10th Bart.*
— Letter to Lord Cecil from Sir G. J. V. Thomas on behalf of Sir A. G. M. Cadogan, 1940. *Signed.* 51089, f. 161.

Thomas (H. Wynne), *of Bromley, co. Kent; member of the Pedestrians' Association.*
— Letter to Lord Cecil, 1943. 51190, f. 105.

Thomas (Hugh Lloyd), *diplomatist.*
— Letter to Lord Cecil from H. L. Thomas, on behalf of Edward VIII as Prince of Wales, 1932. 51168, f. 1.

Thomas (James Henry), *P.C.; M.P.*
— Correspondence between Lord Cecil and J. H. Thomas, 1918, 1934. *Signed.* 51162, ff. 83, 84; 51169, ff. 212-214.

Thommessen (Rolf), *Editor of Tidens Tegn.*
— Correspondence between Lord Cecil and R. Thommessen, 1921. *Signed.* 51163, ff. 19, 20.

Thompson (Alexander M.), *journalist.*
— Letter to Lord Cecil, 1915. *Signed.* 51161, f. 244.

Thompson (Charles A.), *of York.*
— Correspondence between Lord Cecil and C. A. Thompson, 1938. 51181, ff. 88, 90.

Thompson (*Rev.* James Matthew), *former Lecturer in French History at Oxford.*
— Correspondence between Lord Cecil and Rev. J. M. Thompson, 1941. *Signed.* 51187, ff. 22, 36.

Thompson (Merrick Arnold Bardsley Denton-).
— *v.* Denton-Thompson (Merrick Arnold Bardsley).

Thomson (Christopher Birdwood), *Baron Thomson.*
— Correspondence between Lord Cecil and Lord Thomson, 1929. *Signed.* 51099, ff. 173-192.

Thornton (Percy Melville), *M.P.*
— Letter to Lord Cecil, 1909. 51159, f. 74.

Thorop (A.), *Danish correspondent of The Daily Telegraph.*
— Letter to F. Miller from A. Thorop, 1916. 51093, f. 7.

Thurso, *1st Viscount.*
— *v.* Sinclair (Archibald Henry Macdonald).

Thurso, *1st Viscountess.*
— *v.* Sinclair (Marigold).

Thwaites (*Gen. Sir* William), *K.C.B.*
— Letter to A. Webber from Maj.-Gen. W. Thwaites, 1918. *Signed.* 51094, f. 103.
— Letter from Lord Cecil to Maj.-Gen. W. Thwaites, 1918. *Copy.* 51094, f. 166.

Tiedemann (Leo von), *member of German minority from Poland.*
— Letter to Lord Cecil, 1923. *Signed.* 51096, f. 55.

Timperley (Harold John), *of the China Campaign Committee; journalist and author.*
— Correspondence between Lord Cecil and H. J. Timperley, 1940. *Signed.* 51185, ff. 82, 90.

Tiselius (D.), *of the Nobel Foundation, Stockholm.*
— Correspondence between Lord Cecil and D. Tiselius, 1937. *Signed.* 51178, ff. 43, 53.

Titulescu (Nicolae), *Rumanian diplomatist.*
— Letter to N. Titulescu, 1923. *Copy.* 51096, f. 12.
— Letter to Lord Cecil from N. Titulescu, 1937. *Signed.* 51176, f. 1.

Tizard (*Mrs* K. D.), *of Chingford.*
— Correspondence between Lord Cecil and Mrs K. D. Tizard, 1936. 51173, ff. 56, 57.

Toller (Ernst), *German author and exile.*
— Correspondence between Lord Cecil and E. Toller, 1935. *Signed.* 51170, ff. 165-169.

Tollinton (Richard Bartram Boyd), *of the British Council; diplomatist.*
— Correspondence between Lord Cecil and R. B. B. Tollinton, 1939. *Signed.* 51184, ff. 101, 112.

Torre (*Dr.* Andrea), *of the Italian Parliamentary Committee for an Understanding between the Subject Races of Austria-Hungary.*
— Agreement between Dr. A. Torre and Dr. Ante Trumbić, 1918. *Copy.* 51093, f. 107.

Tournier (*Miss* E. A.), *writing from Chelsea.*
— Letter to Lord Cecil, 1912. 51160, f. 136.

Townley (*Sir* Walter Beaupre), *K.C.M.G.; diplomatist.*
— Letter to Sir W. B. Townley, [1918?]. *Draft.* 51094, f. 162.

Toynbee (Arnold Joseph), *historian.*
— Correspondence between Lord Cecil and A. J. Toynbee, 1935. Partly *signed.* 51193, ff. 37-43, 54-57.

Trenchard (*Marshal of the R.A.F.* Hugh Montague), *Viscount Trenchard.*
— Correspondence between Lord Cecil and Viscount Trenchard, 1927-1941. *Signed.* Partly *printed.* 51098, ff. 156-163; 51184, ff. 98, 108.
— Memorandum to members of Watching Committee from Viscount Trenchard, 1941. *Printed.* 51187, ff. 361-364.

Trevelyan (*Sir* Charles), *3rd Bart.*
— Letter to Lord Cecil, 1944. 51191, f. 195.

INDEX

Trevelyan (George Macaulay), *O.M.; historian.*
— Correspondence between Lord Cecil and G. M. Trevelyan, 1935, 1936. 51193, ff. 35, 36, 45-53, 76, 77.

Tribe (*Sir* Frank Newton), *K.C.B.*
— Letter to Lord Cecil, 1927. 51165, f. 144.

Trippel (*Sir* Francis).
— Letters to Sir F. Trippel from G. Wyndham, 1912. *Copies.* 51160, ff. 181, 183.
— Letter to Sir F. Trippel from Sir J. A. Chamberlain, 1912. *Copy.* 51160, f. 182.
— Letter to Sir F. Trippel from A. Bonar Law, 1912. *Copy.* 51160, f. 182.
— Letter to Sir F. Trippel from J. Chamberlain, 1912. *Copy.* 51160, f. 187.

Triscott (*Miss* Lily Yorke-).
— *v.* Yorke-Triscott (*Miss* Lily).

Trumbić (*Dr.* Ante), *President of the Southern Slav Committee.*
— Visiting card, 1918. *Printed.* 51093, f. 106.
— Agreement between Dr. A. Torre and Dr. Ante Trumbić, 1918. *Copy.* 51093, f. 107.
— Memorandum by Lord Cecil rel. to conversation with Dr. Ante Trumbić, 1928. 51099, f. 135.

Tseng Yang-Fu, *Mayor of Canton.*
— Telegram to L. Dolivet from Tseng Yang-Fu, 1938. *Copy.* 51180, f. 37.

Tsouderos (Emmanuel L.), *Prime Minister of Greece.*
— Correspondence between Lord Cecil and E. L. Tsouderos, 1942. *Signed.* 51188, ff. 182, 191, 222-226, 233.

Tufnell (*Mrs* Blanche Beauchamp), *speaker on Central European affairs.*
— Correspondence between Lord Cecil and Mrs B. B. Tufnell, 1940, 1941. 51185, ff. 185, 189; 51187, ff. 318, 323.

Tufton (Charles Henry), *C.M.G.; of the Foreign Office.*
— Correspondence between Lord Cecil and C. H. Tufton, partly on behalf of A. J. Balfour, 1922, 1923. 51071 A, f. 80; 51095, ff. 186, 198.
— Letter to C. H. Tufton from E. Colban, 1923. *Signed.* 51115, f. 25.

Turbervill (Edith Picton-).
— *v.* Picton-Turbervill (Edith).

TURKEY.
— Memoranda by G. A. Lloyd rel. to Turkey, 1918. Partly *signed.* 51071, ff. 52-55; 51094, f. 35.
— Memorandum by H. G. Nicolson rel. to prospects of peace with Turkey, 1918. *Copy.* 51094, f. 37.
— *v. also* Munir (*Bey* Mehmed).

Turle (Aubrey), *Honorary Sec., The Pedestrians' League.*
— Letter, etc., to Lord Cecil, 1942. *Signed.* 51189, ff. 45-48v.

Turner (Arthur C.), *of the University of Glasgow.*
— Correspondence between Lord Cecil and A. C. Turner, 1940. 51184, ff. 335, 342; 51185, ff. 14, 26, 43, 47.

Turnour (Edward), *6th Earl Winterton.*
— Correspondence between Lord Cecil and Lord Winterton, 1918-1943. Partly *signed.* 51094, f. 96; 51180, ff. 106, 115; 51190, ff. 354, 362-364v, 374.

Turton (Ruby Christian), *wife of R. H. Turton, M.P., Baron Tranmire 1974.*
— Correspondence, etc., between Lord Cecil and R. C. Turton, 1943. 51189, ff. 244-247, 253; 51190, f. 381.
Twe (D.), *Liberian, writing from Sierra Leone.*
— Correspondence between Lord Cecil and D. Twe, 1934. 51101, ff. 157, 164-167.
Tweedsmuir, *1st Baron.*
— *v.* Buchan (John).
Tyrrell (William George), *1st Baron Tyrrell.*
— Correspondence between Lord Cecil and Lord Tyrrell, 1925-1942. Partly *signed.* 51079, ff. 143, 164; 51096, f. 6; 51097, ff. 138, 212-214v; 51098, ff. 30, 45-47, 124; 51099, f. 73; 51100, f. 77; 51101, ff. 22-25; 51189, f. 49 ; 51104.
— Telegrams between Lord Cecil and W. G. Tyrrell, 1926. 51104, ff. 70-73.
Tzamoutali (Georges), *Bessarabian landowner in Paris.*
— Letter to Lord Cecil, 1935. *Fr.* 51136, f. 44.

U

Ullswater, *1st Viscount.*
— *v.* Lowther (James William).
Underhill (J. S.), *Sec., Marylebone Constitutional Union.*
— Letters to Lord Cecil, 1904-1909. Partly *signed.* 51158, ff. 14v, 170; 51159, ff. 42, 93.
Union Internationale des Associations pour la Société des Nations.
— *v.* O'Moloney (William).
Unwin (*Sir* Raymond), *town-planner.*
— Correspondence between Lord Cecil and Sir R. Unwin, 1927, 1937. Partly *signed.* 51165, ff. 163, 166; 51175, ff. 62, 67, 76.

Unwin (*Sir* Stanley), *K.C.M.G.; publisher.*
— Correspondence between Lord Cecil and Sir S. Unwin, 1940. *Signed.* 51193, ff. 205, 208.
— *v. also* Allen (George) and Unwin.
Usborne (John), *Editor, Federal Union News.*
— Correspondence between Lord Cecil and J. Usborne, 1940. *Signed.* 51185, ff. 133, 146, 154, 167.

V

Vaisey (*Sir* Harry Bevir), *judge.*
— Memorandum rel. to report of Archbishops' Commission on Church and State, 1943. *Draft.* 51154 B, ff. 126-133.
— Correspondence between Lord Cecil and Sir H. B. Vaisey, 1945. *Signed.* 51192, ff. 183-185.
Vallentin (Antonina), *Editor, Nord und Süd, Berlin.*
— Correspondence between Lord Cecil and A. Vallentin, 1929. *Signed.* 51166, ff. 114, 115, 128.
Vandyk (Arthur), *solicitor.*
— Correspondence between Lord Cecil and A. Vandyk, 1942. *Signed.* 51188, ff. 293, 304.
Vane-Tempest-Stewart (Charles Stewart Henry), *7th Marquess of Londonderry.*
— Correspondence between Lord Cecil and Lord Londonderry, 1938, 1943. *Signed.* 51179, ff. 45, 48, 183, 192, 210; 51190, ff. 327, 346, 361.
Vansittart (Robert Gilbert), *Baron Vansittart.*
— Letter to Lord Cecil from R. G. Vansittart on behalf of J. Ramsay MacDonald, 1929. *Signed.* 51081, f. 75.

INDEX

Vansittart (Robert Gilbert), *Baron Vansittart. continuation*
— Letter to J. R. Clynes from R. G. Vansittart on behalf of J. Ramsay MacDonald, 1929. *Signed.* 51099, f. 199.
— Correspondence between Lord Cecil and R. G. Vansittart, 1931-1933. Partly *signed.* 51100, ff. 80v, 108-112, 165, 169; 51101, ff. 82, 95.

Vasconellos (Augusto de), *Portuguese diplomatist.*
— Memorandum by Lord Cecil rel. to conversation with A. de Vasconellos, 1918. 51093, f. 113.

Vasdias (—), *Dutch journalist.*
— Telegram to Lord Cecil, 1939. 51184, f. 240.

Vaughan (*Capt.* E. G. W.), *Sec., League of Nations Union, Warwickshire and Birmingham Federal Council.*
— Letter, etc., to Col. P. Docker from Capt. E. G. W. Vaughan, 1934. *Signed.* 51169, f. 84.
— Letter to H. H. Stainton from Capt. E. G. W. Vaughan, 1935. *Signed.* 51171, f. 86.
— Correspondence between Lord Cecil and Capt. E. G. W. Vaughan, 1935. *Signed.* 51171, ff. 109, 119.

Vayo (Julio Alvarez del).
— *v.* Alvarez del Vayo (Julio).

Venizelos (Eleutherios Kuriakos), *Greek statesman.*
— Correspondence between Lord Cecil and E. K. Venizelos, 1919-1923. Partly *signed.* Partly *Fr.* 51094, f. 178; 51095, ff. 80, 138, 159-161.
— Memorandum by Lord Cecil rel. to conversation with E. K. Venizelos, 1931. 51100, f. 141.

Venizelos (Helena), *widow of E. K. Venizelos.*
— Correspondence between Lord Cecil and H. Venizelos, 1937. *Signed.* 51176, ff. 7, 8.

Vereeniging voor Volkenbond en Vrede.
— Correspondence between Lord Cecil and Chairman and Sec. of Vereeniging voor Volkenbond en Vrede, 1930. *Signed.* 51167, ff. 13, 14.

Verney (Richard Greville), *19th Baron Willoughby de Broke.*
— Letters to Lord Cecil, 1911, 1913. Partly *signed.* 51160, ff. 31-33; 51161, f. 24.

Vesey (Sydney Philip Charles), *C.B.E.*
— Letters to Lord Cecil, 1912, 1914. *Signed.* 51160, ff. 194, 217, 227; 51161, ff. 29, 34, 35, 39, 53, 56, 82, 92, 99.

Vidaković (A.), *Yugoslav journalist.*
— Correspondence between Lord Cecil and A. Vidaković, 1934. 51169, ff. 125, 135, 144.

Viénot (—), *French politician.*
— Correspondence between Lord Cecil and — Viénot, 1934. 51101, ff. 202, 203.

Villegas Echiburu (Enrique), *Chilean diplomatist.*
— Correspondence between Lord Cecil and E. Villegas Echiburu, 1926. *Signed. Fr.* 51098, ff. 109, 130.

Villeri (Luigi), *of the League of Nations.*
— Letter, etc., to Lord Cecil, 1921. *Signed.* Partly *printed.* 51095, ff. 15-20.

Vincent (Edgar), *Viscount D'Abernon.*
— Correspondence, etc., between Lord Cecil and Lord D'Abernon, 1922. *Signed.* 51095, ff. 85-93.

INDEX

Vincze (Paul), *Hungarian medallist.*
— Correspondence between Lord Cecil and P. Vincze, 1938. *Signed.* 51181, ff. 5, 126, 146.

Vogt (Paul Benjamin), *Norwegian diplomatist.*
— Letter to Lord Cecil, 1925. *Signed.* 51097, f. 176.

Vojtišek (Ota), *Sec., Czechoslovak League of Nations Union.*
— Letters to Lord Cecil, 1943, 1944. *Signed.* 51190, f. 193; 51191, f. 246.

Vyvere (*Count* Alois Jean-Marie van de), *Belgian Minister of Finance.*
— Memorandum by Lord Cecil rel. to conversation with Count A. J.-M. van de Vyvere, 1918. 51094, f. 106.

W

Wadsworth (Alfred Powell), *of The Manchester Guardian.*
— Letter to Lord Cecil from A. P. Wadsworth on behalf of W. P. Crozier, 1942. *Signed.* 51189, f. 100.

Waite (*Mrs* Ethel A.), *of Chelsea.*
— Correspondence between Lord Cecil and Mrs E. A. Waite, 1940. 51186, ff. 182, 199.

Wakefield, W.R., *co. York.*
— Message from Lord Cecil for Peace Week at Wakefield, 1938. *Copy.* 51178, f. 151.

Wakefield, *Bishop of.*
— *v.* Eden (George Rodney).

Wales, *Archbishop of.*
— *v.* Edwards (Alfred George).

Walford (R. G.), *of the B.B.C.*
— Letter to Miss I. M. Butler from R. G. Walford, 1940. 51193, f. 167.

Walker (Douglas G. F.), *of Glasgow; winner of the Cecil Peace Prize.*
— Correspondence between Lord Cecil and D. G. F. Walker, 1943, 1945. 51190, ff. 5, 11, 13-15; 51192, ff. 158, 172, 179.

Walker (John), *Hon. Sec., Hitchin Conservative and Liberal Unionist Working Men's Club.*
— Letter to Lord Cecil, 1918. 51162, f. 67.

Walker (Roy), *of the Peace Pledge Union.*
— Correspondence between Lord Cecil and R. Walker, 1941, 1944. Partly *signed.* 51188, ff. 116-118; 51191, ff. 100, 103.
— Memorandum rel. to the Kershner Plan, 1944. *Printed.* 51191, ff. 31-32v.

Wallace (David Euan), *P.C.; M.P.*
— Correspondence between Lord Cecil and D. E. Wallace, 1939. *Signed.* 51184, ff. 257, 298.

Wallace (Michael), *of the Deuxième Congrès Mondial de la Jeunesse, Paris.*
— Letter from Lord Cecil to M. Wallace, 1938. *Copy.* 51179, f. 144.

Wallinger (*Sir* Geoffrey Arnold), *G.B.E.*
— Correspondence between Lord Cecil and G. A. Wallinger, 1926-1934. Partly *signed.* 51101, ff. 100, 148, 152, 163, 168; 51164, f. 177.

Walshaw (J. D.), *Chairman, League of Nations Youth Group, Ashton-under-Lyne.*
— Correspondence between Lord Cecil and J. D. Walshaw, 1938. *Signed.* 51181, ff. 168, 175.

Walters (Francis Paul), *of the Secretariate of the League of Nations.*
— Letter to J. L. Palmer from F. P. Walters, 1919. *Copy.* 51114, f. 1.

INDEX

Walters (Francis Paul), *of the Secretariate of the League of Nations. continuation*
— Correspondence between F. P. Walters and P. J. Noel-Baker, partly on behalf of Lord Cecil, 1922-1937. Mostly *signed.* 51106, f. 130; 51114, ff. 4-30v, 103.
— Correspondence, including telegrams, between Lord Cecil and F. P. Walters, 1922-1945. Mostly *signed.* 51114, ff. 4-155; 51184, f. 329.
— Letters to J. E. Drummond from F. P. Walters, 1923, 1930. *Signed.* 51110, f. 50; 51112, f. 26.

Walters (*Sir* John Tudor).
— Letter to Lord Cecil on behalf of Sir J. T. Walters, 1914. 51161, f. 148.

Walton (*Sir* Edgar Harris), *K.C.M.G.; High Commissioner for S. Africa, London.*
— Correspondence between Lord Cecil and Sir E. H. Walton on behalf of J. C. Smuts, 1922, 1923. *Signed.* 51076, ff. 102, 103, 115, 116.

Walton (*Sir* Joseph), *Justice of K.B.*
— Letter to Lord Cecil, 1906. 51158, f. 71.

Wandsworth, *co. Surr.*
— Message from Lord Cecil for Peace Week at Wandsworth, 1937. *Copy.* 51178, f. 6.

Wang (*Prof.* Shelley), *of the Chinese People's Foreign Relations Association, Chung King.*
— Letter to Lord Cecil, 1939. *Signed.* 51183, ff. 139, 198.

Wang Ching-ch'un, *President, London Chinese Association.*
— Correspondence between Lord Cecil and Wang Ching-ch'un, 1940, 1944. Partly *signed.* 51191, f. 189; 51193, ff. 186-193.

War Office.
— *v.* Harker (*Brig.* O. Allen).

Ward (*Mrs* —), *wife of Dr. R. Ward, of Torquay.*
— Letter from Lord Cecil to Mrs — Ward, 1937. *Copy.* 51176, f. 56.

Ward (*Miss* Gertrude), *Sec., League of Nations Union, Sheffield District.*
— Correspondence between Lord Cecil and Miss G. Ward, 1935-1945. 51142, ff. 152-219.

Ward (James), *writing from East Finchley.*
— Letter to Lord Cecil, 1914. 51161, f. 125.

Ward (Julia) *afterw.* **Deutsch.**
— *v.* Deutsch (Julia).

Ward (Robert M'Gowan Barrington-).
— *v.* Barrington-Ward (Robert M'Gowan).

Ward (Ronald R. S.), *Appeals Sec., National Parliament of Youth.*
— Correspondence between Lord Cecil and R. R. S. Ward, 1937, 1939. *Signed.* 51175, f. 41; 51182, ff. 207-211, 216.

Ward (Rowland), *physician, of Torquay.*
— Letter to Lord Cecil, 1937. 51175, f. 152.

Wardlaw-Milne (*Sir* John Sydney), *K.B.E.*
— Letter to Lord Cecil from Sir J. S. Wardlaw-Milne, 1939. *Signed.* 51184, f. 82.

Ware (*Sir* Fabian Arthur Goulstone), *K.C.V.O.*
— Letters to Lord Cecil, 1909. Partly *signed.* 51159, ff. 18, 28.

Wargrave, *Baron.*
— *v.* Goulding (Edward Alfred).

Warner (G.), *of the Foreign Office.*
— Correspondence between Lord Cecil and G. Warner, 1940. *Signed.* 51186, ff. 138, 140, 158.

Warren (T. H.), *Sec., Canadian Club of Ottawa.*
— Telegram to Lord Cecil, 1933. 51168, f. 125.

INDEX

Warwick (*Sir* Norman Richard Combe), *K.C.V.O.*
— Letter to Lord Cecil, 1944. 51191, f. 226.

Watching Committee.
— Memorandum to members of Watching Committee from Viscount Trenchard, 1941. *Printed.* 51187, ff. 361-364.

Water (Charles Theodore te), *High Commissioner for South Africa.*
— Correspondence between Lord Cecil and C. T. te Water, 1939. 51184, ff. 75, 183.

Waterlow (*Sir* Sydney Philip), *K.C.M.G.*
— Correspondence between Lord Cecil and S. P. Waterlow, 1925. *Signed.* 51097, ff. 100, 103-105.

Waters (John Dallas), *private sec. to the Lord Chancellor.*
— Letter to Lord Cecil, 1936. *Signed.* 51173, f. 219.

Watson (Robert William Seton-).
— *v.* Seton-Watson (Robert William).

Watt (Raymond G.), *General Sec., League of Nations Union, New South Wales Branch.*
— Correspondence, including telegrams, between Lord Cecil and R. G. Watt, 1936, 1938. *Signed.* 51172, ff. 58, 73; 51179, f. 207.

Waverley, *1st Viscount.*
— *v.* Anderson (John).

Webb (Sidney James), *Baron Passfield.*
— Correspondence between Lord Cecil and Lord Passfield, 1930. *Signed.* 51100, ff. 3, 9-12, 17, 31-34.

Webber (A).
— Letter to A. Webber from J. F. Henderson, 1918. 51094, f. 84.

Webber (Alfred).
— Letter to A. Webber from Maj.-Gen. W. Thwaites, 1918. *Signed.* 51094, f. 103.

Weber (Alfred), *German political economist and sociologist.*
— Letter from Lord Cecil to A. Weber, 1931. *Copy.* 51167, f. 104.

Webster (*Sir* Charles Kingsley), *K.C.M.G; historian.*
— Letters to Lord Cecil, 1938-1946. Partly *signed.* 51187, f. 8; 51192, ff. 109, 111, 237.

Wedgwood (Florence Ethel), *widow of Josiah, 1st Baron Wedgwood.*
— Letter to Lord Cecil, 1943, 1944. 51190, f. 396; 51191, f. 203.

Wedgwood (Josiah), *younger son of Josiah, 1st Baron Wedgwood.*
— Letter to Lord Cecil, 1943. *Signed.* 51190, f. 384.

Wedgwood (Josiah Clement), *1st Baron Wedgwood.*
— Correspondence between Lord Cecil and Lord Wedgwood, 1936-1943. 51173, ff. 182, 203, 241; 51175, ff. 27, 33, 35; 51179, ff. 59, 60, 77; 51188, ff. 124, 332.

Wedgwood (*Sir* Ralph Lewis), *1st Bart.*
— Correspondence, etc., including telegram, between Lord Cecil and Sir R. L. Wedgwood, 1941-1944. Partly *signed.* 51188, ff. 125, 308, 313, 317, 334; 51189, ff. 256, 259-261v; 51191, f. 180.

Weigall (Julian William Wellesley), *barrister.*
— Correspondence between Lord Cecil and J. W. W. Weigall, 1909-1944. 51159, ff. 166, 172, 173; 51160, f. 45; 51169, ff. 200, 207-209, 215-217; 51171, ff. 150, 153, 155-156v; 51191, ff. 232, 237.

Weil (Alain Emile).
— *v.* Emile-Weil (Alain).

INDEX

Weizmann (Chaim), *President of Israel.*
— Letter to Lord Cecil, signed by Archbishop of York and C. Weizmann on behalf of the International Student Service, 1937. *Facsimile.* 51178, f. 45.

Wellesley (*Sir* Victor Alexander Augustus Henry), *K.C.M.G.; of the Foreign Office.*
— Correspondence between Lord Cecil and Sir V. A. A. H. Wellesley, 1929, 1934. *Signed.* 51083, ff. 65-68; 51099, f. 198.

Wells (Herbert George), *author.*
— Letter to E. Beneš from H. G. Wells, 1938. *Copy.* 51181, f. 166.

Wells (Linton), *of New York City.*
— Memorandum by Lord Cecil rel. to interview with L. Wells, 1939. 51182, f. 173.
— Letter to Lord Cecil, 1939. *Signed.* 51183, f. 90.

Wen K.-Y., *General Sec., All-China Comforting Association, Chung King.*
— Letter to Lord Cecil, 1941. *Signed.* 51188, f. 36.

Wertheimer (Egon F. Ranshofen), *journalist and official of the League of Nations.*
— Note, 1944. *Signed.* 51141, f. 227.

West (Margaret), *of The Hogarth Press.*
— Letter to Lord Cecil, 1936. *Signed.* 51193, f. 66.

Weston (*Sir* John Wakefield), *Bart.*
— Correspondence between Lord Cecil and J. W. Weston, 1913. 51161, ff. 33, 46, 52.

Weyl (Carrie S.), *wife of Maurice N. Weyl; of Philadelphia.*
— Correspondence between Lord Cecil and C. S. Weyl, 1937. 51178, ff. 37, 40.

Wheare (*Sir* Kenneth Clinton).
— Correspondence between Lord Cecil and K. C. Wheare, 1942, 1943. 51188, f. 239; 51189, ff. 249, 258; 51190, f. 7.

Wheeler (*Miss* E.), *domestic servant.*
— Letter, etc., to Lord Cecil, 1914. 51161, ff. 198-200.

Wheeler (*Sir* Robert Eric Mortimer), *archaeologist.*
— Letter to Lord Cecil, 1928. *Signed.* 51166, f. 31.

Wheeler-Bennett (*Sir* John Wheeler), *G.C.V.O.*
— Correspondence between Lord Cecil and J. W. Wheeler-Bennett, 1933. *Signed.* 51168, ff. 105, 111.

Wheldon (*Mrs* L. A.), *of Carmarthen.*
— Letter to Lord Cecil, 1941. 51187, f. 153.

Whitaker (Peter), *of the Manchester and Salford Famine Relief Committee.*
— Letter to Lord Cecil, 1944. *Signed.* 51191, f. 58.

White (*Mrs* E. M.), *professional indexer; of Radlett.*
— Correspondence between Lord Cecil and Mrs E. M. White, 1941. 51187, ff. 1, 8.

White (*Miss* Freda), *writer on international affairs.*
— Correspondence between Lord Cecil and Miss F. White, 1935-1941. 51142, ff. 60v-92.

White (John Bazley-).
— *v.* Bazley-White (John).

White (R. A.), *of the League of Nations Union, Harrogate Branch.*
— Correspondence between Lord Cecil and R. A. White, 1940, 1943. *Partly signed.* 51185, ff. 144, 150; 51190, f. 185.

White (Robert A.), *Sec., United Aid to China, Harrogate Committee.*
— Letter to Lord Cecil, 1945. *Signed.* 51192, f. 177.

White (*Mrs?* S. E.).
— Letter to Lord Cecil, [bef. 1919?]. 51162, f. 87.

White (William Hale) *al.* '**Mark Rutherford**'.
— Letters to Lord Cecil, 1910, 1912. Partly *signed*. 51160, ff. 5, 7-9v, 19-26, 116.

Whittingham (Walter Godfrey), *Bishop of St. Edmundsbury and Ipswich.*
— Correspondence between Lord Cecil and Bishop of St. Edmundsbury, 1937. *Signed.* 51175, ff. 102, 103, 107.

Whyte (*Sir* Alexander Frederick), *K.C.S.I.*
— Correspondence between Lord Cecil and Sir A. F. Whyte, 1940, 1941. *Signed.* 51186, ff. 17, 23; 51187, f. 78.

Wickings (Dorothy), *of the Christian Council for Refugees from Germany and Central Europe.*
— Letter to Lord Cecil from D. Wickings, 1940. *Signed.* 51186, f. 118.
— Correspondence between Miss I. M. Butler and D. Wickings, 1940. 51186, ff. 219, 223, 255.

Wigan, *co. Lanc.*
— Message from Lord Cecil for Peace Week at Wigan, 1938. *Copy.* 51179, f. 107.

Wigan (Charles), *solicitor.*
— Letter to Lord Cecil, 1913. *Signed.* 51160, f. 281.

Wigram (Ralph Follet), *C.M.G.; of the Foreign Office.*
— Correspondence, partly on behalf of Lord Cecil, between S. A. Heald and R. F. Wigram, 1934. 51082, ff. 215-227, 232-240, 245-260.

Wilberforce (Octavia Margaret), *physician.*
— Correspondence between Lord Cecil and O. M. Wilberforce, 1940, 1941. 51185, f. 291; 51187, ff. 149, 180.

Wilberforce (Robert), *diplomatist.*
— Correspondence between Lord Cecil and R. Wilberforce, 1922. 51095, ff. 43, 54.

Wile (Frederick William), *U.S. journalist.*
— Correspondence between Lord Cecil and F. W. Wile, 1937. 51178, ff. 33, 41.

Wilkes (G.), *of the League of Nations Union; writing from Wolverhampton.*
— Correspondence between Lord Cecil and G. Wilkes, 1937. 51175, ff. 115, 125.

Wilkinson (Beatrix Frances Gertrude), *wife of Sir Nevile R. Wilkinson.*
— Correspondence between Lord Cecil and B. F. G. Wilkinson, 1940. 51185, ff. 241, 247.

Willert (*Sir* Arthur), *K.B.E.*
— Correspondence between Lord Cecil and Sir A. Willert, 1936. 51172, f. 174; 51173, f. 3.

Williams (Alwyn Terrell Petre), *Bishop of Durham.*
— Letter to Lord Cecil, 1944. *Signed.* 51191, f. 143.

Williams (Aneurin), *M.P.*
— Letters, etc., to Lord Cecil, 1909-1918. Partly *signed.* 51159, f. 51; 51160, ff. 125, 129, 160, 164-166, 172; 51162, ff. 40-56v.

Williams (Dorothy), *wife of A. F. B. Williams.*
— Correspondence between Lord Cecil and D. Williams, 1935, 1940. 51170, ff. 44-48; 51185, f. 192.

Williams (*Sir* Ellis Hume-), *1st Bart.*
— *v.* Hume-Williams (*Sir* Ellis).

Williams (F. D.), *official of the International Peace Campaign.*
— Letters to Lord Cecil, 1937-1939. *Signed.* 51143, ff. 149, 161; 51175, ff. 174, 210; 51176, ff. 73, 87, 128, 146; 51177, ff. 95, 123, 165; 51179, ff. 111, 233; 51180, f. 117; 51183, ff. 187, 230.

INDEX

Williams (*Sir* John Fischer), *barrister.*
— Correspondence between Lord Cecil and Sir J. F. Williams, 1934. 51169, ff. 193, 194, 197.

Williams (W. Philpotts), *author.*
— Letter, etc., to Lord Cecil, 1912. 51160, f. 140.

Williamson (Hugh Ross), *author.*
— Correspondence between Lord Cecil and H. R. Williamson, 1942. 51189, ff. 102-104, 109.

Willink (*Sir* Henry Urmston), *1st Bart.*
— Correspondence between Lord Cecil and H. U. Willink, 1944. *Signed.* 51191, ff. 283, 291.

Willoughby de Broke, *Baron.*
— *v.* Verney (Richard Greville).

Wills (*Miss* M. M.), *Sec., League of Nations Union, Taunton Branch.*
— Letter to Lord Cecil, 1944. 51191, f. 216.

Wilson (Alec), *speaker on behalf of the League of Nations Union.*
— Correspondence between Lord Cecil and A. Wilson, 1939. Partly *signed.* 51136, f. 163; 51184, f. 43; 51182, f. 172.

Wilson (Carine), *Canadian senator.*
— Letter from Lord Cecil to C. Wilson, 1942. *Copy.* 51189, f. 183.

Wilson (Hugh Robert), *U.S. diplomatist.*
— Memorandum by Lord Cecil rel. to conversation with H. R. Wilson, 1931. 51100, f. 139.

Wilson (Joseph Vivian), *New Zealand diplomatist.*
— Correspondence between Lord Cecil and J. V. Wilson, 1942, 1945. *Signed.* 51188, ff. 189, 203; 51192, ff. 136, 149.

Wilson (William Carey), *author.*
— Correspondence between Lord Cecil and W. C. Wilson, 1935. *Signed.* 51170, ff. 200, 215.

Wilson (Woodrow), *President of the U.S.A.*
— Addresses by Woodrow Wilson to Congress at Mount Vernon, 1918. *Printed.* Partly *extracts.* 51093, ff. 60, 79, 80, 188.
— Correspondence, including telegrams, between Lord Cecil and W. Wilson, 1919, 1923. 51094, f. 180; 51163, ff. 171, 172.

Wimperis (Barbara), *Editor, League of Nations Union Youth Bulletin.*
— Correspondence between Lord Cecil and B. Wimperis, 1934. 51169, ff. 110, 146.

Winant (John Gilbert), *U.S. diplomatist.*
— Correspondence, partly on his behalf, with Lord Cecil, 1941-1944. *Signed.* 51187, ff. 253, 259, 262, 282, 370, 379; 51188, f. 300; 51190, ff. 276, 335, 341, 397; 51191, ff. 41, 46, 204, 235.
— Memorandum by Lord Cecil rel. to conversation with J. G. Winant, 1943. 51190, f. 219.

Winchester, *Bishop of.*
— *v.* Garbett (Cyril Forster).

Windsor-Clive (Ivor Miles), *2nd Earl of Plymouth.*
— Letters to Lord Cecil from Lord Plymouth, 1936, 1937. *Signed.* 51174, f. 189; 51178, f. 1.

Wingate (*Gen. Sir* Francis Reginald), *1st Bart.; High Commissioner for Egypt.*
— Letter to Lord Cecil, 1918. *Signed.* 51093, f. 190.

Winnington-Ingram (Arthur Foley), *Bishop of London.*
— Letter to Lord Cecil from Bishop of London, 1911. 51160, f. 29.

Winter (*Dr.* Lev), *Czech politician.*
— Correspondence between Lord Cecil and Dr. L. Winter, 1930. *Signed.* 51167, ff. 106, 109.

Winterton, *6th Earl.*
— *v.* Turnour (Edward).

Winther (H. D.), *of the B.B.C.*
— Correspondence between Lord Cecil and H. D. Winther, 1941. *Signed.* 51193, ff. 258, 259.

Witherow (James M.), *attorney; of Moorhead, Minnesota.*
— Correspondence between Lord Cecil and J. M. Witherow, 1941, 1942. *Signed.* 51188, ff. 79-87, 142.

Wolf (Lucien), *journalist.*
— Correspondence between L. Wolf and Lord Curzon, 1923, 1927. Mostly *signed.* 51096, f. 8; 51099, ff. 88, 95.

Wolff (Dr. Franz), *German refugee in England.*
— Correspondence between Dr. F. Wolff and Miss I. M. Butler, 1939. *Signed.* 51184, ff. 1, 13, 21.

Wolmer, *Viscount.*
— *v.* Palmer (Roundell Cecil).

Women's International Organisations Liaison Committee.
— *v.* Zimmern (*Miss* Elsie M.).

Women's Liberal Federation.
— *v.* Ashby (*Mrs* Margery Corbett).
— *v.* Baerlein (*Mrs* Gladys L.).
— *v.* Harvey (Margaret).

Women's Social and Political Union.
— Leaflet, 'Votes for Women' by the Women's Social and Political Union, 1907. *Printed.* 51158, f. 95.

Wood (Edward Frederick Lindley), *Baron Irwin; 3rd Viscount (1934) and 1st Earl Halifax.*
— Correspondence between Lord Cecil and Sir A. G. M. Cadogan, partly on behalf of Lord Halifax, 1923-1944. Partly *signed.* 51084, ff. 159, 192-194; 51089; 51096, ff. 109-122; 51097, ff. 74-78; 51098, f. 42.
— Letter to E. F. L. Wood from Lord Parmoor, 1924. *Copy.* 51096, f. 149.
— Correspondence between Lord Cecil and Lord Halifax, 1926-1942. Mostly *signed.* 51084.
— Correspondence between Miss I. M. Butler and C. A. C. J. Hendriks on behalf of Lord Halifax, 1938. *Signed.* 51084, ff. 121-123.

Wood (Herbert George), *Professor of Theology, Birmingham University.*
— Letter from Lord Cecil to H. G. Wood, 1942. *Copy.* 51188, f. 238.

Wood (Hugh McKinnon), *Counsellor and Legal Adviser at the League of Nations.*
— Letter from Lord Cecil to H. McK. Wood, 1923. 51096, f. 71.

Wood (Philip), *Town Clerk of Buckingham.*
— Correspondence between Lord Cecil and P. Wood, 1945. *Signed.* 51192, ff. 171, 174, 175, 182.

Woodman (*Miss* **Dorothy),** *Honorary Sec., China Campaign Committee.*
— Correspondence between Lord Cecil and Miss D. Woodman, 1939, 1941. Partly *signed* and *printed.* 51183, ff. 213, 226; 51185, ff. 158, 186, 194; 51186, ff. 101-105v, 110; 51187, ff. 70, 74, 85, 128, 136, 138-142, 193, 199, 337, 400, 406.

Woods (*Col.* **Arthur),** *U.S. Assessor to the League of Nations Opium Committee.*
— Memoranda by Lord Cecil rel. to conversations and correspondence with Col. A. Woods, 1926. 51098, ff. 39, 41, 105-108.
— Correspondence between Lord Cecil and Col. A. Woods, 1926. *Signed.* 51098, ff. 114, 128.

Woodward (Clifford Salisbury), *Bishop of Bristol.*
— Correspondence between Lord Cecil and Bishop of Bristol, 1936. *Signed.* 51174, ff. 19-23.

INDEX

Woolf (*Mrs* Elizabeth Hyatt-).
— *v.* Hyatt-Woolf (*Mrs* Elizabeth).
Woolf (Leonard Sidney), *author and publisher.*
— Letters, etc., to Lord Cecil, 1940, 1941. *Signed.* 51186, f. 97; 51188, ff. 28-30, 38.
Woolley (Mary Emma), *President of Mount Holyoke College, Massachusetts.*
— Letter to Lord Cecil, 1936. *Signed.* 51173, f. 233.
Wootton (G.).
— Letter, etc., to G. Wootton from B. Fitch, 1909. 51159, f. 61.
World Council of Churches.
— *v.* Hooft (Willem Adolph Visser't).
Worsley (Herbert), *of Epping.*
— Letter to Lord Cecil, 1934. 51169, f. 196.
Worthington-Evans (*Sir* Laming), *1st Bart.*
— Correspondence between Lord Cecil and Sir L. Worthington-Evans, 1913, 1922. Partly *signed.* 51095, ff. 100-103; 51160, f. 276.
Wou Sao-fong, *author.*
— Correspondence between Lord Cecil and Wou Sao-fong, 1941, 1943. *Signed.* 51187, ff. 352, 421; 51188, ff. 10, 46, 66; 51190, ff. 215, 277.
Wright (A.), *of the Hitchin Division Conservative and Liberal Unionist Association.*
— Letter, etc., to Lord Cecil from A. Wright, 1918. 51162, ff. 61-63v.
— Letter to A. Wright from Miss M. E. Nicholson, 1918. 51162, f. 63.
Wright (Henry Fitzherbert), *of Yeldersley Hall, Derby.*
— Correspondence between Lord Cecil and H. F. Wright, 1943, 1944. *Signed.* 51190, ff. 295, 306, 315, 323, 326, 389-392; 51191, f. 6.

Wurfbain (André), *Sec. General, Office of the High Commissioner for Refugees from Germany.*
— Correspondence between Lord Cecil and A. Wurfbain, 1934-1936. *Signed.* 51101, f. 136; 51170, ff. 88, 97, 121-125; 51171, ff. 31, 36, 37; 51172, ff. 3-5.
Wyatt (*Col.* G. N.), *of the League of Nations Union, Bristol Branch.*
— Correspondence between Col. G. N. Wyatt and Maj. A. J. C. Freshwater, 1936, 1940. 51136, f. 138; 51184, f. 328.
Wyldbore-Smith (*Sir* Edmund).
— Letters to Lord Cecil, 1917, 1918. *Signed.* 51093, ff. 41-45, 120.
Wyndham (Charles Henry), *3rd Baron Leconfield.*
— Letter to Lord Cecil from Lord Leconfield, 1940. *Printed.* 51184, f. 349.
Wyndham (George), *M.P.*
— Letters to Sir F. Trippel from G. Wyndham, 1912. *Copies.* 51160, ff. 181, 183.
Wynn (John), *detainee under Regulation 18B.*
— Letter to Lord Cecil, 1942. *Signed.* 51189, f. 61.

X

Xirau (J. R.), *of the University of Lyons; formerly Professor of Law at Barcelona.*
— Correspondence between Lord Cecil and J. R. Xirau, 1944, 1945. *Signed.* 51191, f. 314; 51192, f. 9.

Y

Yahuda (Joseph), *author*.
— Correspondence between Lord Cecil and J. Yahuda, 1937. 51193, ff. 85-91, 95-99.

Yehia (M.), *promoter of an Anglo-Egyptian Union*.
— Correspondence between Lord Cecil and M. Yehia, 1939. *Signed*. 51184, ff. 84, 150, 167.

Yencken (Arthur Ferdinand), *diplomatist*.
— Letter, etc., to Lord Cecil, 1923. *Signed*. 51096, ff. 93-96.

Yerburgh (Robert Armstrong), *M.P.*
— Letter to Lord Cecil, 1909. 51159, f. 263.

York, *Archbishop of*.
— *v.* Garbett (Cyril Forster).
— *v.* Lang (Cosmo Gordon).
— *v.* Temple (William).

Yorke (Albert Edward), *6th Earl of Hardwicke*.
— Letter to Lord Cecil from Lord Hardwicke, 1904. 51158, f. 6.

Yorke-Triscott (*Miss* Lily), *Sec., Navy League, Kensington Branch*.
— Correspondence between Lord Cecil and Miss L. Yorke-Triscott, 1936. *Signed*. 51172, ff. 122, 129, 130, 137.

Young (Edgar Philip), *author*.
— Memorandum rel. to visits to Austria, etc., by E. P. Young on behalf of the International Peace Campaign, 1936. *Copy*. 51173, ff. 162-168.

Young (Edward Hilton), *1st Baron Kennet*.
— Correspondence between Lord Cecil and E. H. Young, 1927, 1929. *Signed*. 51165, ff. 100, 118, 121; 51166, ff. 99-102.

Young (H. R.), *Parliamentary Sec., the Postal and Telegraph Clerks' Association*.
— Letter to Lord Cecil, 1914. *Signed*. 51161, f. 151.

Yuka (Musa), *Albanian statesman*.
— Telegram to Lord Cecil, 1941. *Fr*. 51187, f. 389.

Z

Zaleski (August), *Polish statesman*.
— Correspondence between Lord Cecil and A. Zaleski, 1943. *Signed*. 51190, ff. 352, 356.

Zangwill (Edith), *widow of Israel Zangwill*.
— Letter to Lord Cecil, 1936. 51173, f. 234.

Zavalani (Selma), *wife of T. Zavalani*.
— Correspondence between Lord Cecil and S. Zavalani, 1940. *Signed*. *Fr*. 51185, ff. 263, 279, 286; 51186, ff. 129, 150.
— Correspondence between S. Zavalani and Miss I. M. Butler, 1940. *Fr*. 51186, ff. 15, 21.

Zavalani (Trajar), *Vice President, Free Albania Committee in the U.S.A.*
— Correspondence between Lord Cecil and T. Zavalani, 1939-1944. Partly *signed*. Partly *Fr*. 51184, f. 267; 51191, ff. 127, 245; 51193, ff. 230, 233, 237-244, 246.
— Letter to Mrs M. Herbert from T. Zavalani, 1943. *Signed*. 51141, f. 331.

Zetland, *Marquess of*.
— *v.* Dundas (Lawrence John Lumley).

Zhabotinsky (Jeanne).
— *v.* Jabotinsky (Jeanne).

Zilliacus (Konni), *M.P.*
— Correspondence, etc., between Lord Cecil and K. Zilliacus, 1932-1943. *Signed.* 51100, ff. 184-196; 51188, ff. 274, 357-370v, 381; 51189, ff. 2, 8; 51190, ff. 172, 273.

Zimmern (*Sir* Alfred Eckhard).
— Correspondence between P. J. Noel-Baker and A. E. Zimmern, 1923. 51106, ff. 74-76.
— Correspondence between Lord Cecil and A. E. Zimmern, 1931. 51167, ff. 59-62.

Zimmern (*Miss* Elsie M.), *Sec., Liaison Committee, Women's International Organisations.*
— Letters to Lord Cecil, 1945. *Signed.* 51192, ff. 70, 78.

Zionist Federation of Great Britain and Ireland.
— Message from Lord Cecil to Zionist Federation of Great Britain and Ireland, 1942. *Copy.* 51189, f. 148.

Zionist Organisation of America.
— *v.* Rothenberg (Morris).